MAP OF THE JOURNEY OF THE *PANS*

5. 22.12.47. Eight trains with 15,000 Romanian Jews leave for the port of Burgas in Bulgaria. The ships sail from Constantza to Burgas.
6. 27.12.47. The laden ships sail. Their destination: Haifa.
7. 29.12.47. Confrontation with British patrol.
8. 31.12.47. The ships arrive in Cyprus.
9. Paris, Centre for Aliya Bet (unauthorized immigration).
10. The British Navy Command of the Mediterranean in Malta.

VOYAGE TO FREEDOM

VOYAGE
TO
FREEDOM

An Episode in the Illegal
Immigration to Palestine

Ze'ev Venia Hadari
and
Ze'ev Tsahor

VALLENTINE, MITCHELL

304.8
H1250-T

First published 1985 in Great Britain by
VALLENTINE, MITCHELL AND COMPANY LIMITED
Gainsborough House, 11 Gainsborough Road,
London E11 1RS, England

and in the United States of America by
VALLENTINE, MITCHELL AND COMPANY LIMITED
c/o Biblio Distribution Centre,
81 Adams Drive. P.O. Box 327, Totowa. N.J. 07511

British Library Cataloguing in Publication Data
Hadari, Ze'ev
    Voyage to freedom.
    1. Jews—Migrations   2. Palestine—
    History—1929-1948   3. Europe—Emigration
    and immigration—History   4. Palestine
    —Emigration and immigration—History
    I. Title   II. Tsahor, Ze'ev
    304.8'5694'04   JV8749.P3

    ISBN 0-84303-210-6

86·4500

Printed in Great Britain by A. Wheaton & Co. Ltd., Exeter

Contents

List of Illustrations

Acknowledgments

It is our pleasant duty to thank the Ben Gurion University of the Negev which generously allocated the funds for our research; Joseph Tekoa, President of the University at the time of writing, and Shlomo Gazit its current President; the Rectors, Professor Moshe Rosen and Professor David Wolf; the Dean of Humanities and Social Sciences, Professor Ilan Troen; and the Academic Secretary Yair Magen. All showed great interest and offered valuable assistance in our research.

Thanks are also due to the Katzman family whose generosity helped in the completion of the manuscript; to Benjamin Gil for its translation from the Hebrew; to M. Jagendorf and to Ch. Galai for manuscript corrections; and to Jack Israeli of Toronto, Canada, for his constant help.

Z. Hadari
Z. Tsahor

Glossary

Aliyat Noar – an organization dealing with the immigration of children to Israel

Betar – a right-wing youth movement, associated with Etzel (see below).

Dror – a left-wing Zionist youth movement.

Etzel – (acronym) the underground movement led by Menachem Begin, which fought against the British.

General Zionists – a right-wing political party.

Gideons – radio operators in the Mossad Le'Aliya Bet (see below).

Gordonia – a social-democratic youth movement.

Goyim – Jewish term for non-Jewish people.

Ha'aretz – a daily Hebrew newspaper

Hagana – the popular military organization of the Jewish population.

Hamashbir – the distribution and supply organization of the Histadrut (see below)

Hashomer Hatza'ir – kibbutz movement of a revolutionary nature.

Histadrut – the umbrella organization of the labour movement in Israel.

Irgun – shortened form of Irgun Zva'i Leumi (see below).

Irgun Zva'i Leumi – full name of Etzel (see above).

Jewish Agency Directorate – this body acted as the unofficial government of the Jewish settlement.

Joint – shortened form of American Jewish Joint Distribution Agency, a Jewish relief organization in Eastern Europe.

Kibbutz Hameuchad – kibbutz movement of an activist nature.

Lechi – an extremist underground organization which split from Etzel.

Mapai – moderate, social-democratic party.

Mizrachi – moderate religious party.

Moshav – cooperative form of settlement.

Mossad – shortened form of Mossad Le'Aliya Bet (see below)

Mossad Le'Aliya Bet – the organization which operated unauthorized immigration.

Palmach – the organized force of the Hagana (see above).

Palyam – the naval force of the Palmach (see above)

Poale Agudat Yisrael – an extremist religious party.

Poale Zion – an extremist left-wing party.

Revisionist movement – a right-wing party.

Yishuv – the Jews in Palestine up to 1948.

Zim – the national shipping company of Israel

Zionist Congress – conference of the Zionist movement.

Introduction

The wonder that attended the birth of Israel in 1948 has not faded; on the contrary, an increasing number of people seek to understand the events that led to independent statehood. Research into this period has recently revealed the decisive role played by the "illegal" immigration of Jews to Palestine in 1945–48, when the country was under British Mandatory rule. Britain's subsequent withdrawal left the sparse Yishuv – the Jewish Community – to defend itself in its struggle for survival in the War of Independence.

Despite the central function of unauthorized immigration in this story, knowledge of its workings has been scant. The literature has not dealt with the more complex historical analysis of this subject, many of the details of which have still to be revealed when classified files are finally opened. The few studies of the history of unauthorized immigration according to accepted standards of research have been made by non-Israeli historians. Thus, the moving force behind this effort, the Mossad Le'Aliya Beth (organization for "Immigration B", or unauthorized immigration) has not yet been discussed exhaustively. How and why tens of thousands of homeless Jews were conveyed to Palestine, in the face of almost universal opposition, has not yet been clearly explained. How this enormous operation was funded and how it was run by people of no maritime experience remains to be revealed, as do the details of the secret negotiations with governments who permitted the "illegals" to pass through their territory, how the ships were purchased, and more.

Unauthorized immigration began with the end of the Second World War in 1945 and continued until Israel became a state in 1948. It passed through four main periods:

August – December 1945 The first eight boats arrived from Italy and Greece and nearly all their passengers (approximately 1,040) managed to enter Palestine without being caught by the British).

January – July 1946 Eleven boats brought 10,500 immigrants who were interned in the British detention camp at Athlit and released shortly afterwards.

August 1946 – December 1947 The beginning of the expulsion of the immigrants to Cyprus, the U.N. decision and the all-out Arab offensive against Israel. During this time thirty-five ships brought 51,700 immigrants, the vast majority of whom were sent to detention camps in Cyprus. There were heroic episodes during this period, beginning with the *Exodus* affair in July 1947 and culminating in the voyage of the two *Pans*. These were the *Pan York* and the *Pan Crescent* renamed *Kibbutz Galuyot* (Ingathering of the Exiles) and *Atzma'ut* (Independence).

December 1947 – May 1948 Ten boats arrived during the War of Independence with 6,000 immigrants. On 17th May 1948, the two last ships, *Medinat Yisrael* (State of Israel) and *Nitzahon* (Victory) reached the coast of Tel-Aviv to be welcomed by an aerial bombardment.

This book does not try to deal with all the problems, but focuses on one operation out of many – the voyage of the *Pans*. These two boats sailed from Romania in December 1947 carrying 15,236 unauthorized immigrants. They were caught by the British and their passengers transferred to Cyprus.

On the surface, it is a routine story, another account of Jewish refugees making their difficult way home. However, in certain respects the affair of the *Pans* was the climax of unauthorized immigration. The head of the Mossad Le'Aliya Bet, Shaul Avigur, said that the number of immigrants on the ships was greater than the entire annual quota allowed by the British into Palestine. The organization required for the transportation of such a large number of people made it the biggest operation in the history of the Jewish community in Palestine. The drama of the *Pans* was acted out by world leaders at the highest level. In the U.S. President Harry S. Truman and Secretary of State George C. Marshall were involved; in Great Britain, Prime Minister Clement Attlee and Foreign Minister Ernest Bevin, and in the Zionist movement, Chaim Weizmann, David Ben-Gurion, Moshe Sharett (Shertok), Nahum Goldmann and Golda Meir (Meyerson). In addition, the heads of state in Romania, Bulgaria, Turkey, Italy, France and apparently the U.S.S.R. were involved in the affair.

Surprisingly, there was complete unanimity between Western leaders and some of the heads of the Zionist movement in their opposition to the departure of these ships. Nor were the Communist leaders in the U.S.S.R. and Romania happy about the operation; it was receiving too much publicity, influential people were against it and only a small group of Israelis, unknown and without support, obstinately continued to work for this operation which had no political support.

The story took place during the critical time between the UN. decision in favour of the establishment of a Jewish state in Palestine and the outbreak of the War of Independence. The obscure, fluid political situation produced second thoughts in some countries, including the U.S. and made the prospects for the state increasingly doubtful. Bringing the ships at this time, in the face of active opposition by the U.S., Great Britain and, of course, the Arabs, was a crucial decision. This book examines the forces at play in the departure of two refugee ships from Eastern Europe to Israel.

The idea of writing it came from the late Shaul Avigur, head of the Mossad Le'Aliya Bet. Shaul had been involved with the security of the Yishuv for over sixty years and in recognition of his important work, some of which is still classified, he was appointed head of the Mossad Le'Aliya Bet on its foundation in 1938. Even before his official appointment, from as early as 1934, he had been responsible for dozens of ships carrying tens of thousands of unauthorized immigrants from all over the world. After the establishment of the state, when he held a senior position in the Ministry of Defence, he was involved with immigration from enemy countries. And yet, of all the episodes he had participated in, he chose to write a book on the *Pans*.

Before his death, he told some of his close friends about the book and asked for their help. In a conversation with Ze'ev Hadari and others in 1977, he mooted the idea of writing the history of unauthorized immigration as a comprehensive and wide-ranging research project, and showed them the draft outline of a book on the *Pans*. He did not live to write his book and after his death he left a mass of documents, interviews and a draft outline, including twenty lines of notes which were to become the chapter headings for this book.

It is difficult to imagine what form the book would have taken had it been written by Shaul Avigur. It is important to emphasize that it would not have been a collection of memoirs like many books on unauthorized immigration written by immigrants, ship commanders or Mossad emissaries. Shaul was humble, almost ascetic, in his private life and always avoided publicity, and he would not have written a book in order to glorify himself and his exploits. The *Pans* affair was not Shaul Avigur's most important operation and it is hard to believe that he wanted to write an *apologia*. Part of his draft deals with opposition to the voyage of the *Pans* by his beloved brother-in-law, Moshe Sharett, the second Prime Minister of Israel. The close relationship they enjoyed and his sensitivity towards Sharett's historical image and reputation would not have allowed him to do this. Shaul Avigur intended to write a monograph dealing openly and frankly with the *Pans* affair, using documentary sources, in order to explain, by means of one issue in the history of immigration which to a great extent was its climax, the importance of "illegal" immigration to Israel, and the ways in which it was brought about.

In writing this book, Ze'ev (Venia) Hadari, who was at that time Shaul Avigur's assistant and worked with him at Mossad HQ in Paris, has collaborated with Ze'ev Tsahor, a historian specializing in modern Jewish history. This is not a partnership in which the man who "made history" told his story and the historian turned it into a book, but a joint attempt to understand the affair objectively and to produce a complete, integrated picture.

To this end, there were many interviews with Mossad emissaries, ship commanders, immigrants and members of British Intelligence; research literature and memoirs were used as well as newspapers from that time in Israel, Great Britain and the U.S. This material was used mainly for the purposes of illustration, to understand the spirit of that age and to reinforce the story of the operation, but most of the research was based on documentary sources, such as original documents kept in Israel and Great Britain. In some sections of this book these documents are left to speak for themselves and are part of the story. Other important documents are appended in full.

Many people helped in the preparation of this book with encouragement, assistance and reference to documents and sources; evidence of this is the large amount of material on unauthorized immigration and especially on the *Pans* that was collected by the authors.

Thanks are due to the staff of the Hagana Archives, the Israel National Archives, I.D.F. Archives, the Ben-Gurion Institute Archives and the Public Records Office in London for their patience and help. Special thanks for their active cooperation are due to Chaim Sarid, Gershon Rivlin, Chaim Zamir, Dr. Gedalia Jung and Dr. Meir Avizohar.

CHAPTER ONE

In-between Days

A FLUID WORLD

The months leading up to the declaration of the State of Israel in May 1948 were the most decisive in the history of Zionism. It was impossible to predict at the outset what turn events would take. Everything was open. The range of possible solutions to the complex situation in Palestine could have included the whole spectrum of contradictory aims at play in the area, from an independent Arab state to the establishment of a Jewish state in all of Western Palestine.

The most fateful events took place as though in a fog. Everyone was aware that they were living in an interregnum. The Second World War had just ended, leaving mankind shattered and wounded – personally, culturally and economically. The Holocaust inflicted upon the Jewish people showed the depths to which humanity had sunk at a time when education and progress had been expected to bring prosperity to a world where the arts would flourish and human and social relations prosper. Enveloped in this fog were the political processes which everyone could sense but no one could apprehend. The countries of Eastern Europe were under the control of the Red Army, but the process that was to sweep them behind the Iron Curtain was still fluid and the Communist regimes had not yet closed their grip on them. The British were about to give up India, but the dissolution of the Empire was still not apparent. Disturbances and disorder in the Arab countries had not yet attained concrete political significance but contributed to the growing turbulence between two distinct ages.

So did the Holocaust leave turbulence in its wake. The six million – over a third of the Jewish people – who were destroyed in it took with them into the gas chambers the social and cultural traditions and the creativity of a people which had sustained its uniqueness for centuries, enriched the societies around it and contributed to the culture of Europe and America. The Jewish civilization that had been extinguished was also the wellspring of the Zionist movement. Despite its Western organizational structure, Zionism owed its existence to Eastern Europe. Now most of the makers of the Zionist revolution were piles of ashes. Of the six million dead at least two million would probably have been citizens of Israel.[1]

The Holocaust cannot be explained in the conventional terms of reason and history. The Jewish people were too stunned to comprehend what had happened to it. The Yishuv (the Jewish part of Palestine), and particularly the young generation that had grown up in it, were torn by feelings of rage, guilt, helplessness and vengeance. They confronted the destruction uncertain of their way. This uncertainty was shared by the leadership as well. In the face of systematic destruction and the indifference and cynicism of the countries which were not party to it but had refused to offer a shelter to the Jews who tried to escape, there was a feeling of mistrust and a tendency to rely solely on the strength of the Zionist movement. However the movement itself was split into parties which were trying to realize completely different ideological aspirations. Once again there was a stormy controversy over whether to continue to demand a Jewish state in the whole territory of Palestine or to settle for the idea of partitioning the country between the Jews and the Arabs.[2]

Some wanted to fight for a Greater Land of Israel on both banks of the Jordan and others were in favour of a bi-national state. Tensions bristled between David Ben-Gurion, who was then chairman of the Jewish Agency Directorate which acted as the unofficial government of the Yishuv and Chaim Weizmann, who had been president of the Zionist movement for many years. Hostile, even violent, relations brought about a split in the forces in Israel and the establishment of mutually hostile underground movements which, as they struggled against the British, expended time and resources on fighting each other.[3]

Despite the wide range of ideological positions in the Zionist movement, and the internal political struggles in Israel, the scope of activity was desperately narrow. The Holocaust, and the attitude of different countries while it was taking place, proved that Jews had absolutely no influence among the nations and that anti-Semitism was still a central factor in dealing with the Jewish question. The remorse felt towards Jews in post-war Europe was sufficient to facilitate the collection of funds for welfare organizations and medical services, but the limitations of conscience were marked: charity and help for refugees were acceptable, but not at the expense of political factors by which nations might harm their own interests.

The British viewpoint in this matter was traditional and clear. Great Britain, by ruling over a vast empire, was the standard-bearer of progress and culture and therefore brought great benefit to the world.[4] Signs of the dissolution of the Empire, which had started to show before the Second World War,[5] became more pronounced in the light of the changes taking place in Asia and Africa and especially with the decision to grant independence to India.[6] Nonetheless it was still thought that Great Britain, on the basis of its status in the world, had a central role to play among world powers and, particularly, in the Middle East. Great Britain controlled the Suez Canal, oil fields, oil resources, and oil installations and for this purpose she possessed military installations from Iraq to Libya. This whole complex was tenable only by Arab acquiescence and, in an era of developing Arab nationalism, their good will was essential. Great Britain also knew that her very existence as a power depended on her continuing influence in the Middle East, and her influence on good relations with the Arabs who, needless to say, bitterly opposed a Jewish State.

Throughout the history of the Jewish return to the Land of Israel in modern times there had been attempts at reconciliation with the Arabs, initiated either locally, or by the Zionist leadership, or the British authorities.[7] Despite failures and disappointments following continuous Arab violence, the Zionist movement clung tenaciously to the hope of reaching an agreed settlement with the Arabs. However, at this time it was obvious to everyone that Arab opposition to the establishment of a Jewish state was absolute and unambiguous.[8] The Arab leadership was split and torn by internal strife; relations between the Palestinians and the Arab states and among the Arab states themselves were tense, sometimes to the point of open enmity, but they were all united in one matter: their staunch opposition to Zionism. They saw it as an imperialist extension of Europe, and considered the demand for a Zionist state to be an act of European conquest, threatening the fundamental rights of the Arabs. They treated Zionist immigration as a foreign implant, trying arbitrarily and unjustifiably to destroy territorial continuity and to control the Middle East.[9] It became clear that a compromise partition of the country would not be acceptable to the Arabs. Their objection to immigration was unwavering and it was feared that, if it did not stop, there would be an Arab revolt which, like the disturbance towards the end of the thirties, would be directed against the British.[10]

To the Western nations, such a revolt could be disastrous. The U.S.S.R. was giving full attention to establishing Communist regimes in Eastern Europe and creating springboards for intensive Communist penetration in South-East Asia. A horrendous war had just ended and there was already talk of an even more apocalyptic Third World War in which the Western countries would fight the Communist states.[11] Driven by this fear, every country did its best to establish its strength and maintain good relations with potential allies. As a result, the Cold War sabre-rattling between the U.S.S.R. and the West gave birth to the American Marshall Plan which helped rehabilitate Europe. It also eliminated delicate feelings. In face of total war, even Germany, which had so recently and readily accepted Hitler's regime and zealously implemented his evil designs, became the beneficiary of accelerated rehabilitation and generous aid.[12]

The U.S.A. was the main Western power. To counter the Soviet threat it formed an Anglo-American alliance and attempted to establish a firm frontier to stop Russian expansion. Cool political logic also favoured creating a common policy of placating the Arabs. The State Department sided with the British in appeasing the Arabs at the expense of Jewish immigration. However, after much deliberation, the President of the United States, Harry S. Truman, announced that he was in favour of the immigration of one hundred thousand Jewish refugees from concentration camps in German territory.[13] This declaration, which was made on humanitarian grounds, appeared to be influenced by electoral considerations – seeking to obtain the Jewish vote.[14] It created contradictory trends in American policy regarding immigration,[15] and caused tension in relations between Great Britain and the U.S.A. It was also an important way out of the deadlock which trapped the Zionist leadership at that time.

Russian activity after the war may well have been the underlying impetus to British – and to a certain extent – American attitudes to the Arabs and to immigration. It was felt that, in the Middle East, the U.S.S.R. supported the Arabs.[16] Although the U.S.S.R. had not publicly declared its position, its hostile attitude to the Zionist movement and the anti-semitic tendencies revealed during Stalin's regime[17] were an additional reason for thinking so: in 1943 the U.S.S.R. established relations with Egypt, in 1944 with Syria, Lebanon and Iraq and, in 1945–46, supported Syria and Lebanon against the French.[18] Clearly, the U.S.S.R. was also aware of the rising power of the Arabs, the existence of oil fields and military installations in their countries and their potential role in the tense relations between East and West. For this reason, Soviet support for the establishment of a Jewish state, as expressed in Andrei Gromyko's speech to the U.N. General Assembly on 14 May, 1947, was a stunning surprise.[19]

With hindsight, one can understand that the short-lived Russian support for the Zionist movement sprang from the global struggle between East and West; there was a common element in Soviet support for the independence of Egypt, Syria, Lebanon and Iraq and support for the establishment of a Jewish state, namely, an ambition to destabilise the British position in the Middle East.[20] Stalin's attempt to gain support among American Jews for a diplomatic rapprochement between the U.S.S.R. and the U.S.A. and thereby stir up trouble among the Western powers, should also be seen in this light. Possibly Stalin thought that the Zionist state, once established, would remember with gratitude Russian support for its creation and establish friendly relations.[21] In any event, in view of the complicated political situation in the Middle East, the U.S.S.R. considered that the problem of Palestine could act as a catalyst in the breaking-up of the West. The U.S.S.R. thus had an interest in encouraging the flow of Jews from Eastern Europe to the areas occupied by the Allies in Austria and Germany, by this means hoping to ferment perpetual unrest in the Middle East, in the relations between Great Britain and the Arabs, and between Great Britain and the U.S.A.[22] This was done continuously, but indirectly. At that time, the U.S.S.R. was still recovering from the war. It had not yet developed the atomic bomb but wanted to establish supremacy over Eastern Europe and so did not dare openly challenge Great Britain and the U.S.A. When, later, it wanted to answer Israel's desperate appeal for arms, it did so through Czechoslovakia. Prior to this, when it wanted to maintain constant ferment in the Middle East by encouraging the flow of Jews to Mandatory Palestine, it did so with extreme caution through Romania and Bulgaria.

A NON-INSTITUTED INSTITUTION

It was the great misfortune of the Zionist movement that the British Foreign Minister after the war was Ernest Bevin. It is of course impossible to know how a different Foreign Minister might have acted but Bevin's attitude was particularly hostile and extreme. Officially, Palestine was under the aegis of the Colonial Minister, at that time,

Creech Jones, while overall responsibility rested with the Prime
Minister, Clement Attlee. In fact, the Foreign Minister stamped his
imprint on the problem and decided all moves. Golda Meir claimed
that Bevin was possessed by anti-semitism to the point of hysteria,
sometimes resulting in a loss of balanced judgement.[23] His most
striking characteristic was obstinacy. An authoritative historian has
noted that once Bevin took any decision he was subsequently unable to
change his mind.[24] His decisions on the Zionist question were taken
hastily and without understanding[25] the problems. Refusing to retreat
from his position that the solution to the Jewish problem and
Mandatory Palestine were not necessarily connected, Bevin declared
that he was "mortgaging his political future" on his promise to settle
the problem,[26] and he set out to combat Zionism. When the leadership
of the Yishuv realized their solution would not come from Britain, they
turned to activities in which they could depend solely upon
themselves. These included underground movements in Palestine and
forced entry into the country by means of unauthorized immigration.
Bevin did not understand the plight of the Jewish refugees in the
concentration camps in Europe and regarded these developments as a
provocation and an exploitation of their condition for the political ends
of the Zionist leaders. In his view, violent opposition to Great Britain
served to undermine her international position and erode the power of
the West to counteract Communism.

The Yishuv saw Bevin as a hard and wily enemy. He represented the
"perfidious Albion" which, in 1939, had reneged on the Balfour
Declaration by issuing the White Paper which forbade immigration
and the purchase of land in Palestine. It was impossible to forget the
intransigence of Great Britain when it closed the gates of Mandatory
Palestine to beleaguered people attempting to flee Nazi ovens. While
the Zionist leadership was still attempting reconciliation with
Whitehall,[27] the Yishuv had begun treating the local administration as
a foreign conqueror. At the end of 1945 the Hagana (a semi-military
underground organization) joined in the armed struggle against the
British.[28] The revolt did not last long. The explosion at the King David
Hotel, perpetrated by the Irgun (an unofficial right-wing underground organization) in July 1946 caused such enormous loss of life
that it aroused antipathy to violence of this kind.[29] And "Black
Saturday" with mass-arrests of hundreds of members of underground
and political organizations in June of the same year, which coincided
with the establishment of the Anglo-American Committee to find a

solution to the problem,[30] raised doubts about the right method of fighting for a Jewish state. Only in one area was there almost complete unanimity – immigration, and even this was "illegal" from the British point of view. The beginning of this immigration, defined in official documents as Aliya Bet (Immigration "B"), predated the British Mandate since a large proportion of the early settlers had come without authorization from the earlier Turkish administration and were illegal residents.[31] During the time of the British Mandate there was a steady flow of unauthorized immigrants alongside those who were granted official entry permits. Gradually, this hidden immigration became institutionalized. Up to the outbreak of the war some fifty ships had reached the shores of the country, carrying over twenty thousand unauthorized immigrants, organized in the main by the Hagana, the Revisionist Movement (representing right-wing elements) and private elements.[32]

The aura surrounding unauthorized immigration did not stem from its glorious successes but from the dark side of its activities during the war. Between 1939 and 1945 only twenty-four ships, with 16,500 immigrants,[33] sailed from the Black Sea and only a few of them reached the coast of Palestine to land their passengers safely. Some sank on the high seas overloaded with passengers. The names of ships became watchwords in the struggle for independence: the *Struma*, apparently sunk by a Soviet submarine after being expelled from Turkey, and the *Patria*, sunk by the Hagana in Haifa port in protest, became symbols of immigration at any cost. Responsibility for unauthorized immigration was in the hands of the Mossad Le'Aliya Bet (organization implementing Immigration "B" or unauthorized immigration), headed by Shaul Meirov (later Avigur). The Mossad, as it was known, with a daring group of emissaries from Palestine, had built up a complex system of contacts that was to operate most effectively after the war. From the end of 1945 up to the establishment of the State of Israel in 1948, a period of less than three years, it had sent sixty-five ships with seventy thousand illegal immigrants to Israel. One ship, the *Ben Hecht*, was sent by the Irgun.[34] The increased immigration played a key role in the struggle for independence. It became the focus of world attention, necessitating enormous efforts by the British forces in the country. Most important, tens of thousands of immigrants, mostly young, quickly became an integral part of the fighting force defending the young state that was to emerge from a hard-won war of independence. This struggle for immigration demanded great efforts and resources. A widespread system known as the Bricha (escape) operated inside Europe to direct the stream of Jewish displaced persons (DPs) to transit camps near the coast – particularly the Mediterranean coast. Setting up camps and maintaining thousands of refugees required a further system of emissaries, as well as the purchasing and equipping of ships, the locating of professional crews to sail them, the establishment of a sophisticated communication network (known as the Gideons) and the training of commanders. These tasks were carried out in difficult conditions and required large sums of money.

Headed by Avigur, the Mossad created the organizational framework needed to bring in unauthorized immigrants. It sent emissaries from Israel, mainly kibbutz members, to handle the organizational and administrative side of purchasing and preparing the ships, boarding the immigrants and taking them to Israel. The Mossad was, in fact, autonomous. Due to the distance, the secret nature of operations and the need for improvisation and speedy decisions, the Mossad had full authority regarding method of immigration, number of immigrants, countries of origin, level of resistance to the British, and negotiations with governments of the countries from which the ships were to sail, etc. Invested with such a high degree of responsibility, the Mossad went far beyond organization and management to determine the ideology and policy of unauthorized immigration.

Another level of operative sprang from the immigrants themselves. There was a vast distance between their desire to go to Israel and their ability to achieve this goal. Some of them were still in concentration and extermination camps in Germany, while others had escaped along secret routes from Eastern Europe. On their long and arduous route, small groups had emerged who were to share in the exhausting and daunting process of immigration to Palestine.[35] At the centre of these groups were usually graduates of the pioneering youth movements who had been brought up in the Zionist heritage and had bold ideas about building a new sovereign society. On the way from their starting point to the transit camps from which they would leave for Palestine, an internal leadership developed among the immigrants. This helped to consolidate the group and to infuse it with the spiritual strength that would be needed when the ships encountered difficulties on the way, perhaps involving physical resistance to the British. These were the people who were put in charge of food, water, discipline and order in the camps and, later, on the ships.

Another important group was the local Jewish leadership. In France, Italy, and even Romania, pangs of conscience after the war moved some of the surviving members of the community to serve as spokesmen for the plight of the Jews. In the West, most survivors were Jewish businessmen, while in Eastern Europe they were predominantly Jewish members of the Communist Party. Both groups helped the Mossad operatives in different ways, sometimes enthusiastically and sometimes with reservations. A non-Jewish element should also be mentioned: senior officials and local activists who, for a variety of reasons, cooperated in unauthorized immigration, sometimes endangering their own public positions. The stories of many ships are linked to the daring exploits of individuals, some of whom acted to atone for the Holocaust, and others out of hatred of the British. Some acted simply out of a wish to get rid of the Jews in their country and others helped in return for substantial bribes.

The wide range of operatives and collaborators had different and sometimes contradictory aims. These fell into three broad categories. The first involved senior government officials or leaders of the Jewish community in the country of origin; theirs were humanitarian aims such as fulfilling the hopes of the Jews still remaining in concentration camps to go to Israel. They also had internal objectives; the refugee camps were a burden and even a threat to good order in a country trying to rehabilitate itself. There were countries, such as France and Romania, which had a score to settle with the British. The French blamed Great Britain for their expulsion from Syria and Lebanon while Romania, which had become Communist, saw Great Britain as an imperialist power to be challenged.

The second involved the leadership of the Zionist movement which was then fighting to maintain its position. Its strength had, in the past, depended on cooperation with Great Britain and was now being crushed by the force of global interests and the struggle between the Great Powers. Its demands had gradually decreased since the Biltmore Programme, formulated in the U.S.A. in 1942, demanded the establishment of an independent Jewish entity in the whole of Palestine.[36] It was now prepared to accept only a part of the country,[37] and even this had very little prospect of realization at the time. The existence of Jewish refugees was therefore of major political importance. The world that had been silent and indifferent to the destruction of a people now had to solve their problem, and the solution lay in granting them a home for themselves.[38] These refugees were to draw the focus of world opinion on Zionist demands. The Zionist movement successfully drew world attention to the human drama of the ships, harnessing favourable public opinion to the Zionist cause. Looking back, it appears that the role of the *Exodus* in the history of the establishment of the state was no less significant than the many years' work of Zionist leaders or, for that matter, the audacious exploits of the underground movements.[39] Even after the establishment of the state, the immigration myth, as embodied in the *Exodus*, was an excellent propaganda weapon for the young country.[40]

The third ideological area revolved around the Yishuv. The Jewish community in Mandatory Palestine after the Second World War numbered less than 600,000. The struggle against the British and the Arabs had highlighted this numerical disadvantage. Ben-Gurion, who took over the Jewish Agency defence portfolio in 1946,[41] made a far-reaching assumption, later substantiated, that the Yishuv should expect war not only with the Palestinian Arabs, but with all the Arab states. This evaluation served as an excuse for the impatience which typified the Mossad's activities: "We must hurry and send more and more people to Israel, by whatever means we can." "Every extra person is an extra soldier." Training was carried out in the transit camps and in the detention camp in Cyprus where immigrants who had failed to gain entry into Palestine were interned. The Yishuv leaders also wanted to develop the country, and immigrants were the main source of a renewed settlement drive.

Tension flared between the various bodies involved in unauthorized immigration because of the different degrees of importance they ascribed to it. Those to whom humanitarian considerations – the plight of the refugees – were paramount were prepared to moderate their activities and listen to proposals other than immigration to Israel. Those whose prime objective was political wanted to emphasize the drama of immigration. Those who aimed at strengthening the Yishuv wanted immigration immediately and by any means. Clashes between different objectives were inevitable and these were manifest in the affair of the *Pans*.

BLIND ALLEY

The confrontation between the Zionist movement and Great Britain, which held the Mandate over Palestine, took place on three parallel planes; the diplomatic battle in Europe and the U.S.; the armed struggle in Mandatory Palestine; and the conflict between British warships and old, rotting boats filled with refugees on their way to Israel in the Mediterranean.

In the naval war, the British did not have a chance. The powerful image of a British flotilla of destroyers and frigates, armed and ready for combat, attacking a rotten ship crammed with helpless refugees who had survived the death camps and escaped by the skin of their teeth,[42] left the British at a loss to explain their harsh attitude. It was impossible to sink the ships and there was nowhere to send them back to. World opinion supported the underdog and followed the exciting stories of unauthorized immigration faithfully reported in the media. Great Britain was squeezed between the Arab threat and the indirect strength of the Jewish refugees stranded on the water.

The British authorities wanted to avoid this hopeless battle and took preventive action. British diplomatic representatives in the various European countries put pressure on their governments to prohibit the flow of Jewish refugees and the activities of the Mossad; they asked that governments reveal the whereabouts of the transit camps and block the departure of ships from their shores. This pressure was strong and fairly effective. Despite their interest in seeing Jewish refugees leave their shores, and the pleasure they took in Britain's misfortune and in a modest revenge, countries such as Italy and France did restrict such activities.

Another deterrent was the work of the British secret agents who were dispersed throughout Europe in order to locate and disrupt the transfer of Jews to Palestine, and who sometimes even sabotaged installations and ships. Pressure was also exerted on potential immigrants. The British authorities announced that even after their dangerous journey the immigrants would not succeed in entering Palestine. Most of the ships were captured and, from the summer of 1946, would-be immigrants were taken to detention camps in Cyprus. From there, a trickle were allowed into Palestine, according to existing quotas granted to the Jewish Agency. The effort the British put into sabotaging immigration severely hampered its organization. It impeded the transfer of people and the acquisition of ships and professional crews to sail them and it hampered assembly and embarkation. However, this did not weaken the flow of immigrants pushing from below, nor the determination, initiative and resourcefulness of the Mossad emissaries. Great Britain was therefore obliged to tackle the problem on the publicity level.

A reliable British historian attributes the victory of the Zionist movement to its ability to "sell" its ideas to European and American public opinion. He ignores the objective validity of the claims which were made to the public at the time, claiming that the Zionist information system was infinitely better than Arab or British propaganda.[43] As opposed to the plight of the persecuted Jew, languishing in the death camps of Europe and yearning for a home of his own, British propaganda spoke of the "illegality" of his entry into Mandatory Palestine, the contraventions of international shipping laws and the irresponsibility of the immigration operatives in sending people to sea in rotten boats.[44] Sometimes these claims sounded like Balaam's curse which became a blessing for Israel. It was easy to dismiss the British position of trying to protect life at sea as pious hypocrisy. The British argument that immigration would upset the delicate equilibrium in the Middle East[45] could not stand against the poignant image of the Jewish refugee. Public opinion also tended to ignore the British claim that illegal immigration was conducted by doubtful elements at inflated prices through "the Jewish black market",[46] because if the British were trying to stop immigration, it was natural that the Jews should find secret ways where people were ready to take advantage of the situation.

When these arguments had failed, British propaganda adopted a theme calculated to strike fear to the hearts of the public in Western Europe and the U.S.A. – Communism. Thus they claimed that immigration, which came partly from Eastern European ports, was a Russian tool by means of which Communists would stream into Palestine: they were armed and intended to establish a bridgehead for Soviet expansion towards the sensitive installations of the Middle East.[47]

As we have noted, this battle was lost. The revelations at the Nuremberg trials, with their horrific accounts of the extermination camps, coupled with the fact that tens of thousands of Jews were still living in concentration camps one and two years after the war, proved stronger than the British arguments. President Truman, in favouring (despite Bevin's fury) the immigration of one hundred thousand refugees living in these camps, gave expression to the general mood. Britain had reached a dead end.

In this situation, faced with Arab threats and Jewish pressure, the British decided to hand the problem over to the U.N. Referral to this organization seemed a rational move. In 1922 Britain had received

Palestine from the League of Nations as a temporary mandate and not as a British colony with the purpose of developing it for the implementation of the Balfour Declaration. Volumes of commentary have been written on the Balfour Declaration,[48] the way it was obtained and its political and legal significance.[49] It could, therefore, be interpreted according to changing circumstances, but at this time it was absolutely clear that the idea embodied in the Mandate, by any interpretation, had not been implemented and that Britain did not know how to do so. On 2 April, 1947 Britain requested Trygve Lie, Secretary General of the U.N., to call a special meeting of the General Assembly to discuss the problem of Palestine.[50] The U.N. was the natural heir to the League of Nations, and Britain correctly turned to the body that had originally authorized her to now relieve her of the moral responsibility and, more important, of the price in blood and prestige that it was paying in that ungrateful country.

Needless to say, behind this "natural" step lay political considerations. When Bevin brought the matter to the U.N. General Assembly he had no idea it would decide in favour of partition and the establishment of a Jewish state.[51] Every junior official in his department knew that such a decision required a two-thirds majority, and the Arab world, the neutral countries and the Communist Bloc were opposed to it. The appeal to the U.N. was intended to renew international authorization for British control over Palestine and the cancellation of previous obligations, especially that embodied in the mandate to the Zionist movement. There was real pressure on the Zionist movement in this appeal to the U.N. which was intended to force the Zionists to moderate their demands and submit to renewed British dictates. Some leaders of the movement feared a state of complete anarchy which could endanger everything that had been achieved in the Yishuv.[52]

On 14 May, 1947, a year before the establishment of the State of Israel, British hopes of the U.N. suddenly collapsed. The great surprise, and one of the crucial events in the history of the establishment of the state, was the speech of Andrei Gromyko, the Soviet representative to the U.N. Soviet ideology had always been hostile towards Zionism and the rationale of its diplomatic processes suggested a pro-Arab policy. All the more remarkable then, when Gromyko cited the "immeasurable pain and suffering of the Jews in the last war". He deplored the hardships facing them now that the war had ended. Since the West had proved helpless to protect the basic rights of the Jewish people and to defend it from fascist murderers the only solution now was to allow them to fulfil their dream of sovereign statehood.

This development produced the UNSCOP Committee which was sent to Mandatory Palestine to study the problem and submit its recommendations for a solution to the U.N. The Committee returned to New York after over three months of investigations and, by a majority, proposed the partition of the country. On 29 November, 1947 the General Assembly convened and agreed by a decisive majority to the partition of Mandatory Palestine and the establishment of a Jewish State in the Western part of the country. The half-year between the special session of the General Assembly and the decision in favour of the establishment of the state saw the decline of Ernest Bevin.[53] His behaviour as a humiliated and beaten man seeking vengeance affected all areas of government and caused a bitter escalation of the struggle. During this period, the execution of members of Lechi and Etzel (right-wing underground fighters) was carried out by the British and the drama of the *Exodus* took place, when Bevin, against the advice of more balanced officials,[54] decided to return the refugees on the ship to their country of origin, Germany, and finally, in the face of the indignation of the international press and the scorn of the enlightened world, sent them back to the German concentration camps,[55] – the death rattle of the British administration.

However, it would seem that, behind his rage and malevolence, Bevin was trying to obtain political advantage and salvage the trampled honour of Great Britain. There were two discernible stages in this period: the first, up to the U.N. decision for Partition at the end of November 1947, and the second, from that decision up to the establishment of the State of Israel on 15 May, 1948.

In the first stage, which began to gain momentum with Gromyko's speech, it was still impossible to predict how the matter would end. Britain, trying to improve its position in the U.N., wanted to prove that it was in control of the situation. It wished to show the UNSCOP committee, which was then in Palestine, that the prevailing disorder was due to the violent behaviour of the underground movements and the continuation of illegal immigration: the counter-measures became more aggressive and even more provocative.

The second stage, after the decision for partition, was the period of escalation. Bevin, who had exhausted his rage in the *Exodus* affair, decided to adopt a policy of non-cooperation in the implementation of

the U.N. decision on partition. This could have been an expression of
his deep personal frustration but, beyond that, there were once again
political considerations. The reports from the British ambassadors in
the Arab states were unequivocal; they warned Bevin of increasing
ferment directed against Britain.[56] The Arab complaints, as revealed in
those reports, were against the compromising and even favourable
attitude[57] of the administration towards immigration and they
contained a clear threat. Bevin, defeated and disgraced, had turned his
resentment of the U.N., America, and of course the Jews into a
political rationale. The U.N. had decided in favour of partition but
there was no reason why the British should pull their chestnuts out of
the fire. Time and events would tell, he warned; the Jews had made
their bed and they must lie in it.[58] His political reasoning was that if
Britain did not implement the decision of partition it would
demonstrate distance from the idea of establishing a Jewish state and
thereby maintain good relations with the Arabs. This would avoid
endangering British interests in the Middle East and save the lives of
soldiers: Britain had had enough of the unhappy role of policeman
between two implacable groups. Beyond this rational consideration
there might have been hidden hopes of revenge. If Great Britain
remained opposed to and did not help to implement Partition, it would
have no chance of becoming an established fact. The plot hatched by
the U.S. and the U.S.S.R., which Bevin regarded as an act of
treachery, might even fall. If this happened, they would come back and
beg Britain to restore order in the Middle East and then Bevin would
be able to dictate his own terms and restore his honour.[59] It is difficult
to ascertain whether this was the decisive reason, but there was clearly
a combination of political judgement and a feeling of personal insult.
In any event, the British policy of "non-cooperation" with Partition
included meticulous observance of the *status quo* in Palestine:
continuation of the strict prohibition against military organization and
arms purchases and, most important, the blockade of the coast against
Jewish immigration. But these were a matter of life and death to the
emerging state. Despite the U.N. decision on partition, the Arabs had
initiated violent actions against the Yishuv[60] and despite Ben-Gurion's
earlier prediction that such actions were to be expected, the Yishuv
was not prepared to deal with them.[61]

There was a real possibility that, with the actual establishment of the
state, the armies of the Arab nations would invade and Israel would be
stillborn. The prospects of defence and even victory depended on the

acquisition of weapons and additional manpower for the army, now being built up. There were glorious exploits in the area of arms purchase and in the organization of groups of Jewish fighters,[62] but most important of all were the reserves waiting in the transit camps in Europe and the detention camps in Cyprus.

All the parties – the Arabs, the British and the Jews – ascribed prime significance to immigration. During the critical year from the middle of 1947 to the establishment of the state all the diplomatic decisions and processes had been made and carried through, but the contradictions and conflicts of interest remained and the final outcome would be decided only by physical combat. In the anticipated conflict every extra man would count, because the Yishuv was a minuscule fraction of the combined Arab population of Palestine and the neighbouring states. In Europe was a potential force of hundreds of thousands of Jews which could determine the outcome of the war.

Thus, the Yishuv was obviously concerned about maintaining unauthorized immigration, despite the fact that a state would soon come into being, when they would be able to bring in as many immigrants as they wanted without breaking the law. However, for the very same reasons, the Arabs wanted to prevent immigration, and since the issue was so important from their point of view the British were also compelled to combat it to the very end, on grounds that Bevin considered to be in the British interest.

All moves and considerations by opposing sides during that fateful year were concentrated on the affair of the two ships, the *Pan York* and *Pan Crescent*.

From the Arab point of view they contained an extremely significant addition to the Zionist forces; the 15,236 immigrants on these ships numbered more than the population of Ramat Gan, which was then a relatively large urban settlement with 12,500 inhabitants; each one of the two ships carried more people than Natanya, another urban settlement which then had 6,500 residents;[63] the whole cooperative agricultural Moshav movement comprising 63 settlements had only 8,000 members.[64] It should be noted that when independence was declared, the whole mobilized force, including members of front-line settlements, only numbered 29,900 soldiers.[65] The number of passengers on the *Pans* was equal to the number of all the unauthorized immigrants that had reached the country on the twenty-four immigrant ships that had sailed from Europe during the whole of the Second World War.[66] Clearly then, the Yishuv demanded that great efforts be made to bring these immigrants in. According to the logic of the complex Palestinian triangle, British political advantage lay in maintaining the *status quo* and preventing the arrival of these ships at any price. Those other aspects already mentioned, which produced such bitter confrontations over illegal immigration, were magnified because of the particularly large number of immigrants and because of the timing. Now that the U.N. had decided in favour of establishing a Jewish state the British could claim that Palestine was in the hands of the U.N. and the problem was nearing a solution; therefore the continuation of illegal immigration constituted wrongful pressure which could place the diplomatic processes at risk. As will be seen below, this argument produced reactions in the Zionist camp – and so these ships, sailing to Israel on the eve of the establishment of the state, embodied and typified the drama and the ideology of all immigration to Israel.

CHAPTER TWO

Banana Boats

"FIX THE BRITISH, INC."

In the Israeli consciousness, America was the rival of Zionism. Immigration activists were mostly children of the first generation of pioneers who had left their homes in Eastern Europe and gone to Palestine. This was in the opposite direction to the main-stream which immigrated westwards from the Jewish Pale of Settlement to America. The decision to immigrate to Palestine signified a rejection of temptation to the fleshpots, and the attitude to those who had opted for America[1] was duly scornful. Even after the Second World War, when it was obvious that, with the gates of the U.S.S.R. closed, American Jewry had become the main reservoir of its people and the central power in organizational and economic terms, their brothers in Palestine were unable to overcome the feeling of scorn and mistrust towards them.

Leaders of the labour movement such as Ben-Gurion and Ben Zvi,[2] Berl Katznelson,[3] Chaim Arlozoroff and even Enzo Sereni,[4] who had spent some time in the U.S., contributed to this attitude. Their letters and reports described a business-oriented Jewish life-style as well as alienation from and coldness towards Israel and its emissaries. These emissaries, who had been brought up in the warmth of traditional Eastern European Jewish fellow-feeling, and the close companionship of kibbutz and the Zionist movement, conveyed their misgivings about American Jewry to the immigration operatives.

The new focus on America was due to the transition from small boats to larger vessels. In two years they had progressed from the fishing boat *Dalin* of twenty-five tons displacement and thirty-five passenger capacity to the *Pans*, each with a displacement of 4,500 tons and carrying over 7,500 passengers. This development demanded a basic change in the approach to unauthorized immigration.

In post-war Europe it was difficult to buy ships. Control over their purchase was in government hands and the supply of big ships was limited. For this reason small fishing boats were first used, either hired or purchased by the Mossad. Costs were relatively low and it was hoped that small boats would have a better chance of dodging the British blockade. However when nearly all these boats were caught by the British and calculations showed that the cost per passenger was very high, it was decided to bring in larger numbers of immigrants in bigger ships. This would create more difficulty for the British because of the strong political impact created by thousands of homeless immigrants. In addition, larger numbers of them would exceed the quota of certificates that had been allocated by the authorities. British figures for the total permitted to enter were to exclude the number of illegal immigrants caught, thus reducing the significance of entering by force.

When the Mossad decided to buy large ships, some of the emissaries set out for the unexplored shores of America. The metamorphosis of the Mossad emissary, the kibbutznik clad in khaki shorts and plucked straight from the fields, into the button-down-collared, pin-stripe-suited American ship buyer became the subject of great mirth in the kibbutz and American shipping circles.

Ze'ev Shind was an example of the ploughman-cum-shipping-magnate. A member of kibbutz Ayelet Hashachar, he was sent by the Mossad to buy ships in the U.S. In New York, he established a Pan-American shipping concern, the F.B. Shipping Company, and though F.B. stood for "Fuck the British", a business-like, respectable image belied its purpose. Everything was run according to the rules, thanks to Shind's "collaborators" from the powerful American Jewish community. In the affair of the *Pans* three people must be mentioned – Morris Ginsburg, owner of the American Foreign Steamship Company, Joe Buchsenbaum and Paul Shulman.[5] When describing Mossad members there are certain characteristics that spring to mind. They were generally young, kibbutz-affiliated, confident of their mission, loyal to the Mossad, discreet and utterly dedicated to their work. They were willing members of a society with collective values and a staunch belief in the authority of the group. Their American partners came from an individualistic free-enterprise society which placed great stock on status symbols and was reserved in its attitude to ideologies, but the three Americans who took part in the adventure of the *Pans* did not conform to this image. They were ready to do the practical work connected with unauthorized immigration, they had an appetite for adventure and were Zionists at heart. Involved in shipping, an occupation where there were very few Jews, they were ideally placed to help.

In his report after the sailing of the *Pans*, Ze'ev Shind described them:

> Buying the two ships, checking them professionally, eliciting the promise that we would not be caught (which would be very easy), running the whole undercover operation in America, getting the supplies and the people to work the two ships, setting in motion the complicated machinery of looking after them – we did not use the set-up that we had in America and which had worked with all the other ships that we sent. In this operation we were helped by a number of friends who are an integral part of our set-up and of our group although they are not with us now. I must mention them and express our appreciation for their help because without it we probably could not have got the ships out of America when we did.
>
> At that time, when we were in a very difficult situation as a result of the *Exodus* and other ships, we had to start working on the two ships and get them going. There is a man in America that nobody here knows, apart from the Americans. His name is Morris Ginsburg and it is impossible to imagine how much time and work he put into this. In America time is more precious than money. He gave all his time, his contacts, his knowledge and professional experience to this task unreservedly.
>
> I also want to mention a second friend who some of our people have already met, Paul Shulman. He is a young war veteran, a graduate of the most important naval college in the world, Annapolis. He supports us and does everything he can to help. In America there are many Jews who are prepared to help Jews – they give one or ten thousand dollars but nothing else. Very few Jews are prepared to give more than dollars. Shulman is a rare phenomenon. He has wealthy parents and studied for six years at the best college in America and he has let us use his name in our work. He is the official owner of the two ships that we bought and his name has come in very useful. He is a well-known financier and did not come to us as a stranger. He has a house in Stanford and a factory and other very important holdings. This helps us fool the English because no emissary from Israel has such advantages. Paul Shulman entered into this with complete dedication and worked with us up to the last moment even though this was very difficult

without knowing Hebrew, which became so necessary later on.[6]

There were others who played vital roles in this operation. The brothers Morris and Kalman Ginsburg, owners of a shipping company, referred potential clients to the new firm, giving it a further stamp of legitimacy. Ralph Goldman helped recruit crew members and Captain Ash, as head of the professional association of engineering officers, found the necessary members to complete the crews of the two ships. Their dedication and, above all, the confident, orderly and professional way in which they worked amazed the heads of the Mossad. The influence of this contact with American men of action, prepared to run risks for the sake of the Zionist ideal and to take an active part in areas of security, went beyond the affair of the *Pans*. After a long tradition of suspicion by the defence heads of the Yishuv towards the Americans, who were considered stony-hearted and mercenary, their acquaintance with the group of Americans who were active in the *Pans* affair altered this perception considerably. After the affair was over Ben-Gurion sent a cable to Moshe Sharett in the U.S. asking him to send "two or three Jewish shipping experts" and added, "Can Paul Shulman come at once?"[7] Shulman arrived soon after and in November 1948 Ben-Gurion made him a general. Although he did not know any Hebrew, he was appointed the first commander of the navy.[8]

Cooperation between Ze'ev Shind and the Americans had begun before the purchase of the ships. Two relatively new Corvettes were bought and refitted in the U.S. and one of them, the *President Garfield*, sailed to Israel from France in July 1947 and became known to the whole world as the *Exodus*. By the time the *Pans* were purchased, the kibbutznik Ze'ev Shind had become an expert on shipping, marine insurance, armament of ships and the recruitment of seamen. He now wanted to be even more audacious than before, to buy larger ships, refit them more effectively and carry many more immigrants. However, at this stage the operation became more complicated. The world economy was beginning to recover from the post-war depression, the demand for ships increased and so did their price. At the same time, the British had learnt about the big ships, how they were bought and operated and how significant a number of immigrants they could bring into the country. They decided to concentrate on preventative action – disrupting the purchase, preparation and refitting of the ships.

In order to utilize large vessels and overcome British pressure in the U.S., Ze'ev Shind needed the help of another American Jew, Sam Zemurray, an exceptional figure in this band of "conspirators" for the Zionist cause. Zemurray personified the American success story, rising from penury to ownership of the United Fruit Company, the largest importer of bananas in the world with land in Central America, vast banana plantations and of course a shipping company to carry the produce. Ze'ev Shind applied to this company to buy two banana boats. He was assisted at this time by Davidke Nameri of Kibbutz Ashdot Yaakov, a Mossad representative in the U.S. Shind showed great perspicacity regarding immigration. He chose banana boats because of their internal structure, designed to transport as many bananas as possible and provide proper ventilation. He felt that what was suitable for the safe storage of ripening bananas would be suitable for his kind of cargo – immigrants. Another important factor was that the ships were high in the water, making it difficult for the British to board them at sea as they had done in the past by suddenly approaching them with a destroyer or a corvette. Shind and Nameri thought such action would be impossible with these ships because they were higher than the British craft that would be waiting for them in the Eastern Mediterranean.

Shind and Nameri's political and military judgement were astute but they lacked business acumen. They bought the ships at the fairly steep price of $200,000 each.[9] At the time of the purchase, when they appeared as directors of the F.B. Company, they did not think of hinting to the Jewish owners what these initials stood for, since the negotiations were handled by the director of Zemurray's shipping company who was, inevitably, an Englishman who had served in British naval intelligence on the American coast during the Second World War.[10] This patriotic Englishman could not have fathomed that he was selling ships that would cause considerable trouble for his country, and the efforts to prevent them from sailing would involve his former colleagues in the intelligence service in an intensive operation throughout Europe that would place his government in contact with half the countries of Europe as well as the U.S. In any event, this piquant aspect of the negotiations almost certainly cost a great deal of money because Shind eventually met Zemurray himself and had to tell him why he wanted to buy the ships. Although in his report to the Mossad, Shind claimed that Zemurray would not have lowered the price even if the negotiations had been conducted with him directly, some of the Mossad operatives estimated that they could have saved at least $100,000 on the deal.[11] The meeting between Shind and Zemurray took place in dramatic circumstances. It is described by Meir Weisgal, the flamboyant and charismatic lobbyist for the Zionist cause:

> On one of my rare Sabbath days of rest I was interrupted by the intrusion of a young Jew, Danny [his underground name] Shind,[12] who was one of the most remarkable people involved in this business and in all activities connected with illegal immigration into Palestine. It was to Danny Shind, in fact, that Weizmann had given over the first £500 after the war for the renewal of illegal immigration. He died, unfortunately, shortly after the establishment of the state.
>
> Danny's interruption was curt and decisive: "We're going to New Orleans." The idea did not immediately appeal to me. "When?" I asked. "Right now," he answered. As I reluctantly packed my toothbrush he explained the purpose of our mission. Three ships had been purchased in South and Central American countries and refitted in Philadelphia for illegal immigration. Under some kind of pressure from the Americans or British, or blackmail – no one knew exactly – they were not allowed to move out of Philadelphia. The man who could help us was a Jew from New Orleans by the name of Samuel Zemurray. I happened to know Zemurray – which was not his major asset, but happened to be mine at the moment. He had started out in life peddling bananas on a pushcart, and at this juncture in history was the President of the United Fruit Company, which practically owned half of Central America. He knew all the ins and outs of Central American shipping, including the "bosses" at the docks and the government officials who could be persuaded for a consideration. It was clearly a matter which we could not conduct by telephone from New York, so off we went.
>
> It was as miserable a trip as I ever made, sitting up all night in a plane trying to figure out how we could locate the man as it was Sunday. When we arrived in New Orleans we could not get a room at a hotel, so we conducted our negotiations from a phone booth. There was no answer from Zemurray's home; we tried several of his friends, but no one knew where he was spending the weekend. We stood for hours in a suffocating phone booth, pleading with

operators and exchanges not to give up the search. Finally we learned that Mr. Zemurray was at his retreat, sixty miles from New Orleans, in a lodge with an unlisted number. At this stage I was informed by the head telephone supervisor that he was forbidden to reveal the number. I told him that it was a question of life and death for thousands of people. I said to him: "Don't give me the number if it's against the rules. You can call him and tell him who is at the other end of the line. If he refuses the call, nothing is lost. If he agrees, let him call me here in the phone booth." In about ten minutes the phone rang; it was Zemurray, and I experienced an ecstasy of deliverance. By this time Danny was so agitated that I had to support him physically into the car which I hired at Mr. Zemurray's insistence and expense. We were on our way. We finally arrived after surviving sixty miles of a suffocating humidity compounded by a deluge. Zemurray heard us out, snorted a few times, and finally said: "Give so-and-so $10,000, so-and-so $5,000," and after a brief pause, "and so-and-so $7,500." He explained: "It's less than $10,000 and more than $5,000. That's his place in the hierarchy."[13]

In writing his memoirs over the distance of many years and events, Weisgal omitted a few details in his story, such as the fact that the ships purchased (two, not three) were Zemurray's. However, Weisgal's dramatic style does not obscure the nature of the operation, the degree of improvisation, the cooperation between different Jewish elements and the use of various methods, including bribery.

The many people who participated in the widespread operation of buying and equipping the ships, as well as those who helped with the organization of the immigrants and their transportation, were divided into two groups: those who had some ideological connection with the operation and those who hoped to gain some material advantage from it. Ze'ev Shind had misgivings about the meeting because Zemurray was not known for his Zionist beliefs and he had no need of the pitiful rewards the Mossad could give him. Shind revealed afterwards that he had conducted all the negotiations about buying the ships "without contacting him because he was afraid Zemurray would ruin the whole business".[14] But, added Shind, at that dramatic meeting,

when I told him the whole story, he called one of his slaves (I want to tell you that in the Southern states of America there really are slaves) and told him to bring his best whisky from the cellar (and it was!) and started to talk to me half in Yiddish and half in English and told me his life story, from the childhood in a small town in the Ukraine up to his buying the company in America. It was a long story and after he had finished he said that I should realize that despite everything he was still at the mercy of the 'goyim' (gentiles).[15]

Such Jews, cut off from their heritage but full of longing to recapture it, sometimes played a decisive role in the critical stages of illegal immigration. The problem was to locate them.

The ships were purchased and registered in the names of their new owner on 17th March, 1947,[16] under the Panamanian flag. Panama, like Liberia, "owned" one of the largest merchant fleets in the world, but this was only a technicality. The large private shipping companies preferred the Panamanian or Liberian flag because those countries had more liberal registration and taxation procedures. This was to their advantage because the registration of hundreds of vessels provided them with considerable revenues. There were no problems with registration because both the ships had previously flown the Panamanian flag. Their voyage to Palestine began several months later in 1947. This meant a long, expensive and problematic delay. During this period there was an escalation in the struggle against the British in Mandatory Palestine. Bevin's obstinacy had reached new heights. The *Exodus* saga was headline material in newspapers throughout the world. The U.N. had decided in favour of a Jewish state in Palestine and the War of Independence was already raging. The ports of France, Italy and Greece were closed to illegal immigration (Yugoslavia had been closed earlier) and complicated negotiations were underway with Romania to permit the immigration of fifteen thousand Jews from a Bulgarian port. The Mossad was taking stock of its own aims and functions at this time,[17] which led to a later dramatic turn in the affair of the *Pans* – the clash between the Mossad and the political leadership of the Jewish Agency. Meanwhile the ships were not standing idle. The young emissaries were not concerned with abstract questions; they were burning to carry out the mission for which they had been called – effecting the immigration of Jews to Israel, quickly and in large numbers. To this end they had to prepare and equip the ships, find crews for them, sail them to Europe and evade the watchful eyes of British intelligence agents.

Increased British pressure in Europe was affecting the Mossad's ability to equip and fuel the ships and so they turned to America, although the way fund-raising was traditionally done there contravened the rules of secrecy that were a basic condition of unauthorized immigration. For example, in order to raise funds to feed the 7,500 passengers on one ship for two weeks, the Jewish community in Philadelphia put on a gala entertainment evening in a magnificent ballroom. Posters were printed, invitations sent out, a tombola was held and at the event itself, the master of ceremonies called out: "Mr. X has donated 30,000 cans of meat for our brothers on their way to Israel" and "Mr. Y has pledged to equip an operating theatre on the ship".

Shind, who attended this function,[18] must have felt far out of his element. In any event, the ships were equipped and provisioned as no immigrant ships had ever been before. Almost a year later, the surplus provisions were still being used by the guards on the ships for an occasional banquet.[19] Needless to say, the existence of the ships was no longer a secret although both sides continued to play the secrecy game.

SABOTAGE IN VENICE

Ships were not, after this, provisioned in the U.S. The reason seems to have been the lack of consensus about immigration and the function of the Mossad. The operatives wanted to repair all the damage done to secrecy and were not keen to answer questions asked in public such as "Why should a banana boat carry thousands of life jackets, life boats and equipment when every stevedore can see they are not needed to rescue bunches of bananas?"[20] F.B. Shipping, the owner of the two Panamanian-registered banana boats, contacted the shipping company of T. J. Stevenson and proposed to carry cargo on their behalf to the Mediterranean. The company advertised that two cargo boats, *Pan York* and *Pan Crescent*, were sailing to Europe and were available for shipping. In fact, the voyage to Europe was a commercial success. The holds were filled with phosphates and the deck cargo was buses for Europe. The owners were paid the substantial sum of $200,000.[21] The *Pan York* continued for some time to carry freight between Europe and North Africa while the *Pan Crescent* began her transformation in anticipation of her great mission.[22]

The "commercial voyages" were conventional both in terms of the operating company and the methods. Even the crew consisted mainly of professional seamen. Paul Shulman who recruited the crews knew from the start that it would be difficult to find a sufficient number of professional sailors who would want to take part in the adventure that was in store for these ships. Each ship needed eight officers, and for a ship operating between Central America and the U.S., crossing the ocean and taking aboard thousands of passengers, even without the anticipated military problems, was a complicated matter. How many Jewish naval officers were there in the U.S. altogether, and how many of them were experienced? Out of these, how many were Zionists, prepared to immigrate to Israel? And how many of these were ready to take part in an unauthorized operation which could cost them their careers?

A few young Jews were finally recruited to serve on the ships. Some of them immigrated to Israel, fought in the War of Independence and later joined ZIM Lines, the Israeli shipping company, or the kibbutz movement. Most of the crew were recruited in the normal way to sail the ships to Europe where they signed off. When they arrived in Europe the Mossad had in its possession two large and impressive ships. They were well provisioned and to all appearances they were capable of getting through, but that was all: there was no crew, they were not yet fitted to carry passengers, there was no clear plan, there was no port of call, although everyone knew that the *Pans* had come to Europe in order to take unauthorized immigrants to Israel. The British were close on their heels and made no attempt to hide this fact.[23]

Thus, the Mossad had to deal simultaneously with the problems of fitting out the ships, hiring the crews, deciding on the destination, country of origin, selection and preparation of the immigrants, and always be alert to the obstacles that the British were setting up at every step along the way.

These obstacles made themselves felt as soon as the refitting of the *Pan Crescent* began. Only a few dockyards were suitable for this size of ship and of these, still fewer were prepared to take risks. As was customary with unauthorized immigration, contacts were needed outside conventional channels and this time they were found by Ada Sereni, the Mossad emissary in Italy. Ada, the widow of Enzo Sereni, who had parachuted into Occupied Europe during the Second World War and was a unique personality in the history of the Yishuv,[24] had become the coordinator of Mossad activities in Italy. When she was given this task in April 1947,[25] the Allied military administration in Italy had ended but the British Ambassador, the representative of the victorious power, was still very much in control. She had to utilize the whole range of her personal contacts to facilitate the refitting of the *Pan Crescent* and then use them once again to overcome the difficulties that arose in its wake.

An Italian dockyard had to be used because there were no suitable facilities for the two ships in Romania, and the Romanians did not have materials to provide for fifteen thousand people, despite their need for the foreign currency such a transaction would bring them. After frantic searching, a dockyard in Venice was found, the owners of which agreed to fit out one ship. The place was not ideal from the point of view of the Mossad – it was adjacent to an active British military installation. On the other hand the Italian owners, who had great respect for the dollars they were promised, did not investigate Paul Shulman's story about needing extensive alterations to prepare the ships for carrying flocks of sheep from Australia. They might have been convinced if it had only been a question of providing numerous water containers and ventilation in the enormous holds. They might, with difficulty, have believed that the layers of bunks were required for the comfort of the sheep, but even a "rich and eccentric American" like the young Paul Shulman, who acted as the ship-owner, found it hard to explain why the sheep needed advanced operating theatres and so many showers and toilets. . . . The British had no need to make guesses about the *Pan Crescent*. The ship was under constant surveillance[26] and pressure on the Italian government was not long in coming.[27]

The *Pan Crescent* came to Italy just when the *Exodus* affair had exploded; Bevin's rage against illegal immigration was at its height and he was prepared to do anything to throttle this movement. Ada Sereni could not have been happy with Shaul Avigur's request to handle such a prominent ship which simply invited trouble. The Mossad brought together people from different backgrounds, mentalities and ideologies and the tensions this produced were not restricted to the *Pans*. It should be emphasized that Ada Sereni's reservations stemmed from her desire to maintain good relations with the Italian authorities in order to be able to continue unauthorized immigration from that country. The problems arising from the special circumstances of the *Pans* were, in Ada's view, liable to finish Italy as an important base for future operations, from assembling Jews for immigration to buying and transporting arms.

Shaul Avigur, for whom the *Pans* represented a new peak in Mossad activity and a decisive breakthrough in mass immigration to Israel, wanted to ignore "local" considerations. In fact, the possibilities of fitting out the ships were getting smaller, as were the number of supply bases, sources of fuel and assembly points for the illegal immigrants to board the ships. The Mossad people who witnessed the friction between Ada and Shaul[28] point out that it did not affect the actual preparations – the fitting of the ships was carried out energetically under the supervision of Avraham Zakai and Dov Magen – but it did lead to a compromise to cut short the *Pans'* stay. From August 1947 the bulk of the work consisted in acquiring supplies and equipment which were to be transported on deck as soon as possible to Constantsa in Romania where the work was to be completed.

Since there was sufficient manpower in Romania and all the necessary supplies which were unobtainable there[29] had been purchased in Italy, down to the last nail, it was decided to accede to Ada's proposal and sail from Italy earlier than planned. The British got wind of this decision, and the scores of Italians employed on the ship immediately stopped working. According to Ada, the British had a direct source of information in one of the ship's officers who was in the pay of British Intelligence[30] and had told them the sailing date.

For the British, despite their complaints and the pressure they put on the Italian authorities, there was advantage in the Mossad operating in Italy. They were able to keep track of the ship, plan their moves and, if necessary, bring all their influence to bear in forcing the Italians to do their bidding. For this reason, the British reaction to the fitting out of the *Pan Crescent* in Venice was relatively mild.[31] However, when it became obvious that the ship was about to sail and that the destination was Romania, where the British did not have the same freedom of action as in Italy, they decided to take firm measures.

This time they tried a new approach which was uncharacteristic of traditional British methods and indicated a loss of direction and a feeling of desperation. There was no diplomatic activity, no political pressure or economic or legal action. Instead there was an undercover move carried out by the intelligence and security branch – an attempt to prevent mass immigration to Israel by sinking the ship. On the night before the sailing, a small rowboat circled the ship and a frogman swam under water to her bows and attached a mine.[32] If the ship had sailed at the appointed time, the mine would have exploded at sea and the ship would certainly have sunk; however the sailing was several hours late and the mine went off when the ship was still in shallow water near the coast. The blast smashed two large plates in the bows and made a hole a

metre and a half wide. Water rushed into the hold and the ship began
to sink, settling finally in the shallows with most of the hull above
water.

The problem facing the Mossad operatives was enormous. Damage
to the ship in a neutral port was a new startling turn of events. They
had no real information about the perpetrators of this act or their
objectives. The British were silent, and only the Arab League hastened
to take credit for what seemed like an act of Arab sabotage.[33] Only the
confession of the naval officer who had been planted by British
Intelligence made it possible, some time later, to uncover their
culpability.[34]

The *Pan Crescent* became the subject of open discussion as it lay,
with its bows gaping open in the waters of the port of Venice. When
Shaul Avigur heard about the sabotage he realized that any decision
about rescue work on the ship would affect the continuation of
immigration. There was an oppressive atmosphere at the meeting of
immigration workers in Milan two days after the explosion. They had
all seen the sunken ship but only a few grasped the technical
implications. The only "professional" was Paul Shulman, who was not
steeped in the same traditions of improvisation and dedication as the
Israelis. According to the other participants at the meeting, he threw
up his hands[35] and declared that the ship was lost. Ada Sereni, who
from the start had had strong reservations about bringing the ship to
Italy, saw Shulman's reticence as an opportunity to solve her own
problems with the Italian authorities and she seconded his urging to
abandon the ship. She realized that insistence on salvaging and
repairing the ship would place a great strain upon her and that she
would have to stretch beyond the limit her very delicate relations with
the authorities.

However, Shaul Avigur stood firm and his decision to salvage the
ship exemplifies his methods and his personality. He was not a seaman
and knew nothing about maritime matters. Most of his work in
immigration was carried out in a small room in the Metropole Hotel in
Paris, where he coordinated clandestine political activity through a
wide network of operatives from Israel who in turn maintained their
own contacts. Opposing him were a naval officer, the graduate of a top
naval college and qualified to command large ships, and Ada Sereni,
with her intimate knowledge of the local scene. Shaul Avigur was
adamant, and thanks to the spontaneity that typified the whole Mossad
ethos he found support at that meeting in the Milan hotel in the person

of Binyamin Yerushalmi, a young man of Turkish origin who, in his own words, "had lived there as a peasant, ignorant of Judaism",[36] and was later to become "a fervent believer in immigration".

There are many wonderful stories in the long and difficult struggle for the establishment of the State of Israel and the fight for her survival. One of the most intriguing, and one which still cannot be fully revealed, concerns this man who, until recently, was still being sought by many countries in the region. Journalists and agents involved in matters affecting security had different names for him in a number of complicated and unsolved cases, but they never succeeded in identifying him. "The Turkish Merchant" of the "Uranium Plot" in the 1970s, or the "Gnome from Geneva" (in another context) were some of the nicknames which for over thirty years were pinned on that same young man to whom Shaul Avigur had revealed the meaning of practical Zionism.[37] In 1943 he threw himself into the work of the Palestine rescue committee in Istanbul, placing at their disposal his dedication, his knowledge of the language and the country. He became involved in smuggling Jews out on the trains travelling east from Turkey. In Aleppo, the Jews left the train, went to the synagogue and then crossed Syria in small groups and infiltrated across the border into Palestine. Binyamin joined the Hulda Kibbutz and thought he had found his place, but he was not to be left in peace. Just as he was about to immigrate to Palestine himself, he was "recruited" into the Mossad. He began to work in Greece and later in Spain and Italy and in all the small ports where there was illegal activity. After Israel's establishment he remained in the Mossad and continued to work in other areas for more than thirty eventful and danger-filled years. His comrades, all of them men of action, held him in the highest regard.[38] He was best characterized by his dedication and his skill in finding amazingly simple solutions to difficult problems. It is difficult to define exactly what Binyamin Yerushalmi's work was in the Mossad, and this is inherently true of its other operatives as well. This lack of definition was disadvantageous in terms of accuracy, order, organization and discipline, but it also had distinct advantages. Working underground against powerful and sometimes unforeseen forces, ingenuity and a willingness to take on new repsonsibilities were essential.

On his way from Spain, after one of his missions, Binyamin Yerushalmi found himself in Italy. Since he wanted to meet Shaul Avigur who was rushing to the meeting in Milan to discuss the future of the *Pan Crescent*, he went along. He could not understand the feeling of despair at the meeting. "There's been an explosion? All right, let's repair the damage." Shaul Avigur was full of admiration for him. When everyone else had written off the ship, here was somebody with positive ideas. Yerushalmi was considered one of the veterans, greatly experienced and deeply involved in the organization. In view of the hesitancy of the "professional", Shaul asked him if he would accept responsibility for the repairs. Yerushalmi agreed, and in the dramatic tradition of those days, added "Right now", and left in the middle of the meeting for Venice.

Thirty years later Binyamin Yerushalmi described his first view of the sunken ship and the dejected faces of Paul Shulman and David Zakai – but, as he said, "I am a bit of a Turk.[39] I had no patience for this kind of attitude. I went to the owner of the dockyard and hired divers. We fixed wooden plates on both sides of the hole in the bows and began to pump the water out." The ship began to float but just then a fire broke out in the engine room. His resourcefulness came into play as Yerushalmi, who was organizing the pumping operation from the hold, turned the hose onto the raging fire and was thus able to deal with both acts of sabotage at once.

In the chaotic atmosphere of the time, these acts of sabotage went unnoticed. There is no record of the fire aboard ship and it was only during the interviews for this book that the incident was remembered and dredged up from oblivion. The ship had not yet carried out her mission, after having cost a fortune, making a long voyage, standing a considerable time in Europe and suffering an explosion and a fire: she was the subject of heated controversy and she had not yet carried one person to Palestine.

In the meantime, Binyamin Yerushalmi had thrown himself into his task. On inspecting the ship, he found that the air conditioning units were unsuitable and sorely inadequate to provide sufficient oxygen for the thousands of people who were expected to occupy the hold. The fuel tanks that were intended to contain drinking water for the passengers had been damaged when the ship sank and had been flooded with sea water; some of the equipment was ruined by sea water and smoke. While he was trying to handle the repairs, Ada Sereni was trying to get the ship into dry dock. Even when the water was eventually pumped out and the fire extinguished their troubles were by no means over. Years of hardship, failure, frustration and adversity had produced a certain wry humour among the Mossad operatives. It probably helped them on their long and exhausting obstacle course. When they had finally recovered from the sabotage and other problems and were trying to put the ship into dry dock, the way was blocked by a British warship. It was not an overt blockade because Venice was a port in a sovereign state, but the positioning of the ship and the attitude of the sailors left no doubt as to its purpose. Paul Shulman, who could see the British captain on the bridge peering through his binoculars at what was happening on the *Pan Crescent*, followed the rules he had learnt at naval college. With great ceremony, he drew close by the British warship and following naval custom, lowered the Panamanian flag to half-mast. The proud British captain was momentarily confused but hallowed tradition impelled him to reply by lowering his flag, as befitted ceremonial occasions. The entire crew of the warship, ranged at battle stations, stood at attention on deck and saluted as the ship blasted out a greeting.[40] Thus, honoured by the British warship, the *Pan Crescent* went into dry dock. While the repairs were being rushed, the British were looking for other ways to stop her. They applied to the management of the port of Venice and requested that they confiscate her papers which, in accordance with regulations, had been deposited with the port management on going into dry dock. The pressure was strong and it seemed that the port officials had decided to hold the ship's papers. Paul Shulman notified them that as the owner he was not very happy about sailing anyway because hostile elements wanted to sabotage the ship – he preferred to stay and pay for the extra time in dock.[41] Since this was the only dry dock in Venice, it threatened to paralyse the port, so despite British pressure the documents were returned and the ship left the dock.[42]

Suddenly a new problem arose – the Italian captain disappeared. It should be explained that on Mossad ships there were three separate command structures. The Palyam crew (the naval arm of the Palmach) was responsible for security, for problems arising from contact with the British and for communication with the Mossad and headquarters in Palestine. The head of this crew was commander of the ship. He was generally an experienced commander but without naval training. The second crew consisted mainly of immigrants themselves and included group leaders responsible for various activities, including kitchen duties and water distribution. It was responsible for solving the personal problems of immmigrants arising during the long journey to Palestine. The third crew consisted of the actual seamen – officers and sailors whose task was to sail the ship and run it in an orderly fashion.

There were few qualified seamen in Israel and even fewer authorized to work on large ships; international rules in this field were very strict. Recruiting a professional crew in Italy to replace the American crew that had brought the ship over had been extremely difficult and required considerable bribery. And then, two days before the departure from Venice, the intended captain disappeared.

Three years later, in 1951, an Italian captain came to Haifa and asked to meet Paul Shulman. He confessed that he was the man who had run away and left the ship. He related how he had been caught by the British, who had discovered that his family lived in Trieste which was not then Italian territory. They told him bluntly that if he did not disclose everything he knew about the ship and what was happening aboard, his family would be arrested. He told them everything he knew and in return for his promise to leave Venice at once and not return to the ship his family's safety was assured.[43] This was but one incident in the sea of intrigue and subterfuge surrounding the *Pans*, in which a handful of operatives had to fight for their cause against a tide of foreign hostility and British intransigence.[44]

A similar mishap, although not as drastic as an explosion on board ship, befell the *Pan York*. After five successful commercial voyages from North African ports to France, where the possibilities of fitting her out as an immigrant ship were investigated in every port, the Mossad realized that there was no chance of finding a shipyard that would do the work. Since there was no alternative, the *Pan York* sailed for Romania after taking on all the necessary supplies and equipment for the work.[45]

The voyage to Romania highlighted the degree of attention being paid to the ships; a British destroyer was assigned to shadow them[46] but from the Bosphorus onwards into the Black Sea they were left alone. The inability of the British to maintain constant surveillance in the Black Sea would be of great significance later on, during the voyage from Constantsa. They found it difficult to delay the ships' departure when they were loaded with immigrants due to a series of international conventions concerning the Bosphorus and the Dardanelles. The conventions of Monterrey and Detroit were of particular importance since they forbade the entry of warships belonging to nations not bordering on the Black Sea. There were no British destroyers in the Black Sea but there were mines and depth charges left over from the Second World War. The ships' commanders wondered whether the British warships or the mines were more dangerous.[47]

At the beginning of October 1947 the two ships met in Constantsa[48] harbour and the largest operation ever undertaken by the Yishuv on its road to independence began – preparing the ships and assembling their passengers.[49]

"LUXURY LINERS"

The two ships were anchored side by side in Constantsa for nearly three months. Over three hundred people worked on them full time and another forty-five were engaged solely in guarding them. Although Romania was outside the British sphere of influence, the troubles the ships had undergone and the amount of attention that had been focused on them aroused the fear that there would be attempts at sabotage or that one of the workers or an outsider might conceal explosives in the engine room. The Romanian authorities also provided surveillance on the ships and there were occasions when the Mossad guards encountered suspicious "loiterers" in the port area who were obliged to show papers proving they were Romanian police agents working alongside the Mossad.

The preparation of the ships cost over half a million dollars and enormous resources of planning and execution. It was not easy to embark 7,500 people on a dangerous voyage in a banana boat. These were not young immigrants who had undergone pioneer training and were ready for adventure and hardship, but families with old people and young children, for whom it was necessary to ensure more comfortable conditions than was customary in Mossad vessels. Furthermore, on smaller ships, lighting, loudspeakers and ventilation were not so crucial. In an emergency everyone went up on deck. On a large ship problems with ventilation would be disastrous; by the time the passengers reached the deck which was limited in size in any case, many would have been trampled. This also applied to lighting, loudspeakers, medical facilities, water, food, the galley and even an apparently simple problem like stairways. It was not easy to plan stairways to facilitate the smooth flow of thousands of people through the holds of a banana boat. Dov Magen, in trying to illustrate some of the difficulties he faced in fitting out the *Pan Crescent* chose the toilets as an example. The norm for toilets in installations that were in use twenty-four hours a day was one toilet for thirty people, which meant that each ship needed 250 toilets. "When it became obvious that this was impossible technically and spatially we solved the problem by reducing the number by half and simply sawing up the wooden floor at the end of the decks, laying down long boards in which holes were drilled at close intervals and separated from each other by wood or canvas screens."[50] The preparation of the living quarters was more complicated. Geda Shochet, who was responsible for the work on the *Pan York*, and Dov Magen of the *Pan Crescent*, had transformed freighters into passenger ships that continued to serve Israel after it was established by bringing over tens of thousands of immigrants. Neither Geda nor Dov had had any engineering training and they solved their problems by sheer ingenuity. When, for example, Dov Magen was wondering how to provide sufficient ventilation in the lower hold where over a thousand people would be living, he turned to the proprietor of the largest cinema in Bucharest who became a "consultant" on ventilation.[51] According to Dov Magen, when this "consultant" came aboard and discovered that there were four levels below the deck where so many people would be living, he claimed that it was impossible to provide sufficient ventilation and "resigned" from his position. The improvised solution of square funnels projecting downwards from the deck with a smaller diameter on each level to maintain an even flow of air to each level did not work, even though the mouth of the tunnel was curved and was turned into the wind manually throughout the whole voyage. Finally they had to instal large fans to force air into the different levels and another set of fans to expel the air from the hold. In addition to operating these fans, the generators had to provide power for lighting and cooking. Additional generators were acquired and the electrical system was boosted but even so they could not illuminate the whole ship and lighting was installed only in passageways and corridors, often being cut off during peak hours in the galley.

The galley in each ship was divided into three sections, each one catering for an average of 2,500 people. One hot meal was provided daily, cooked in enormous tubs. Breakfast and supper issued by the galley consisted mainly of biscuits and tinned sardines. David Wolf, a passenger who was then a boy of fifteen, and is now the Rector of Ben-Gurion University of the Negev, said thirty-two years later that he has not eaten sardines since. He was not sure whether this was due to the excessive ingestion, or being squeezed with 7,500 other people inside the banana boat "like sardines in a tin".[52]

This sensation of being packed like sardines was well founded. Originally, seven thousand bunks had been built on the four levels and were known as "beds". Each "bed" was allocated a width of half a metre, a length of 1.80 metres and a height of 60 centimetres. When the number of passengers increased the width of each bunk was reduced, first to 47.5 centimetres and then to 40 centimetres per person.[53]

Professor Wolf tried to illustrate his shock on first seeing the hold of the ship filled with bunks by moving towards the shelves of books in his office at Ben-Gurion University. "This is how the bunks were built, one on top of the other, narrow and cramped." There was no room for personal effects and it was difficult to squeeze into them to sleep. This is one of the reasons for the strict decision to limit personal luggage, which was sparse enough to begin with.

These conditions did not promise great luxury but they showed a concern for basic needs, especially the supply of water and provision of medical care. After the special tanks of the *Pan Crescent* had been damaged in the explosion in Venice, Binyamin Yerushalmi proposed sealing off the front section of the bow of the ship. This was done and the sealed-off section became a water tank. Eight distribution stations working around the clock were set up and each group of immigrants reported for their water ration according to a fixed timetable.

Medical facilities were given priority because of the fear of violent confrontation during the voyage and the experience of previous voyages when most of the passengers had been survivors of Nazi extermination camps, many of them seriously ill. A forty-five bed hospital was set up on the bridge, the most convenient part of the ship, in what were originally the officers' quarters. An isolation ward was prepared for infectious diseases as well as a maternity unit. Next to them was a fully-equipped operating theatre. In addition, a surgery was provided on each level with a team of nurses and doctors – altogether there were forty-four nurses and twenty-two doctors on each ship.[54] For the purposes of better organization, each ship was divided into three sections which cut across the four levels. The installations were separated so that each section consisted of only 2,500 people, operating independent ventilation systems, toilets, water and galley. Each one of these was further subdivided into groups of forty-five, and a leader was appointed for each group. There were 160 group leaders on each ship and fifty-five to sixty-five groups in each section. This was planned to make it easier to control the distribution of food and water, because only group leaders had access to supplies. The loudspeakers were needed to maintain order, keep the timetable and notify group leaders when to come for food and water, etc.

All the accumulated experience of previous voyages went into these preparations– it was a case of being prepared for everything but not knowing what to expect. The Mossad workers were in charge of the operation and were expected to carry it out to the best of their abilities and judgement. For example, when Geda Shochet and Dov Magen were asked to prepare the ships, they were told that there would be six thousand passengers on each. Later this number increased to seven thousand but together they anticipated that the final number would exceed the original estimate, although this was supposed to be a most meticulously organized operation. For this reason they did not install the full quota of bunks. They only fitted the original six thousand requested and left the central area of each level free of the frames supporting the bunks. This space, as a result of long experience, stood them in good stead when they learned that each ship was to take on a further seven hundred immigrants above the maximum plan. The judgement of these non-professional kibbutzniks was based on one objective – more and more immigrants. Other considerations were less important and they sometimes showed a lack of sensitivity towards the plight and desires of the people whose fate was entrusted to them. They did not think of providing space for the storage of personal effects – on the contrary, as will be seen later, they discussed at length the construction of a "loading system" whereby they could confiscate and jettison the immigrants' possessions. But when the ships were ready, and after Pino Ginsburg, the Mossad treasurer, indicated that the money raised greatly exceeded the price paid for them,[55] Geda Shochet, the kibbutznik from Kfar Giladi, and Dov Magen, the kibbutznik from Ramat Hashofet, turned to Pino Ginsburg, the kibbutznik from Ramat Hakovesh, and said, "This is going to be immigration *de luxe*".[56]

CHAPTER THREE

Who were the Immigrants?

THE WHOLE HOUSE OF ISRAEL

The history of immigration reached its apogee in the *Pan* affair. It was the largest operation in terms of organization and the most problematic politically. It also marked the transition from the furtive and hazardous byways of illegal immigration to the open, legal, full-scale, mass immigration that would soon be implemented by the Jewish state. The organizational system used in the *Pans* operation was handed down to the Mossad.[1] This system, which was about to be transferred from undercover activities to the management of Israel's national shipping company ZIM Lines, was then used to handle the mass immigration which was to bring nearly 700,000 immigrants to Israel between 1948 and 1951.[2] The organizational effort was so intense that the *Pan* operatives saw it as a highly specialized field. Some of them later rose to senior government positions, and saw Israel through many a stormy sea, but in retrospect they all cited the *Pan* affair as the high point in their careers. Yet from the point of view of their wards, the immigrants, it appeared to be a deceptively simple undertaking. David Wolf, who a month before the voyage learned that he and his family were to be among the passengers and was asked by his youth movement, Bnei Akiva, to help in the preparations, relates that he did not feel that any great efforts were being made. He was unable, during the whole journey, to identify one emissary. He and his family could not distinguish, out of the thousands of people they met in the town, on the way to the ship and on the voyage, who were the emissaries and commanders; he had the feeling that the whole operation was so efficient, it was simply running itself.[3]

A proof of the successful organization was that in one operation, the final stage of which lasted only ten days from start to finish, 16,000 people left their homes, livelihoods, social milieux, language and background, placing themselves in the hands of a few nameless youths, some of whom could not even speak their language, and went on their way unquestioningly.

Unauthorized immigration prior to the *Pans* had a special character. The potential immigrants had usually been organized in preparatory groups (hachsharot), which were a kind of collective of young people, based on the traditions of the Jewish youth movements in the diaspora and Palestine. These groups, assembled in transit camps in Italy, Romania, Germany, Bulgaria and France, underwent basic training in ideological, physical and even military teamwork.

But now, the situation was different: political regimes had changed in the countries of origin, and the transit camps were gone. The focus had shifted from the problems of running the voyage, to screening and assembling the people who were to undertake it.

In May, 1947, Moshe Agami and Yosef Klarman met Bodnares, the key figure in the Romanian government and explained to him their plan to bring the *Pans* to Constantsa in order to take 15,000 Jews to Palestine. Bodnares asked for twenty-four hours to consider the matter and went to the Russian ambassador in Bucharest, Kaptaradze. Two days later Bodnares called Agami and Klarman and told them that the *Pans* operation was approved and also hinted that the ships might sail from a Bulgarian port, not from Romania.

In October, 1947, a special team, called the "operative section",[4] assembled in Bucharest with the task of coordinating organization in Romania. This section was headed by Yaakov Salomon, commander of the Hagana mission in South East Europe. It included thirty men, Hagana commanders and members of local movements, with Hagana activists in Hungary and Czechoslovakia who took their instructions from Moshe Auerbach, known by his underground name "Agami". Auerbach, a member of Kibbutz Kfar Giladi, performed a central part in the *Pans* affair, chiefly in the sensitive political negotiations with the Romanian authorities. In this area he was assisted by Yosef Klarman, a member of the Revisionist party and its representative on the committee for rescuing Jews that operated in Istanbul during the Second World War.[5] This cooperation between Auerbach and Klarman was an innovation in internal political procedure and, as a transitional stage in the shift of power from the Mossad to the State, it was decided to extend this cooperation so that contrary to established custom the *Pans* would take people from all the Zionist movements as well as non-members of movements; the screening would be done by special committees in the different areas and not by the Zionist party offices selecting on a percentage basis according to political affiliations. The decision to ignore the Zionist parties in Romania was a daring one and it met with some resistance. Heavy pressure was put on Auerbach to give quotas to the parties and, when he did not comply, serious complaints were lodged against him to the Jewish Agency in Jerusalem.[6] Moshe Sneh, a member of the Jewish Agency directorate, was in Romania at that time and he took the matter up and produced a party index, with percentages for each party, as had been done in the past. Auerbach did not give way. He called the Mossad office in Palestine: "Do not make me act like a Chinese general: without an explanation of your lists I will not send one candidate . . ." and then he pointed out that on the lists he had received there were people who did not have priority and "whose immigration we cannot justify".[7] With the cooperation of Yaakov Salomon and the help of Amos Manor, who had also joined the "operative section", he managed to get his own way. This group, consisting of Hagana commanders and led by one of the veterans of the Palmach, was put at the disposal of a fully national operation; they ran it by ignoring political divisions for the first time in the history of immigration. In view of the intense disagreements in the Yishuv and within the Zionist movement, especially the dispute between the labor movement and the Revisionist movement and its offshoots, Betar and Irgun Zvai Leumi, this was a genuine revolution.[8]

When it became apparent how complex the mission was, the task was broken down into stages. First, in October 1947, members of the section went out to survey the Jewish communities in Romania. At this stage it was decided that the immigrants should come from various places and not just from Bucharest and other large cities. This decision was made with long-term consequences in mind even though it complicated matters. The Mossad knew that they had two ships and a one-time agreement from the Romanian authorities for the release of a large number of Jews. They did not know when they would be able to send further ships to Romania or whether the Romanians would allow the Jews to leave. The problem of obtaining permission from a regime that was in the process of becoming Communist, and which was inspired by the U.S.S.R., will be discussed later. The Mossad's decision to "leave traces" throughout Romania was prompted by the feeling that doing so might prove to be a ray of light – their efforts would help to create an undercurrent of hope and longing among Romanian Jewry. If the operation were concentrated on one location it would be easier organizationally but that place would merely be vacated, without repercussions for Jews elsewhere. But if the operation were to touch Jewish communities all over Romania, links would be maintained betweeen those who had gone to Palestine and those who had stayed behind, who could always hope to join their compatriots.

The Hagana representatives did not decide upon who was to go in an arbitrary fashion. Local selection committees were established in conjunction with the Zionist political movements and the various communal organizations. Preference was given to the many orphans in the community and to young people, and the candidates' health was carefully checked. The Hagana visited the training groups and collectives of the pioneering youth movements and chose eight hundred to act as leaders and orderlies.

The organizational difficulties were considered so serious that nine-day crash courses were held at different locations for the youngsters who were given leadership tasks. The training programme and instructors were chosen by the "operative section" and the courses were a great success. The operation now possessed a framework of leadership spread throughout the different communities which would be responsible for the movement to the ships and for routine organization on board them.[9] In the idiom of that time, this framework was called a "cadre". Most of the people returned home and waited to be notified of the sailing date, but a small number joined the operative section which was then engaged in planning.

The long planning meetings had all the appearance of an official, recognised body.[10] Discussions involved senior Romanian government officials including representatives of the Ministry of the Interior, the Police and Customs, Health Ministry officials and, of course, directors of the railways. On the advice of the local authorities and following the structure of the railway system in Romania, the country was divided into seven districts, from each of which 1,500 – 2,000 immigrants were chosen; in each of these districts a train was scheduled to leave from the most distant station and collect the candidates for immigration at set points along the way.

This seemed a simple idea but various requirements complicated the planning of the journey. For reasons which will be discussed later the Romanian government refused to permit the embarkation of passengers in Constantsa. The ships sailed to Burgas in Bulgaria and the immigrants had to change trains at the Romania-Bulgarian border. The Bulgarian government was only willing to allow a short time for this so that the "loading" of the immigrants had to be carried out from the trains straight to the boats. There was no place to stay in Bulgaria and each train had to arrive within a certain period of time, "unload" its "freight" and leave according to a precise timetable to make way for the next train. Another requirement was the date. For reasons typical of an unauthorized movement which had to take advantage of special situations in timing and location and also had to pay bribes, the Mossad decided that the ships should pass through the weakest point, the Bosphorus, which was under Turkish surveillance, on Saturday evening between 5:00 and 6:00 pm. This calculation was based on the twenty-four-hour journey from the port of Burgas to the Bosphorus, the forty-eight hours for loading the ships, and a further forty-eight hours for the journey of the final train. Since the operation employed a large part of the Romanian transport system and it was intended to minimize its effects and save time, the reserve time was reduced to only twelve hours.

A precise operation like this, which had one important unknown factor – the behaviour of the thousands of immigrants – demanded planning down to the last detail. The members of the operative section studied maps of the railway and the different areas, measured times and distances and briefed the "cadres" in the communities until they felt that everything was ready and accounted for. As for the anticipated behaviour of the immigrants, the situation of the Jews in Romania at the end of 1947 had created a powerful drive to emigrate which meant that it was essential to ensure that only authorized people boarded the trains. This was not an easy matter. The Jews had gone through a period of extreme hardship when their survival had depended on their ability to cope and even, occasionally, to cheat the authorities and they were quite ready to cheat the Mossad in order to get to Palestine. Members of the operative section had come to understand the feelings of the Romanian Jews and realized that a reliable means had to be found to check the passengers at each station.

The Romanian authorities had their own reasons for checking the passengers. Besides the Soviet-inspired political interest in undermining the British Empire by sending Jews into a sensitive part of it, Romania had a definite social and economic interest in the exodus of Jews. It would clear the country of a "foreign element" with divided and uncertain loyalties and wide contacts with the outside world, working in occupations they hoped to see transferred to a new generation better indoctrinated in the ways of the regime.

The Romanians were also well aware that emigrating Jews would leave behind houses and property, not to mention the ransom of a dollar per Jew. Multiplied by the thousands leaving the country it amounted to a considerable sum with which to line the empty coffers of the Romanian government in those days.[11]

With the assistance of the Romanian Ministry of the Interior an office was opened in each area where people were selected, given instructions about the journey and provided with travel documents, stamped in large letters to prevent forgery, and to which were attached control coupons for different laps of the journey. The selection phase was extremely problematic. A report written later by Auerbach indicated that "there were many disruptions in the organization because of us".[12] As this report stressed, government representatives were present but they rejected only a few of the candidates – the main difficulties came from the Jewish side. There was strong pressure both from the various political movements and from individuals wanting to immigrate, and threats from the Jewish Communists whom the Mossad called "collaborators". They were not collaborating with the government at this time, however, but pressing to prevent this immigration to Palestine and they were supported by the fear that the Romanian government would change its mind at the last moment and consider the people who had registered as deserters. Over 400,000 Jews remained in Romania after the Holocaust; it was the largest Jewish community to have survived in a country dominated by Nazi Germany. The majority wanted to leave the country with its strong tradition of anti-Semitism. The hope of securing a berth on the *Pans* beckoned to the members of the political movements, the Zionist activists and youth organizations and the ordinary traditional Jews with a deep longing to return to Zion.

The selection committees were guided by many considerations, the first of which was the "Palestine factor". The Mossad emissaries and Hagana leaders came from Palestine and knew that the struggles they had seen there were only the beginning. Yaakov Salomon was commander of the first Hagana naval training course and was one of the Palmach battalion commanders. He understood the strategic importance of such a large number of Jews, when it was possible to choose the young members of the pioneering movements who were several times more numerous than all the ranks of the Palmach, Irgun and Lechi combined.

However, this was not to be the decisive factor. There was a long-standing conflict between the desire for selective immigration, which would create an elite pioneering group in the country and in time help absorb the general mass of the Jewish people, and the demand to allow any Jew who wished it to emigrate to Palestine.[13] In this conflict the Labour movement, which ran the Mossad, could not support a policy of preference and selection.[14] In addition, the political function of illegal immigration was tied to the "presentation" of the image of the immigrants as representing the whole House of Israel, young and old, men and women, whoever yearned for home and country. The Mossad believed that these ships, like the *Exodus*, would attract world attention. Questions would be asked and there was no more convincing answer than the classical Zionist response that this was a genuine mass movement surging up from below and carrying the whole House of Israel with it irresistibly, and not just organized youth groups "brainwashed" into Zionism, as the British claimed.[15] The Romanian authorities, whose cooperation was essential, were also interested in "family-based" immigration. The organized departure of groups of young people only would produce a demographic imbalance. Obviously a state moving with full force towards socialism would not find this acceptable. There was also the economic factor – the homes that were to be vacated by family-based immigration – so that there was no prospect of creating a different selection system because the authorities simply would not permit it.

The inevitable decision, therefore, was to take the immigrants with their wives and children from all over Romania and thereby turn the *Pans* into an organic link between the hundreds of thousands of Jews remaining in Romania and Zionist fulfilment in Palestine. The 15,000 immigrants, gathered from every community, would be the harbingers of further immigrations from their country. All this, assuming, of course, that Romanian Jewry was prepared to immigrate. The overwhelming majority were more than prepared – they were anxious to go with all their hearts.

ROMANIAN JEWS, 1947

On 30th December 1947, the day the *Pan York* and *Pan Crescent* entered the Mediterranean loaded with immigrants, King Michael was expelled from his country and Romania became a people's republic under a Communist regime. Since the end of the war in the summer of 1944, there had been four governments, each growing successively more Communist. In 1947 the opposition had been almost completely eliminated. Anna Pauker was the Foreign Minister and, although she was Jewish, she bitterly opposed Zionism while Bodnares, the Minister of War, supported the emigration of Jews from Romania.

The number of Jews in Romania in 1947 is estimated[16] at between 350,000[17] and 430,000.[18] In relation to the devastation that had struck the Jewish communities of Europe this was an astonishing number; yet almost half a million Jews from Romania and Transylvania were slaughtered in the Holocaust.[19] Many of the survivors were refugees with no papers or definite legal status and almost all of them had had their homes and possessions confiscated. The process of personal rehabilitation was long and difficult, the main obstacle being that even after the horrors of the war, the old anti-semitic stereotypes still raged,[20] untouched by the flames that had consumed so much of Europe.

The new Communist-inspired regime was supposed to eradicate anti-semitism and all other forms of discrimination, which were counter to the Marxist world view. But the heritage of anti-semitism was not to be uprooted; rather it was strengthened by the presence of large numbers of Jewish refugees who had gathered in Romania and a widely-held view saw a connection between the Communist take-over, which had been carried out forcefully and with Soviet intervention, and the predominance of Jews in the leadership of the Communist party, of whom Anna Pauker was the most prominent.[21] The rise of the Communists only aggravated the Jewish problem. It increased popular animosities towards them as a group that had abetted the process of establishing a foreign regime in opposition to Romanian national traditions, while this very regime, they claimed, influenced by Jewish Communists, was opposed to Judaism because of its negative attitude towards organized religion and above all because of its ideological opposition to Zionism.

The Jewish Communists, who belonged to the "Jewish Democratic Committee", were the spearhead of the struggle against Jewish self-organization which they portrayed as nationalistic and reactionary. The status of the central body, "The Association of Romanian Jews", established after the war by Dr. Wilhelm Philderman, eroded rapidly and its functional ability weakened; it was dissolved in the summer of 1947.[22]

The attempt to set up a central federation did not succeed but Jewish urban life provided a wide base for far-reaching secondary organizations, the most important of which was the Zionist movement. This movement had some 100,000 members in 1946[23] and most of the

Jews in Romania maintained some kind of contact with it.[24] As was customary, the Romanian Zionist movement was marked by internal political divisions along the lines of the party political divisions in Palestine,[25] although the actual relationship between the Romanian Jews and the Yishuv was weak.

The first Romanian Zionist Congress since the war met in the spring of 1946 and the Left, known as "Labour Palestine", acquired a powerful position in the Zionist movement. In the elections to the Congress this party gained 45 per cent of the votes, the General Zionists gained 33 per cent, Mizrachi 16 per cent and the Revisionists only 4 per cent.

The Romanian Zionist movement was unable to produce a leadership acceptable to everyone. The internecine fighting among the various parties and the arguments among the general public due to the difficulties of this post-war period did not inspire a feeling of belonging and purpose. This situation strengthened the position of the emissaries who worked chiefly with the pioneering youth movements, which were the active element in the Zionist movement. The fact that these emissaries served as the liaison with Palestine and later were in charge of immigration, placed them in a decisive position in the Zionist parties.

This influence on the Zionist movement became increasingly important towards the end of 1947 with the escalation of the struggle in the Jewish community between the movement and the Jewish Communists. This struggle has been described as "a conflict on every front and on every subject".[26] In the course of this struggle the Zionist movement gained growing support in the community and by the time of the U.N. decision on the establishment of the Jewish state on 29th November, it had become a surge of enthusiasm, combined with disenchantment with the Communist regime.[27]

It would not be correct to claim that the entire Jewish public wanted to immigrate to Palestine at any price. There were many whose objective was America and many others who had no Zionist sympathies. People with means – and there were some in the Jewish community – were not in a hurry to immigrate to that Asian backwater of the Mediterranean, or at least not until they had consolidated their assets. At that time the chances of taking large sums of money out of Romania were slim. There were also the young and the intellectuals, who believed that genuine change was on the way in Romania, which would offer them a personal opportunity to take part in a promising new enterprise in the country of their birth.

Immigration was a personal solution for stateless refugees from the U.S.S.R. who were looking for an easy haven, and the weak and orphaned. It was also the driving force behind the pioneering youth movements. But time was to dampen the ardour of potential immigrants, especially the refugees and the weaker sections of the community. Many of them had struck roots, finding jobs, homes and families. Restricted immigration quotas, anticipated difficulties on the way and lack of knowledge of what was happening in Palestine shifted the focus from immediate immigration to adjustment and assimilation into the places where they lived.

From this point of view the importance of unauthorized immigration was immeasurably greater than the numbers involved would seem to indicate. The air of courage, initiative, pride and participation in personal and Jewish independence which accompanied immigration produced a sense of unity and belonging and a new-found prestige. This radiated outwards to the immigrants' friends and families who had remained in Europe and became a source of hope. During the post-war period of unauthorized immigration, these immigrants revived the Zionist movement and gave it the strength to confront the Jewish community at a difficult time and in all its facets, particularly the Jewish Communists. In view of the domestic situation in Romania, the idea of unauthorized immigration served as a kind of bridge over the gap between Communism and Zionism. This gap split the Jewish community and could have endangered the Zionist movement, since Zionism was diametrically opposed to Communism, as the Jewish Communists claimed, and since the regime was Communist, the Zionist movement could therefore be condemned as reactionary by this contradiction, as had already been done in the U.S.S.R. However, in this case there was clearly a common interest between the Communist regime's malevolent stand towards British imperialism and the Jews' yearning to go to Palestine. The Zionist movement was the catalyst for the attainment of this goal.

Covert support for immigration was not unequivocal. When the immigrant ship, *Max Nordau*, sailed in the spring of 1946, the Romanians provided active assistance including arms for the captain in the hope that an armed clash would erupt between the immigrants and the British.[28] The regular meetings between Bodnares, Klarman and Auerbach produced a broad agreement on the aims and methods of immigration, and it was decided that 50,000 Jews should leave in one operation towards the end of 1947.[29] However, such undercover activity has its own dynamics which a regime aiming at maximum centralism may find difficult to control.[30] The mass exodus of one population group from a country is liable to foment unrest and demands from other minority groups while hampering the integration process. When these risks have ideological underpinnings, the matter becomes even more complicated.

Ideological support for the opposition to immigration came, predictably, from the Jewish Communists. It was assumed that Judaism was opposed to Communism.[31] The Return to Zion, the basic principle of Zionism, was a romantic melange of religious nostalgia, and a rejection of the revolutionary mission. Anna Pauker strenuously opposed the Zionist ideal and the exodus of Jews from Romania precisely because she was Jewish herself. The British thought that the strengthening of her position in the country, after she had been appointed Foreign Minister in July, 1947, would prevent Jews from leaving Romania.[32]

On several occasions in modern Jewish history a Jew appointed to a senior position in his country has become an opponent of Zionism, either in order to prove his "loyalty" or else because Zionism has been used by his enemies to remind him that his "natural" place is elsewhere.[33]

In Romania there was an interval of about a year and a half between the departure of the *Max Nordau* and the renewal of immigration. In September, 1947, the *Geula* (Redemption) and *Medinat Ha Yehudim* (Jewish State) sailed with four thousand immigrants aboard, but from Burgas in Bulgaria and not from a Romanian port.[34] The Romanians' willingness to allow such a large number of Jews to leave could be seen as an agreement in principle to the immigration of Jews to Mandatory Palestine. However, their extreme caution in not allowing the ships to sail from Constantsa was an indication of the Romanians' lack of real freedom of movement. The contrast between Zionism and Communism enhanced the image of immigration but the contact between the two was very weak. The firm supporters of cooperation were the pioneering youth groups in the Zionist movement, and Bodnares in the Romanian government, both of whom worked towards the immigration objective. In the wider strata of Romanian Jewry, Zionist ideals were dormant and, of course, Anna Pauker in the government was firmly opposed to them.

Two distinct groups of Jews emerged in Romania during the first three years after the Second World War. One took full part in the Communist revolution and tried to fit into the local government, the party, the economy and society. The revolution offered a new chance for the Jew, as a person and as a citizen. The other side comprised the active part of the Zionist movement, the youth groups striving to fulfil the Zionist dream. Most of the Jews in Romania were ranged between these two camps. They were not active members of any party or movement. The fulfilment or deferment of the return to Zion would be determined by historical circumstances, often economic processes. In this case, the crystallization of the Zionist camp and the process that turned hope into action were related to the grave economic situation in Romania. The Jews, like the general population, were the victims of famine, poverty, inflation and unemployment. In August, 1947, monetary reform was announced, the currency was changed, it was forbidden to hold gold or foreign currency and bank accounts were frozen. The reform rendered a large proportion of private assets worthless or unsafe. For the Jews, whom history had taught to keep liquid assets which were easy to carry at times of expulsion, pogroms or other disasters, this was a hard blow. It also affected the Jewish relief organizations such as the Joint Distribution Committee, which supported 75 per cent of the Jews in Romania.[35]

This economic blow which struck Romania came in the wake of a long war, after an important part of the national wealth had been confiscated by the U.S.S.R. and the nation had undergone an accelerated process of social and political radicalization. However, the Jews were more vulnerable to its vicissitudes. Many of them were refugees who had returned from concentration camps broken and ill, exposed and helpless. Others had been evicted from their homes and lost their possessions during the war, or had been dismissed from their jobs. Some of the unemployed were involved in smuggling or in the black market in order to make a living – these were very few,[36] but the popular anti-semitism which had forced the Jews into marginal economic activities was happy to revive the image of the "Jewish exploiter".

The anti-semitism and the desperate economic situation combined with the fresh memories of the Holocaust to arouse longings for Jewish national independence. Romanian Jewry was fertile ground in which to sow the seeds of Zionist fulfilment. Wide sections of the Jewish community which had hitherto shown no interest in the Zionist movement began to join its ranks and it gained popular force

Exodus at Haifa

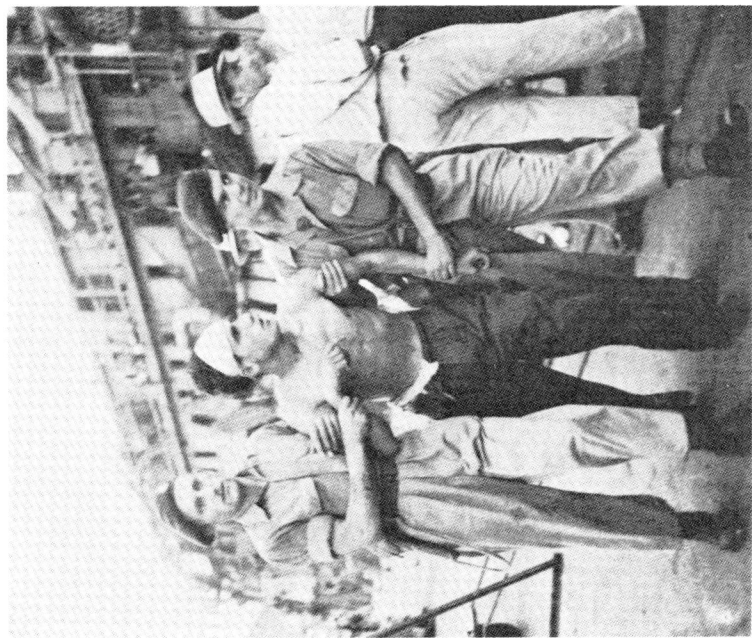

Injured immigrant being taken off at Haifa

In the hold of an immigrant ship

unparalleled elsewhere at the time. The main objective was immigration – so much so that Mossad emissaries and operatives in Romania began to react, instead of activating. The enthusiasm with which the Romanians threw themselves into the work of implementing the departure for Palestine swept away all those who wanted to control and organize the process. Mass participation at different levels was rapid and powerful. From the point of view of the emissaries this was an impressive achievement which justified their own efforts and self-sacrifice. They knew they were dealing with a huge wave but it could roll back just as easily if there was any amelioration of the economic situation, or if the gates of Palestine were to be completely closed to immigration. If the Zionist movement were to fail in its efforts to facilitate the departure of the Jews, they would seek their personal rehabilitation in Romania and over the years forget the Zionist dream.

The emissaries who stood at the centre of events in the Romanian Jewish community were henceforth to be the people who pressed for immigration even in opposition to the views of the Zionist leadership. Without realizing it they were acting on behalf of the Romanian movement to the Palestinian leadership and to their own superiors. They were not just advocates but an integral part of this new enthusiasm which they carefully nurtured. When they saw that world leaders, the heads of the Jewish Agency and their own commanders were trying to prevent them and stop the immigration they would find a way round them and let the surge of Zionist fervour force its way into Palestine.

This situation compelled the selection committees to impose basic restrictions and criteria. However, they were not always clear-cut because there was only limited central supervision and the committees had been appointed in haste. In general terms the restrictions mainly concerned the assurance that candidates were in good health; they had also to show some kind of financial ability by paying an "immigration tax".[37] The criteria aimed at selecting candidates who had been active in the life of their local communities and preferably, in Zionist institutions. However, as customary in the Zionist movement, the intention was to leave behind the leadership of the community in order to guarantee its survival until the complete termination of the Romanian diaspora.

There is the question of whether, in the haste and pressure of the operation, the selection was always fair and free from the private considerations of the local leadership in various places. People were discovered on the train who had always been hostile towards the Zionist movement in their community but who were related to members of the selection committee.[38] In general, however, most of the immigrants on the *Pans* were from lower-middle-class families who had shown some degree of activity in local Jewish organizations or who were known to have ties with the Zionist movement, as well as many orphans from the various communities. Special attention was given to young deserters from the army but this subject, referred to in later cables, is not properly documented.[39]

The selection committees reported to the "operative section" on the heavy demand to immigrate and assumed that many of the people they rejected would find other ways of joining the immigrants. In planning the journey much time was devoted to the problem of "illegal" immigrants who were attempting to join the "legal" immigrants on their "illegal" journey to Palestine.

On each of the nine trains there was a special car for the "stowaways" whom it was planned to remove. The train commanders were very strict about checking the travel documents prepared by the selection committees and indeed, they found many forgeries. Diversionary tactics were drawn up, with false timetables and incorrect collection[40] points but despite all this and the attempts to get rid of the "illegal" immigrants, in the end some four hundred unauthorized but determined immigrants managed to get aboard the ships.[41]

CHAPTER FOUR

Ships or a State . . .

CHANGES

Fired by the rebirth of the Zionist idea, at the end of the 19th century tens of thousands of young immigrants had streamed to the Land of Israel to pioneer its fulfilment. But this Zionism sprang from different, sometimes contradictory ideological and spiritual sources,[1] from which emerged a variety of political frameworks, the divided leadership which represented a wide spectrum of views and aspirations. In the 1940s there was, for example, an essential difference between the approach of Menachem Begin, commander of the Irgun Zvai Leumi and that of Chaim Weizmann who, although not in office at the time, was the recognized spokesman in the corridors of international diplomacy[2] for the establishment of a Jewish state. The argument between Weizmann and Ben-Gurion, who was then chairman of the Jewish Agency directorate, had reached a climax shortly before and revealed a deep spiritual gulf between them.[3] There were social and ideological tensions even between apparently kindred groups, such as the two radical underground organizations, Etzel and Lechi. Both were isolated in the Yishuv, and externally their methods seemed alike, yet the conflicts between them sometimes reached crisis point.[4]

And finally, within the groups themselves there were different views. Lechi, an underground movement that was small, even by the standard of the diminutive Yishuv,[5] fluctuated between opposing concepts[6] – from the establishment of a "Kingdom of Israel" to a blending into the "Semitic region". There were as many ideas as there were countries of origin among the immigrants. And at a time when the eyes of the world were on Palestine, as the Jewish state was about to be reborn, these differences were glaringly conspicuous.

The ideological rivalry between groups struggling for national independence was a source of both strength and weakness to the Zionists in Palestine and elsewhere. Weizmann's approach, which attached the greatest importance to diplomacy, often clashed with Ben-Gurion's, which insisted that top priority belonged to establishing the Yishuv. They both struggled against Etzel and Lechi who wanted to acquire national leadership for themselves. In addition, the Yishuv found itself in conflict with the ultra-orthodox Jews in Palestine, a sizeable and well organized group,[7] and with some members of the American Zionist leadership.[8] If internal strife can weaken a people fighting for their independence, it seems it may also have certain advantages. Weizmann was trying to gain the support of world leaders for the idea of Zionism,[9] and Ben-Gurion wanted to establish a defence force in the country;[10] Etzel and Lechi were making it difficult for the British to stay in Mandatory Palestine and kept the Palestine question on the agenda in Whitehall. While the historical process was leading irreversibly to the establishment of the state, the need to consolidate forces became more urgent. Local and group initiative, which was adequate when matters were fluid, now needed to coordinate efforts and establish priorities.

With the fulfilment of the dream of national independence drawing near, this situation would reach a climax in the affair of the *Pans*. The Mossad was at the height of its powers. By the end of 1947 it had brought tens of thousands of people into Palestine, providing a vital new source of strength to the Yishuv. They had instilled a new purpose in the shattered lives of the European refugees by bringing them to their own country. In the course of all these adventures, the Mossad had sharpened their skills and their daring. Their exploits in the field of immigration were widely acclaimed because the idea of taking Jews to Israel, although not strictly legal, was legitimized by public opinion in Europe and America. In disputes on the subject, the idea of a Jewish state was continually raised. Vast numbers of Jews saw this as the solution to their own plight and others, especially in the U.S., agreed to give their financial support to the costly immigration operations. It was natural that the organization handling immigration should acquire great prestige and its head, Shaul Avigur, became increasingly powerful as the organization gained additional autonomy. In an operation demanding unwavering dedication, absence from family and home for long periods and the acceptance of danger, survival depended upon total identification with the mission at hand. Immigration operatives were an organic part of a system which had an ideology and a purpose sometimes exceeding the bounds of reasonable action. Their identification with the task of embarking Jewish immigrants on their secret journey to Palestine was strengthened by personal contact with them and their plight.

This sense of urgency and purpose led Shaul Avigur and his team to perceive the Mossad as an independent entity invested with a prophetic mission. While Moshe Sharett, who was soon to become the first Foreign Minister of the State of Israel, was involved in painstaking diplomatic negotiations aimed at implementing the option granted by the United Nations to the Jewish state, and David Ben-Gurion was concentrating on creating an army in the face of impending war, the Mossad felt that the battlefield of immigration had been left solely in its hands. Since Shaul Avigur saw immigration as the principal goal and understood that the people who had sent him into battle were too busy with other matters to realize this, he gradually, albeit ruefully, began to act independently without reference to the overall system of "the emerging state". This was a source of conflicts that were soon to erupt between the leadership of the Yishuv, which found itself facing a new situation, and the groups of activists who had brought it about. The leadership wanted to construct a centralized system, under its control, while the various groups, whose objectives had yet to be achieved after the state was established, if indeed it was, challenged this supremacy.

The conflict between Moshe Sharett and his brother-in-law and close friend, Shaul Avigur, focused on the issue of whether to bring in the 15,000 Romanian Jews who had been chosen to immigrate aboard the *Pans* or to cancel the sailings from Romania. It centred on issues overriding that of helping thousands of homeless Jews to reach their goal.

In the turbulent period from the purchase of the ships in the spring of 1947 to the end of that year, there had been many events that placed the problem of unauthorized immigration in a different light. The *Exodus* affair had been a moral victory for the idea of immigration. It had gained attention and sympathy throughout the world but had also caused a crisis when the immigrants were returned to Germany and British Foreign Minister Bevin had made clear his determination to prevent illegal immigration. After the *Exodus* there was no point in further publicity of this kind because the repercussions had been widespread and unambiguous, and additional activity could only be harmful. If, for example, the British could prove that the ships were carrying Soviet agents, all these achievements would be rendered meaningless and the justice of the British claims upheld.

The decision to establish a Jewish state, taken in the U.N. on 29th

November, 1947, included a recommendation to open a free port for immigration on 1st February, 1948.[11] This should have placated the Jews remaining in the transit camps in Europe because it meant that soon their problems would be solved legally and without their falling prey to international scandals and rotten, unseaworthy boats.

The uncertainty of the international political situation, the recalcitrance of the State Department[12] and the war with the Arabs in Palestine placed onerous pressures on the leadership of the Yishuv. Anything could happen; caution was essential to avoid further problems on top of the grave ones already at hand.

At the height of these events, which were being acted out in the corridors of the U.N. and the White House, and at the same time in Prague and Amman,[13] the problem of the *Pans* erupted. It had begun to seethe before the decision to establish the State of Israel. The Jews of Romania were chosen for immigration for several reasons. Western Europe was ruled out because of the relative success of the British Foreign Office pressure there against Mossad activities especially in France and Italy. The hundreds of British intelligence agents haunting the ports of Europe on the trail of immigration operatives were able to report the various assembling points, broadcasting stations, location of headquarters and even names of principal emissaries. It would have been impossible in any case to conceal such a large and complex operation.

In one case the French government wanted to track down some British agents in Paris and a member of the French secret service asked the Mossad to help. An atmosphere of feverish activity was faked at Mossad headquarters as several operatives suddenly rushed out and drove off in different directions. These were followed, as expected, by carloads of the ubiquitous British intelligence agents who stayed on the trail of the Mossad cars, unaware that they were being followed in turn by the French. Enjoying their little joke, the Mossad operatives drove around the lovely avenues of Paris, watching in their rear-view mirrors the grim expression on the faces of the British agents and behind them the French agents. One of the Mossad people drove out to a remote suburb with no cars in sight and pulled up in front of a deserted cafe. The British car stopped a short distance away and the French car pulled up on the pavement behind it. One by one they gathered inside the cafe and ordered wine in different French accents; one of them raised his glass to the others who couldn't help sharing in the absurd humour of an otherwise all-too-grave situation.[14]

The British used as many as five hundred or more agents,[15] according to one estimate, in Europe and Turkey,[16] including demolition experts and frogmen.[17] There were signals and radio experts[18] whose task was to locate the Mossad broadcasting stations and even agents who infiltrated the ranks of the Jewish refugees in the transit camps to familiarize themselves with the workings of the Mossad.[19] There was also a different type of agent: immigrants who spied for British Intelligence. For example, on board of the *Af-Al-Pi*, which nevertheless sailed from Italy in September, 1947 there was a British Intelligence agent called Betty Fidler. The boat managed to get close to the coast of Palestine camouflaged as a freighter but was caught when this agent signalled to the British destroyer that it was carrying illegal immigrants.[20]

Such efforts illustrate Bevin's determination to combat Zionism and stop the flow of Jewish refugees who were pressing to immigrate to Mandatory Palestine. In the case of the *Pans*, this determination was significant, as the ships sailed after the U.N. decision on the establishment of the Jewish state and the British had begun to accept the decision. Unhampered by Bevin's dogged determination a way could probably have been found to ease the tension[21] since the struggle was already an anachronism, the Palestine problem had been taken out of British hands, a solution had been found and was about to be implemented and there was no point in investing manpower, energy, money and prestige on such a scale to prevent the passage of refugees to the country which was soon to become their sovereign homeland.

BEVIN: A CUNNING ENEMY

The obstinacy which was Bevin's most striking characteristic[22] was a major factor in the relationship between the Mandatory authorities and the Zionist movement from the time the Labour government was elected in Great Britain in 1945 up to the establishment of the State of Israel. In the case of the *Pans* it should be emphasized that while the actual sailing to Palestine took place in the last week of 1947, when the situation demanded a reassessment of political positions and tactics, the whole affair had begun when the struggle was at its height. When it was planned to purchase the ships in the U.S., at the beginning of 1947, the British had not yet returned to the U.N. and they intended to hold on to the Palestine Mandate for many years.[23] The purchasing of the ships was carried out while the Jewish Agency maintained contacts

with Eastern European countries. The British knew, to their conster-
nation, about the ships and the plans to take Jews out of Romania and
possible other countries.

When the British learnt, at the end of September 1947, that the
Mossad had succeeded in repairing the *Pan Crescent* and that it had
slipped into the Black Sea, they decided to launch an all-out initiative
to stop the ships from leaving Constantsa.

On 30th September, 1947, the British press published a report
issued by the Foreign Office about two large ships which had been
purchased in the U.S. and had come to Europe in order to carry illegal
immigrants to Palestine. The *Daily Telegraph* even printed a
photograph of the *Pan Crescent*.[24] From then on, the battle for the *Pans*
was waged on two different fronts: in secret, involving diplomatic
contacts by the British, the Mossad and the Jewish Agency heads; and
in public where reports and articles on the ships were published by
both sides.

British diplomacy was aimed in three directions: the U.S., Panama
and Romania. Directly after it became known that the *Pans* were
anchored in Constantsa within the Soviet sphere of influence and thus
removed completely from the area where Britain had the power to act
or even influence – Britain began urgent discussions with the U.S. On
28th October, 1947 the American Ambassador in London, Douglas,
sent Secretary of State Marshall an urgent cable after he had spent an
hour with Bevin, discussing Great Britain's attitude to the
recommendations on Palestine taken by the U.N. Among other things,
he said, Bevin had expressed his concern over the fact that two
American ships, the *Pan York* and *Pan Crescent*, were in the Romanian
port of Constantsa and intended to take eighteen thousand illegal
immigrants to Palestine.[25]

The British knew there was no point in seeking direct American
action against immigration, so they chose to work in three stages. First,
the Americans were to be persuaded to stop their direct and indirect
assistance in Europe to the movement of Jewish refugees towards
Palestine.

A special memorandum sent on 31st October, 1947, by the British
Ambassador in Washington to the State Department expresses the
resentment towards this assistance:

> It is possible that as many as 17,000 illegal Jewish immigrants will
> arrive in Palestinian waters from the Black Sea in the very near

future and the camps in Cyprus will become completely full. It is therefore important that none of the 28,000 Jewish refugees now in Italy should immigrate to Palestine in the next few months. His Majesty's Government in London has come to an agreement with the Italian government to examine the transfer of additional refugees from Austria to Italy. The British delegate in Vienna [at that time the committee of the four powers was based in Austria] has received instructions to clarify this matter with the American and French delegates to the inter-power committee. The British representative in Paris has also been asked to clarify this matter with the French authorities. As regards the French Zone in Austria, the main problems are:

(1) to prevent Jewish refugees crossing the border in the direction of Italy from their zone and to return to Austria those refugees who had crossed the border.

(2) to increase inspection on the border of the American and French Zones in Austria.

(3) according to the latest information, the French Zone is not strict about Jewish refugees crossing the border and this is chiefly because the Americans do not seriously check the movement of refugees from their zone to the French Zone.

(4) the largest concentration of Jews in Austria is in the American Zone. It is understood that the policy of the authorities of the American Zone in Austria in the matter of the movement of Jewish refugees is not to help and not to hinder this movement. The authorities of the American Zone will not alter their attitude until they receive clear instructions from Washington.

(5) His Majesty's government is worried by the fact (and would like it stopped) that the Joint Distribution Committee and other American Jewish organizations, which were attached to the U.S. Army, are using vehicles and equipment for refugees. At the end of May [1947] five hundred Jews came to the border between the American and French Zones in Austria. They arrived behind a jeep belonging to the Joint in which there sat a man dressed in U.S. Army uniform. This man threatened the Austrian gendarmes with a machine gun when they tried to stop the convoy of vehicles with the five hundred refugees. We suggest that the Joint paint its vehicles in a special colour and does not use the U.S. Army colour in order to move refugees.[26]

Yielding to British pressure, Secretary of State Marshall initiated a series of phased talks between the Administration and Jewish Agency representatives. At first, the ground was cleared by informal meetings; for example, Dean Rusk of the American delegation to the U.N. met with Lionel Gelber, who was acting as aide and consultant to the political department of the Jewish Agency. This was a relaxed, almost intimate meeting, due perhaps to the fact that they had been friends in their student days at Oxford. Rusk reported to Marshall: "Our talk was personal, not political." However, as though by chance, Rusk raised the problem with Gelber and later told Marshall:

> I took the opportunity to express our deep concern about the continuation of incidents such as bringing illegal Jewish immigrants to Palestine. The view of our administration is that the Jews should allow the U.N. to deal with these problems without the difficulties that such incidents can cause. I asked him to speak formally with the heads of the Jewish Agency along these lines.[27]

As for diplomatic discussions, the phrasing was harsh and unequivocal. Gelber reported this to the beleaguered Moshe Sharett, Director of the Political Department of the Jewish Agency. He knew the mood of the State Department and realized that Marshall would do everything to prevent a U.N. decision in favour of the establishment of a Jewish State. However, to do this, it would be necessary to change Truman's position. Marshall's idea was to utilize the *Pans* affair to the full to prove that the Jewish Agency was irresponsible and could not be relied on to control matters, making partition a dangerous step. On his own authority Sharett asked Gelber to inform Rusk that "the Jewish Agency had reached an agreement with the Jewish underground". Rusk reported:

> After my conversation with Gelber the Jewish Agency continued to clarify matters on Saturday and Sunday. Gelber told me that he was authorized to say that he had no information on sailings from ports on the Atlantic or the Black Sea during the next five or six weeks. He informed me that the Jewish Agency would do everything in its power to avoid such "incidents" but that it did not have complete control over the underground.[28] He requested that I provide him with the information at our disposal about sailings so that the Jewish Agency could use its influence to prevent incidents. I repeated what I had said at our previous meeting when I asked that the Agency exert its influence on the underground.

Sharett could promise some degree of restraint on immigration as opposed to the activities of the underground in Palestine. Unauthorized immigration was totally in the hands of the Mossad under the command of his brother-in-law, Shaul Avigur, who had agreed not to disturb the sensitive moves that were taking place at the U.N. in preparation for the vote on the partition plan. Rusk could have suggested to Marshall, on behalf of the Jewish Agency, cooperation in the field of intelligence concerning the movement of the ships suspected of carrying refugees to Mandatory Palestine.[29]

The talks between Rusk and Gelber were exploratory. The agreement that they reached paved the way for the meeting between Marshall and Sharett. It was a crucial period. Sharett was engaged in feverish effort and it was forbidden to miss even a single opportunity to persuade the nations of the world and particularly the U.S. to support the partition plan. To this end Sharett was prepared to give Marshall far-reaching promises. Marshall reported to his British counterpart, Bevin:

> These two ships are flying the Panamanian flag and are at present at anchor in Constantsa, Romania. The State Department is taking steps regarding the status of these ships. The information is not complete but these remarks affect the understanding that exists between the U.S. government and His Majesty's government concerning the illegal movement of passengers to Palestine. We can provide the British Foreign Office with secret information because we are in communication on this subject with representatives of the Jewish Agency in New York, especially regarding the sailing of the two ships, *Pan York* and *Pan Crescent*. They have no information on the illegal sailing of any ship to Palestine in the next five to six weeks. We have been told by a representative of the Jewish Agency that they will do everything in their power to prevent such sailings but they have no control over the Jewish underground. A representative of our State Department has told a representative of the Agency to restrict the activity of the underground.[30]

The Secretary of State spoke personally with the leaders of the Jewish Agency and with the heads of the American Jewish Congress and asked them to stop these illegal activities; otherwise the State Department would deal with the matter in public.[31] The Jewish Agency kept its promise and the Mossad maintained the moratorium on immigration. But when the U.N. voted for the establishment of a

Jewish state, there was pressure again from below to continue with immigration. This pressure was significant because of the lack of clarity and the instability of the situation.

On the day after the trains in Romania had started moving the immigrants to the ships, a meeting took place in Washington with the participation of representatives from the British Colonial Office and Foreign Office and the American State Department at which a kind of summary of the talks between Bevin and Marshall was brought up. The British demanded that the Americans put pressure on the Jewish Agency to stop immigration and that the U.S. denounce illegal infiltration into Mandatory Palestine. The possibility of reaching an arrangement with the Agency to transfer future immigrants straight to Cyprus was raised.[32] In the frequent meetings between British and American representatives after the U.N. decision, the British revealed a kind of blind rage in the face of what they considered Jewish audacity and their helplessness to crush it. The British enjoyed a modicum of support from State Department officials and the Secretary of State himself, but in their view it was lukewarm, verging upon indifference. They urged the Americans to act and in particular to use their influence on the Jewish Agency as well as on the governments of Panama and Romania.

Reliance upon the U.S. became increasingly desperate. British contacts with the Panamanian and Romanian governments proved ineffectual. Time after time the Panamanian representative in London was summoned to the Foreign Office and the British envoy in Panama knocked on the doors of the government of this Central American nation with the demand that they withdraw their protection enabling passenger and cargo ships to fly the Panamanian flag. The British hoped that by removing the flag they would be able to prevent the passage of ships through the Bosphorus, and even if they managed to get through, with no flag and no protection, they would be "illegal", possibly even "pirate" ships.[33] As long as the *Pan York* and *Pan Crescent* flew the Panamanian flag they were ordinary ships belonging to the F.B. Shipping Co., Panama, like thousands of other ships, belonging to various companies and flying the flags of sovereign states. The repeated British appeals to the governments concerned to arrest the ships in their ports were always rejected. There was no legal reason to arrest or to interfere with the activity of ships following normal procedures and obeying maritime law.[34]

In order not to turn the British away empty-handed the Panamanian

Consul announced that when the current agreement expired six months later, in April 1948, they would seriously reconsider whether to grant protection to the ships.

Even Great Britain refrained from actions of this kind because of legal considerations. Thus, for example, on 29th September 1947, members of the Admiralty staff on Gibraltar stood gnashing their teeth as they watched the *Pan York* pass through the straits which they controlled. They knew she was sailing for the Black Sea but were helpless to stop her.[35]

In conversations with the Consul General of Panama in London, the Panamanian authorities were given precise details about the ships, the company that had bought them, the names of the directors and proof of their Zionist connections.[36] The British Foreign Office surmised that the Consul had no intention of taking this matter up; they were actually afraid that he was not even going to pass on this information to his government. After the ships had already left the Mediterranean ports a full memorandum was sent directly to the government of Panama with details of the request based on the fact that eleven ships flying the Panamanian flag had already taken illegal immigrants to Mandatory Palestine.

The memorandum emphasized that this case was especially grave. Each ship could carry eight thousand passengers but the conditions were unsuitable and the voyage could be dangerous. These facts combined with a long series of illegal acts carried out under their flag obliged the government of Panama to withdraw its protection from the ships.[37] When no answer to this arrived, Bevin personally called the Panamanian consul in London, Dr. Demetrio Puras, to the Foreign Office. In vague diplomatic language he promised to deal with Bevin's request. This time the Foreign Office decided to force Panama to react effectively and notified the media about the meeting.[38]

The government of Panama was forced to respond to this demand, and it came to a courageous and even provocative decision. As a small country that earned large revenues from granting its flag to thousands of ships throughout the world, Panama decided that it could not withdraw its flag from ships operating within the bounds of the law. Bevin must have been enraged when he received this answer which he interpreted as the cynical, mercenary reaction of a country enriching itself on the suffering of others.[39] His relentless pressure bore results only after the end of the affair, in connection with the confiscation of the ships which were anchored in Cyprus.[40]

At the same time Bevin tried to act in Bucharest. In 1947 the Communists had become the ruling party in Romania and in July of that year Bodnares, the man with whom the Mossad had conducted most of the negotiations, had been appointed Minister of War and the hostile Anna Pauker had become Foreign Minister.[41] It was a Moscow-inspired Communist regime. In the escalating Cold War between the U.S.S.R. and the West, control over sensitive regions was of critical importance. When the Russians succeeded in gaining a foothold in a certain country, they would become entrenched and firmly block the entry of any rival – in this case, Great Britain and the U.S. The Russians saw their entry into Romania as politically justifiable. Under the terms of the agreement reached in October 1944 between Stalin, Churchill and Roosevelt, Eastern Europe was to be divided into spheres of influence. Great Britain was given "influence" over Greece, and the U.S.S.R. over Romania. This agreement was limited to a three-month period but the Russians had always taken the view that if an agreement suited them, it should be permanent.[42]

The Communist takeover in Romania was accompanied by growing hostility towards the West which left Great Britain helpless in her contacts with the authorities there. Dozens of secret telegrams and reports were sent from the British legation in Bucharest to the Foreign Office in London testifying to the humiliation they were subjected to in their discussions with Romanian officials.[43] In these abortive attempts the British representatives used different arguments at different levels. The political reasons – the need to moderate the conflict between the Jews and the Arabs and the chance of settling it by peaceful means, provided there was no unnecessary friction such as illegal immigration, were not relevant. The Romanians, following the U.S.S.R., had no interest in preventing trouble in the British Middle East. The British approaches to the Russians reveal how desperate Bevin was. In all his appeals to the various European governments, and to the U.S. in particular, he took pains to explain that the *Pans* were an instrument of the Russians and the immigrants aboard them were Communist agents who intended to bring chaos to the Middle East. Now he himself turned to Russia and asked for help in maintaining order; however, his legalistic arguments, based on the U.N. decision and the existence of official committees to deal with the subject, were equally ineffective. Romania was not yet a member of the U.N. and strict observance of the fine points of the law was not typical of the new regime. Neither were they impressed by the British claims that these ships, carrying thousands of passengers, were dangerous. On reading through the reports of these discussions, one is almost sympathetic to the British spokesmen forced to go from appeals to entreaties and from wheedling to threats.

British intelligence also ran an extensive operation inside Romania. They gathered up-to-date information on the selection of Jews in the various towns, the state of readiness of the ships, the problems of recruiting crews, the establishment of training camps for the group leaders and the planned timetable for the trains.[44] They attempted to utilize this information in the most cynical manner, typical of intelligence services. They "leaked" information to the Romanian authorities about possible Jewish deserters from the army, forged documents, attempts to smuggle property and cash, collaboration with Western intelligence agencies, corruption and deceit. At the same time the British were "leaking" contradictory information to Washington in particular, about the high concentration of Soviet agents among the immigrants, weapons training by Communist experts, collaboration with the U.S.S.R., etc.[45] In their pressure on the Romanian authorities the British were not ashamed to resort to the tactic of stirring up trouble between different elements of government. One of their more Machiavellian moves was to drive a wedge between Bodnares, the War Minister, who was in favour of the departure of Jews from Romania and actually encouraged it and Anna Pauker, the anti-Zionist Foreign Minister.[46] Supporters of the Communist idea had always claimed that their revolution would provide the solution to the Jewish problem. Communism, the great equalizer, would put an end to all forms of discrimination and persecution.[47] The Jews would have no reason to seek a haven elsewhere and could devote themselves to building the new society in their countries of origin.

Such arguments, long forwarded by the Communist parties, were pressed forcibly, especially by their Jewish members, who were obliged to justify their senior positions in a country where even loyal members of their own party regarded them as outsiders.

It was natural that the opposition of the Jewish party leaders to Zionism should be stronger than that of the party itself which, in this instance, supported the idea of the establishment of a Jewish state in Palestine.[48] Thus the strengthening of Anna Pauker's position offered a ray of hope to the British representatives who tried to persuade her to stop immigration on ideological grounds.

Activity in Eastern Europe reached a peak when the British Foreign

Office appealed directly to Moscow[49] to prevent a situation which could bring disaster to the Middle East. At one point the Romanian position softened. Either due to the strength of Anna Pauker's opposition to the departure of the Jews, or because the Romanians wanted to avoid an open rift with Great Britain, and perhaps because at this very time the U.S.S.R. was planning a revolution in Greece which, according to the tripartite agreement, was in the British sphere of influence, the Romanian authorities decided to make a concession to the British.[50] They would not permit the *Pans* to board Jews in Constantsa and the ships would sail empty from Romania. But this was a meaningless diplomatic exercise; the ships would sail to Bulgaria and the Romanian Jews would leave the country, not on Mossad immigration ships but by train, and not to Israel but to Bulgaria. Everyone knew that the same ships would be waiting for them there, but Romania could disclaim responsibility for this.[51] In a document dated 3rd October, 1947 which was classified as top secret and circulated only among members of the cabinet, the chief of the Naval Staff in the Middle East and British representatives in Russia, Romania and Bulgaria, it was stated:

> The Bulgarians will not prevent the sailing of the ships, nor will the Romanians. The only hope to stop it is by Turkish action. Action towards the Turkish government is required. It should be pointed out to them that the sailing of these ships will have a negative influence on the Arab countries. The Turkish authorities should be obliged to take joint action with the British Ambassador in Ankara in efforts to prevent the ships from passing through the Straits.[52]

The British continued to appeal to the Turkish authorities but the Turks hesitated because of the Monterrey Agreement which forbade the passage of British warships into the Black Sea and the arbitrary closure of the Straits. They were chary of the Russians, who had shown extreme sensitivity towards the Straits and the conduct of the Turks. The British cited moral and other obligations but these did not move the Turks.

The South-East Europe Department of the Foreign Office had in fact guessed from the start of their contacts with Romania that Bulgaria would be involved in the operation. On 2nd October the British representative in Sofia requested a meeting with the Bulgarian Foreign Minister and this possibility was discussed. His chagrin was reflected in his report to London. The Bulgarian Foreign Minister had expressed astonishment at the idea. Throughout the conversation he pretended that he did not understand what was being discussed and was able to promise the Englishman facing him, with a degree of feigned innocence, that Bulgaria would always act in accordance with international law.[53]

In Bulgaria the Romanian situation was repeated. The British had up-to-date information; they continually requested, pleaded and pressed and were given ingenuous and placatory replies – the Bulgarians promised that everything would be above-board. However, the British were well informed enough to know that in legal terms the ships were legitimate, the Jews were travelling voluntarily and there was no international law to forbid it.

The British invested great efforts in their attempt to prevent the passage of the ships from the Black Sea through the Straits which were under Turkish control. This was a convenient point since the ships could not pass through the Bosphorus without permission from the Turkish authorities. This was granted only after an inspection during which it was possible to stop "illegal" ships which did not comply with international maritime standards as to registration, safety and hygiene. However, the Turks, like the British, were restricted by the Monterrey Agreement permitting the free passage of civilian ships through the Bosphorus and the Dardanelles.

In the protracted discussions between the British and the Turkish authorities, it emerged that the Turks were prepared to stop the ships if a satisfactory reason could be found. It was decided that if the ships appeared without a flag, they would not be allowed to go through. But the British did not place much trust in Panama, which was supposed to withdraw their flags, and they tried instead to find a way of stopping the ships in the Black Sea.

The Foreign Office suggested two alternatives to the Turks: to hold the ships for an extended period in a Turkish port or to force them to return to their port of origin. The Turks refused immediately even to discuss the possibility of arresting the 16,000 refugees, and, as for the second alternative, they were afraid that the commanders of the ships would refuse to obey. They announced that they would under no circumstances open fire, rendering this idea impractical. British reports on the discussions with the Turks reveal signs of increasing reservations, giving rise to suspicion that the Turkish officials in Ankara and those responsible for the passage of ships in Istanbul had been bribed.[54] In November the reports from Ankara contained a note of despair about the prospects of the Turks closing the Straits. Finally, when no solution was to be found in the countries of origin or the passage through the Straits, pressure was again concentrated on the Jews themselves, through the Jewish Agency. This was in fact the only body that could stop the *Pans*.

The British were in no position to apply pressure to the leaders of the Yishuv who nurtured a deep sense of betrayal. The White Paper of 1939, the pro-Arab inclinations of the British administration in Palestine and above all, the closure of the country to the Jewish refugees escaping from the holocaust in Europe had aroused bitter hostility towards Great Britain in the Yishuv and its leaders. Even Chaim Weizmann, who was considered moderate and pro-British in his view, regarded the present British government as hostile.[55] Although at this time Weizmann did not hold any official position in the Zionist movement, he was still its best-known leader and had wide influence in the Jewish world. When he was called upon to help the movement at this crucial time his base of operation was the U.S. Ben-Gurion, who even before the Biltmore Conference in 1942 had realized that America would be the decisive factor in the Middle East,[56] focused the diplomatic activity of the Jewish Agency on Washington, and the head of its Political Department, Moshe Sharett, went there frequently with his aides, headed by Eliahu Elath.

Parallel to their activities throughout Europe, including attempted sabotage of the ships and pressure on the governments concerned, the British concentrated on the U.S. which, from the summer of 1946, had begun to play a role in the Middle East. This increasing involvement was imposed upon the U.S. against its will as it was manoeuvred by Bevin into a more central position in the arena.[57] The bold manoeuvre referring the question of Palestine to the U.N. was intended to force the Americans to increase their involvement. When the U.S. supported the establishment of the State of Israel at the historic session of the General Assembly on the 29th November 1947, they found themselves in an unpleasant situation – Great Britain was liable to abandon a vital and sensitive area where a war was being fought which had every likelihood of escalating. The West, struggling to establish spheres of influence, ran the risk of losing its hold in the Middle East because of this unwanted war.

The problem of Mandatory Palestine was complex, extremely sensitive and involved interests vital to the Great Powers. Delaying the U.N. decision on Partition and the establishment of the Jewish state would mean the freezing or quashing of the decision until it was no longer possible to establish the state. Everyone, including the Zionist leadership, realized that the situation which led to the U.N. decision was special and perhaps unique. Non-implementation of the decision would show that it had no prospects and would condemn it forever. In such a case the British would willingly agree to remain in Mandatory Palestine and it would be easy for them to maintain their hold on the Middle East. This would be sufficient to remove the Soviet threat to Western control of that part of the world.

The State Department has never been known for its excessive love of the Jews. The special sensitivities of the President of the U.S. in Jewish affairs, stemming partly from electoral considerations (mainly the need for Jewish money in electoral campaigns), did not affect the cynical and realistic calculations of the people responsible for international relations during the Cold War. Secretary of State Marshall probably assumed that just as American Jewry had become integrated into their society, the surviving Jews of Europe would be absorbed into the countries in which they were living. In any event he did not have much sympathy for a refugee movement which was liable to upset the alignment of the Arab states, and certainly not for a few thousand Jews from Communist countries who were performing a Communist mission, even if they were doing so unconsciously.

Although the proposal to delay the process which had begun after the U.N. decision on the establishment of the state was the easiest in the complicated Middle East situation, it was not simple to carry out. The decision was passed by a decisive majority, including the U.S.S.R., the U.S. and thirty-three other nations. Public opinion in the West favoured the decision and the existence of the Arab threat did not make withdrawal easier, especially after the Holocaust, the horrifying scale of which had stunned the Christian world and aroused feelings of guilt. Thus, the steps taken by the State Department, indicating a slow but clear diplomatic process towards blocking the U.N. decision, were hesitant. This was further evidenced by Marshall's cautious attempts to obtain the tacit agreement of President Truman and, if possible, the support of public opinion.[58]

The *Pans* affair offered the State Department a convenient instrument in its complicated manoeuvres aimed at delaying the process of Jewish statehood. Bevin took care to emphasize the role of the U.S. in the affair and reminded the American ambassador in London, as well as the Secretary of State directly, that the ships had been purchased in the U.S. with American money raised by appeals in the U.S. Some of this money came from Communist countries and the ships would be used by Soviet agents to infiltrate the Middle East.[59] Bevin challenged Marshall: if illegal immigration to Palestine continued, the war between the Jews and the Arabs would intensify and Great Britain would withdraw at the height of the conflict. In this case, would the U.S. care to intervene?[60] Marshall must have been horrified by such a possibility. The Middle East, and Bevin himself, had to be pacified. The State Department would undertake to try to stop the sailing of the *Pans*. Marshall's office sent a request to the Treasury Department in Washington to find out how the Jews were collecting money in the U.S. and whether the way it was transferred to Europe and used there was legal.[61] The American press began to protest that American money was being used to help Communists split the Western alliance, and even the revered *New York Times* claimed that the U.S.S.R. was placing Soviet agents under the guise of Zionist infiltration into Palestine.[62]

To justify the possible use of arms against the ships, the British Admiralty publicized the fact that they were "surrounded by barbed wire, some of the crew were armed, they had torpedoes, they could ram the destroyers, they could travel at a speed of twelve knots and they had instructions from the Jewish Agency to resist by force".[63] This reached the American press, and British naval intelligence were able to conclude, to their satisfaction, that the mood of senior officials in the administration was to stop the ships which would only bring danger and problems and that "they were now discussing means of stopping the transfer of American Jewish money to Romania. This is because they are convinced that the organization of immigration from Romania to Palestine is being carried out with Russian approval and mainly with money from the Joint."[64] Moshe Sharett collated the diplomatic events in the State Department and was afraid that a terrible plot was being hatched in secret to undermine the U.N. decision on the establishment of the state and to render it meaningless. He remembered the British Peel Commission which had decided ten years earlier in favour of Partition and the establishment of a Jewish state in Mandatory Palestine. Within a few months the opponents of that decision had succeed in turning it into a worthless scrap of paper. Had the decision taken in 1937 been implemented, many of the Jews who subsequently perished in the Holocaust would have been saved.[65]

Sharett, who was afraid of a similar plot, suggested setting a new target date to which the sailing of the *Pans* would be postponed, as it had been during the debate in the U.N. General Assembly. This time he proposed the end of January 1948, on the grounds that the Security Council was due to meet for a final discussion of the Palestine question earlier that month, and it was absolutely out of the question to give the plotters an easy excuse for blocking the partition plan.[66]

The Admiralty was drawing up its own plan to combat the ships, although some of the ideas were speculative. One proposal was to return the ships to the Black Sea under British escort despite the Monterrey Agreement. Some wanted to transfer the passengers to Germany, as with the *Exodus*, and others suggested taking the ships to Beirut, placing the immigrants on trains and sending them back to Bulgaria via Syria and Turkey. The assumption was that since these were Moslem countries, they would gladly cooperate in driving the Jews back to the countries they had come from. All these were vague proposals rather than operational orders; the operational orders of the Admiralty were simpler. A joint plan was prepared with the R.A.F., the ship *HMS Mauritius* was put in charge of the interception operation and orders were given to set up a regular formation of a destroyer and two frigates at the opening of the Aegean until the ships steamed out of the Black Sea. The orders called for a state of alert from the moment the ships sailed, ending with all the destroyers of the Eastern Mediterrranean fleet at the mouth of the Dardanelles.

On 29th December, 1947, the Commander of the British forces in the Middle East issued an "operations order" for the arrest and boarding of the *Pans* with a clear directive: under no circumstances should the ships be allowed to approach the coast of Palestine. The British fleet was to be deployed during the capture of the ships. The stage was set for the struggle.

CHAPTER FIVE

The Mossad *versus* the Establishment

David Ben-Gurion: There is a conflagration.
We must act with caution.

Elhanan Yishai: Are these two ships really endangering
the fate of the Jewish people?

FRIENDSHIP AND DISAGREEMENT

The longstanding friendship between Moshe Sharett, head of the
political department of the Jewish Agency, and Shaul Avigur, head of
the Mossad Le'Aliya Bet, was based on mutual respect and on the
public responsibilities they shared. As younger members of the second
wave of immigration to Palestine (between 1903 and 1914) they had
created a kind of political pact against the older generation of that
immigration, which included David Ben-Gurion, Berl Katznelson
and Yitzhak Ben Zvi. The difference in age between these two
"generations" was small, and ostensibly less significant than the
ideological differences within the same generation-group (e.g.
between Ben-Gurion and Yitzhak Tabenkin). For psychological
reasons and because of the value placed on 'camaraderie', friendship
was a more vital factor within the group than mere ideological
agreement.

The friendship between Shaul Avigur and Moshe Sharett was a
profound one, a social and family link. They differed markedly in
personality and belief. Shaul was modest, introverted, avoiding the
limelight – and valuing action above all; Moshe Sharett was a smooth
diplomat, with a high regard for political negotiation. Despite the
contrast between them, and perhaps because they complemented each
other, they were able to work in mutual agreement and harmony.

The *Pan* incident was a severe test of their friendship.[1] Shaul, head of the Mossad, was the prime mover behind the idea of using large ships to bring immigrants, thereby not only expediting Jewish immigration to Mandatory Palestine, but also creating a powerful political tool. He was responsible for the complete operation of purchasing the ships in the U.S. and transferring them to Europe. Now, in Constantsa, he was setting in motion the involved plan that was to constitute the impressive culmination of this project.

Moshe Sharett was spending most of his time in the corridors of the United Nations. He was involved deeply in negotiations with the British and Americans. At a time when Shaul Avigur succeeded, through his emissaries, in reaching agreement with the Romanian authorities on the emigration of Jews from there, Sharett was playing a leading part in the process that led to the United Nations decision on the establishment of the state. A clash between the brothers-in-law seemed inevitable but they preferred to conduct their conflicts in a way that avoided personal confrontation – through Ben-Gurion.

From October 1947 onwards, the press covered the story of the two ships. It was widely known that the Mossad was trying to bring a large number of Jews from Eastern Europe. At the end of that month Sharett reported to Ben-Gurion from the U.S. that George Marshall, the American Secretary of State, would be ready to support the establishment of a Jewish state but was asking the Zionist leadership to put a halt to illegal immigration in order not to create difficulties for the Americans *vis-à-vis* Great Britain. This would enable Washington to rectify its pro-Zionist image. Marshall apparently threatened Sharett that if this request was not complied with, the U.S. would publicly denounce illegal immigration and fight it.[2] Sharett asked the Jewish Agency Executive for authorization to assure Marshall that the Executive would do its best not to hinder diplomatic activity at the United Nations in anticipation of the debate on the establishment of the state. Ben-Gurion, who had always bitterly objected to any agreement to halt immigration even partially, assented this time.[3] And in fact, in this period, just before the United Nations decision, no immigrant ships embarked for Palestine. There were, of course, other reasons as well for this slow-down, after the furore following the *Exodus* affair.

Now that the decision had been taken to establish the state, the political situation changed. There was also a shift in the mood of the leadership of the Yishuv as a whole. In the course of the long, tortuous negotiations that led to the U.N. decision, Sharett discovered the power of diplomacy and personal influence. He discovered the advantage of personal contacts, the role of negotiation or deliberations, and the power of persuasion. As he established strong ties with powerful statesmen, he became increasingly indebted to the good will of the politicians and states that had supported the idea of Partition.

He now preferred the classical methods of informal meetings and give-and-take attitudes to violent conflict or provocation. If negotiations were to succeed, personal credibility was of cardinal importance and this depended on the ability of the negotiator to prove that he had the authority and power to keep his word.

Sharett demanded Ben-Gurion's backing and help, particularly in restraining unauthorized immigration – the activity that most infuriated the British. This was the pre-condition for negotiations; and the "freezing" of unauthorized immigration would allow Sharett to prove that he was the responsible representative of an organized body, able to implement its promises. Ben-Gurion acceded to this demand and was probably ready even for a confrontation with the Mossad and with Shaul Avigur.

Ben-Gurion had struggled all his life for the consolidation of effort and the establishment of an overall authority over the varied organizations of the emerging state.[4] This was not an easy task. The institutions of the Yishuv were of a voluntary nature and did not always accept sovereign control. This was obviously true of the Irgun Zvai Leumi and Lechi, but even certain bodies that were not considered to have "seceded" from the Yishuv did not always accept Jewish Agency authority. In the case of the Mossad, the lack of a direct chain of command was ostensibly to the advantage of the Jewish Agency Executive, because they could evade outside pressures, and claim to have nothing to do with unauthorized immigration, which was the spontaneous action of Jews wishing to return to their country.[5]

However, beyond this external reason, Ben-Gurion wanted to be involved, and even, perhaps, to be the key figure in the most important area in the struggle against the British – the battle for free immigration. From the beginning of 1946 he tried to take an active part in the main decisions of the Mossad.[6]

When the Mossad advocated large ships, Ben-Gurion proposed concentrating on small boats each carrying up to 200 immigrants.[7] Throughout this period Ben-Gurion reiterated the proposal. His experience had taught him that when the subject came up for decision he would be able to get his own way, and subsequently to gain control of the whole issue of unauthorized immigration.

Shaul Avigur was well acquainted with Ben-Gurion and his organizational methods. He realized that if the ideology and strategy of unauthorized immigration were made the subject of public debate, Ben-Gurion would win the day. Immigration would then be controlled by Ben-Gurion through his young followers who would be content to bring in a number of small boats to Palestine. The aim of immigration would be to harass the British, and it would come to play a marginal role in the struggle for national independence.

At a meeting of the Mapai secretariat on 9th December 1947, Ben-Gurion said,

> For a year and a half I have been saying to the people dealing with this matter that it is necessary to change the methods of immigration . . . I am not for large ships but for small boats, 200 people to a boat! Many such boats! . . . The tragedy is that they did not argue with me, they merely did the opposite . . . Every time I was in Paris I spoke about this to Shaul, but they went their own way.[8]

The fact is that Shaul simply avoided direct confrontation with Ben-Gurion. Ben-Gurion was preoccupied with many problems; his visits to Europe, where the Mossad was operating, were few, and Shaul had gained a wide degree of autonomy. In order to challenge it, Ben-Gurion would have had to launch a long, obstinate struggle. As he said, "I did not want to give orders in this affair so matters proceeded as they did."[9]

As soon as the moratorium in the Mossad's activities had ended, and the decision to establish the state was taken on 29th November 1947, the Mossad announced the renewal of immigration on an unprecedented scale. The *Pans* were ready to sail and a date had been fixed – 14th December 1947. This information was brought to Palestine by Moshe Sneh.[10]

Sneh was a member of the Jewish Agency Executive; his operational experience as commander of the Hagana made him an authority on clandestine military activities. As such, he was the liaison officer between the political leadership, i.e. the Jewish Agency, and the Mossad. In theory he was in charge of the Mossad because he held the immigration portfolio on the Jewish Agency Executive.

Sneh wanted to make the decisions in the Mossad. Twenty years after the affair of the *Pans* he claimed that he had reached a status where he was consulted on every subject, from the purchase of ships (for which, he claimed, he had personally obtained money from an American bank) to determining their destinations.[11] However, he does not, in fact, seem to have succeeded in obtaining control over what took place in the Mossad. He visited Romania at this time but the documentary evidence records his contacts with local Zionist leadership and the various political parties on one matter alone: the allocation of places in the ships among the parties.[12] And even in this matter his contribution was marginal because, in the end, most of the immigrants were chosen by selection committees to whom party considerations were irrelevant.

During his brief stay in Romania, Moshe Sneh was the senior Palestinian emissary there. He asked to meet Bodnares, the Deputy Premier, and was able to see him with the help of Moshe Auerbach and Yosef Klarman. For a long time, Sneh claimed that this conversation had paved the way for immigration from Romania,[13] but here too the job had already been done. The decision on immigration from Romania had already been reached, and the ships were already waiting in Constantsa harbour. The decision of the government of Romania to allow 20,000 Jews to leave its territory had been finalized even earlier between Klarman, Auerbach and Bodnares,[14] with the agreement of the Russians. When they decided that the moratorium was over, it was they who informed Moshe Sneh of the new date of sailing. They had arranged it without consulting him even though he was in Romania at the time. Furthermore, the eventual reckoning between the Jewish Agency Executive and the heads of the Mossad was a direct confrontation between Ben-Gurion and Shaul Avigur. Moshe Sneh did not take part in the discussions and decisions.

These facts do not so much reflect Sneh's standing in the Jewish Agency and his personal power, as the degree to which the Mossad felt independent, and the considerable autonomy it had acquired. In a letter to Moshe Sharett, Shaul Avigur wrote plainly: "The Executive [of the Jewish Agency] has never claimed that it manages illegal immigration and that it is able to stop, direct or renew it as it wishes. For it to say so would be untrue . . ."[15]

Further on in his letter, Avigur emphasized that "organized immigration is now headed by people who comply with the discipline of Zionism", but that this compliance had limits, at which he hinted quite clearly: "Immigration will not be stopped – cannot be stopped by force of an Executive decision."[16]

When Sneh brought the information about the expected sailing of the ships to Ben-Gurion, it was obvious that a sharp clash was imminent. Members of the Jewish Agency Executive in Jerusalem, who were beginning to digest the significance of the General Assembly decision on the establishment of the state, and who were dividing their time between public rallies and celebrations and intensive activity for the implementation of the decision, debated the information. This was the first session summoned since the partition resolution and there were many complex political and defence matters on the agenda. For this reason a sub-committee of six people including Ben-Gurion was appointed, and met the same day (30th November 1947). Only two members, Eliahu Dobkin and Moshe Sneh, were in favour of sending the boats. The four others, Golda Meir, Moshe Shapira, Yitzhak Greenbaum and Ben-Gurion himself, were opposed.[17] Moshe Sneh (who was already in the throes of the political transition which was to lead him from Zionism into the Israeli Communist Party) resigned. This act of resignation against the background of the *Pans* affair marked the end of the brilliant defence career of a unique personallity who had played a major role in the struggle to establish a Jewish state. The reasons for his resignation reflect the start of his political erosion. He later stated that then, at the end of 1947, he had already sensed that the ban on the sailing of the ships was "an act of ingratitude towards the Romanian government and an act of surrender to the Anglo-American dictate ... I saw it as auguring our dependence on the Western powers in violation of the concept of national independence and the national interest of the future state."[18]

DOUBTS AND HESITATIONS AT HOME

Ben-Gurion, who was afraid of the Mossad activists and of Shaul Avigur, and who knew that Sneh's resignation would make it difficult for him to control unauthorized immigration, toned down his opposition. He sought a decisive argument, to be voiced by Moshe Sharett. The argument should be blunt and unambiguous. "The sailing would endanger the State of Israel."[19] For this reason the debate did not end with a clear decision, but with an appeal to Moshe Sharett in New York. Ben-Gurion cabled him on 1st December 1947, asking how to react to the Mossad's notification that the boats had sailed,[20] and at the same time cabled Avigur to delay the ships. The cables were sent in code from the Mossad office in Israel, whose secretary was Moshe Carmel. The cable read as follows:

1 December 1947
To Ben Yehuda [Shaul Avigur's code name in the Labour party]
From Ovadiah [Ben-Gurion's code name in the Labour party]
Departure from Agami [code name for both Romania and for
Moshe Auerbach, head of the Mossad there] discussed by [Jewish
Agency] Directorate, opinion favours cancel or reduce or
postpone.[21]
The decision passed to committee which will decide in consultation
with your brother-in-law [Sharett].
Meanwhile decided that departure will not take place unless
Directorate signals agreement, you must notify Agami of this.[22]

1 December 1947
To Or [Shaul Avigur's code name in the Mossad]
From Arnon [Mossad code name in Palestine], Berg [Geneva, or
Pino Ginsburg, Mossad treasurer there]
Further to Ovadiah's memo
According to Zahava [Golda Meir] we should continue with vessels
from west [Italy, France].[23]
Re Agami awaiting opinion of Ben Kedem [Moshe Sharett].
Probably will await his return. Try to contact him and influence his
reply . . . Essential you come here immediately to take part in
debates and decisions. Debates started.[24]

2 December 1947
To Or
From Arnon, Berg
Ami [Ben-Gurion's code name in the Mossad and the Hagana] of
opinion activity from west should continue and even increase. Re
Agami, Ami knows and fears situation there. He is awaiting further
news from Ben Kedem to take decision. Ami has told this to Ben
Kedem.[25]

4 December 1947
To Agami
From Or
Further to the negotiations taking place between the Jewish Agency
Executive and all outside parties concerned, it has been decided to
begin large-scale immigration in the immediate future. We have
received orders from the authorized bodies to delay the departure of

the two vessels from Agami. The order to delay is valid solely for sailing of the 2 vessels from Agami![26]

This cable from Shaul Avigur, sent to Romania three days later, was a severe blow to the Mossad workers. The effort that had been invested in the *Pans* was the greatest ever made by the Yishuv. Each obstacle that these dedicated people had overcome bolstered their enthusiasm. The scale of the operation was enormous, the financial investment was the heaviest ever made by the Yishuv and even more important was the actual significance of the task.

They thought along the same lines as Shaul Avigur, who had said on several occasions: "I am thinking of Kvutzat Kinneret [where he lived for a while]. Every ship like this is twelve or thirteen times the size of Kvutzat Kinneret."[27] Most of the young people involved in the operation were kibbutz members; they knew how a kibbutz was founded and what its strength was. These ships were conveying the equivalent of the population of twenty-five large kibbutzim at a critical moment when the small Yishuv was fighting for its life and every kibbutz was a powerful living barrier against possible Arab invasion.

As Moshe Sharett, as a result of his activities and achievements, was attaching increasing significance to the power of diplomatic negotiations, so these young people, whose dedication had enabled them to organize a large immigration movement which had made an impact on all the Jewish communities in Europe and on world public opinion, were convinced that their achievements were the most important and decisive at this sensitive stage in the struggle for statehood. Because they had outwitted hundreds of British agents and overcome complex British diplomatic pressures, they belittled diplomatic considerations or regarded them as merely the sequel to their own field work. Diplomacy was intended to further the goal of bringing Jews to Israel, and not the reverse.

The emissaries of the Mossad had good reasons for thinking that diplomacy was motivated not by ideals but by pragmatic calculations. The Mossad people believed that in addition to political interests, bribery played a key part in negotiations. The many obstacles to the voyage of the *Pans* to Romania, and in Romania itself, were overcome mainly by means of bribes. Venia Hadari, reporting to the Mossad on the preparations for sailing, wrote: "Attempts by the enemy to interfere continue all the time – but up to now, they have not succeeded. You know that this is costing us a lot of Stephens [dollars][28] and perhaps in retrospect it is good that this is the basic factor in the attitude of the government people there. But it is a strain on our budget!"[29] Thus, it was possible to solve problems: it was always possible to urge, to promise, to bribe or to persuade, but immigration must never be halted.

The Mossad agents viewed the decision of the Jewish Agency as the irresponsible act of people detached from public opinion, remote from what was happening "in the field". Scorn for diplomacy and suspicions regarding "professional politicians" had brought the hard-pressed and embattled kibbutz members working for the Mossad to explosion point. Moshe Auerbach hastened to cable Shaul Avigur:

> Urgent – Secret
> 4.12.1947
> to the Mossad
> from Romania
> Received from Sh . . . [Shaul Avigur] the decision of the directorate re postponement departure of "big ones".
> Please notify Directorate [of Jewish Agency] and David [Ben-Gurion].
> 14,000 people left with no means of support, having liquidated their affairs and sold possessions. They cannot remain here during winter, since no preparations made for heating or supplies.
> Please note that the gates are wide open here but can close with this consignment. We have been asked to remove from the list of immigrants all technicians, engineers and skilled industrial workers.
> The Jewish collaborators [in the Romanian Communist Party] will exploit the situation to destroy our standing with the government by holding us responsible for the fate of 14,000 people. The postponement can destroy the whole Zionist movement in Romania. The immigrants have already packed because the departure date has been fixed for 14th December.
> Please discuss this question again and cancel decision.[30]

Moshe Auerbach did not stop at sending the cable but, through friends in Israel, arranged for a copy of the cable to be sent direct to Ben-Gurion. The ships were standing ready in Constantsa harbour and the whole operation was primed to go. Moshe Auerbach was convinced that he could not leave Romania at this time but he was not certain that the politicians in Tel Aviv understood the situation. His confidence in Shaul Avigur was weakening. What was happening there? How could they abandon this most vital matter at such a critical time?

Moshe Auerbach decided at his own discretion to go to Tel Aviv at once, to bang on the table, to shout, to explain. They would surely understand. They were certain to change the decision and then he would return at once to be in Constantsa to give the signal to sail. Without consulting his superiors, he cabled:

4.12.1947
Immediate
To Arnon
From Morris [Auerbach himself] (Constantsa)
Advise immediately if Agami can come at once to Israel by air[31]

Shaul Avigur knew his people, their dedication and commitment. It took precedence over their loyalty to him as their commander and to the national leadership. He sensed that he was liable to lose control over them. The Palmach and Mossad representatives might take the law into their own hands and decide to disregard his order and take the ships out of Romania. They would not call this mutiny, but would create a situation where it would appear that they themselves had lost control over events and had been compelled to let the ships sail because of pressure from thousands of passengers.

Avigur had acquired power and a great degree of autonomy by virtue of being the man on the spot. He knew that because of difficulties in making contact with home and because, in the special conditions of unauthorized immigration, the people actually doing the work gained considerable authority, an inner clique was being formed among the Mossad emissaries, including people very close to him. At the decisive moment they would decide for themselves, even contravening his views. The ships were destined to sail!

The head of the Mossad Le' Aliya Bet was no weakling. Avigur had been convinced that he was acting correctly when he was party to the order to hide a load of explosives on board the *Patria* and when he called for a fight on the high seas between rickety illegal immigrant boats and Royal Navy destroyers. But this time his doubts made it difficult for him to reach a decision. He appealed to his subordinates to exercise self-restraint and found himself having to explain the reasons for the delay. He did not do this willingly, and it was evident that he had been influenced by Moshe Sharett (his brother-in-law and friend). Again he advised the emissaries:

> There are negotiations on immigration. Nothing is certain, there is a recommendation that the British leave on 1st February and immigration will commence. Meanwhile negotiations are going on about Monia [Monia Meridor, active in arms purchase] and other matters. The law is on our side and we must obey the law.[32]

It was clear that these "legal" arguments would not convince Avigur's subordinates. Trust in the British had long since vanished and there were reservations about negotiations with other countries. Avigur therefore attempted to cite security arguments. It was essential to bring arms to Israel. Several of the unauthorized immigration agents, such as Ehud Avriel, had been recruited for arms acquisition. At that very moment Avriel, together with Monia Meridor, was in Prague about to sign a large-scale agreement for the supply of arms to the Yishuv.[33] The departure of the ships at this stage could harm these negotiations, and hence delaying them was part of the immediate security objectives of the future state.

This time, Shaul did not sound his usual self, but the tone was blunt: "Like or not, we have to postpone the sailing." Yet, in addressing his superiors, he faithfully represented the views of his own agents. Since Ben-Gurion's cable, calling for delay, had asked that the decision on sailing be taken only after consultation with Sharett in the U.S.,[34] Avigur appealed to his brother-in-law in a long, emotional letter.

After an affectionate "Shalom, dear brother", he launched into an impassioned appeal not to stop the ships. "I suspect that you do not physically experience the real, daily life in the shadow of the fears and the compulsion and the dangers of the thousands of people who you do your best to serve." In fact, he writes, "you ignore the human side of Zionism. Perhaps you do not understand the urgency of immigration. It is not just a political exercise or demonstration. The moment the Executive halts unauthorized immigration, without being immediately able to organize legal immigration in its place, it simply strengthens our enemies." And Shaul Avigur, the man of action, doubts whether diplomacy will really be able to arrange legal immigration or whether the promises to open a free port will be implemented in the near future. Furthermore, "Does the Executive have the power to stop unauthorized immigration? I don't think so." This was a grave statement. Avigur wrote to his close friend, "The matter is not in your hand, nor perhaps even in mine. . . . It is not a

The *Pan Crescent* at Cyprus

The Pan York

question of imposing discipline. The organized unauthorized immigration is headed by people who accept the discipline of Zionism. But immigration will not stop – cannot stop – because of a decree of the Executive."

This brought Shaul Avigur to a new and painful subject – the Revisionists. Since unauthorized immigration would continue regardless, it might be resumed by others. "It will seek other channels and other operatives and will find them either among people we want or those we do not want – this is a word to the wise." At a time when the whole Yishuv was worried about how the Lechi and the Irgun would behave when the state was established, and when civil war could break out at any moment,[35] it would be folly to abandon such a central position of power as the organization of immigration to Israel.

Shaul Avigur went on to write that the gates of Eastern Europe were open but could close again at once. The Romanians were showing signs of regretting their agreement, and "the Jewish Communist vulture is working and pressing constantly from every direction" to cancel the agreement on the departure of the *Pans*. And what will happen to the Jews? "We have alerted 14,000 of them . . . they are already packed, most of them have sold the remnants of their possessions, the Romanian winter is approaching and we shall be responsible for them, their tragedy and their destruction."

The firm tone of the letter abated towards the end. Avigur repeated his warning – it was impossible to cancel the sailing – but it could be postponed, though only for a short time, "otherwise the masses of people will storm the ships and our comrades will not desert them; they will take them aboard and sail".[36]

In this conflict, waged on two fronts, Shaul tried to stop Moshe Auerbach from leaving for Palestine;[37] he himself would fly there at once from Paris, but first he extracted a promise from Venia Hadari, then coordinating the unauthorized immigration operations from the Paris headquarters of the Mossad, that he would not cooperate in attempts to remove the ships from Constantsa. He was aware that the Mossad operatives were up in arms and he was afraid they would do something rash. And in fact some daring schemes were being bruited in exploratory conversations between operatives, and hinted at over the telephone and in the flow of cables from Moshe Auerbach in Bucharest to Ehud Avriel in Prague,[38] from Prague to Pino Ginsburg in Geneva,[39] from Geneva to Venia Hadari in Paris,[40] and then back again through the unauthorized immigration operatives in Italy, Turkey and Bulgaria.

While Shaul Avigur was meeting Ben-Gurion, Golda Meir, the heads of the Hagana and leaders of the Jewish Agency and trying to persuade them to allow the ships to depart, a parallel campaign was being conducted by the younger generation of Palestinian fighters and operatives in Europe, who were seeking a solution whereby the ships could sail.

Shaul Avigur was walking a tightrope. He needed the help of his agents to bolster his demand for the departure of the *Pans* and he wanted to cite the arguments of the Yishuv leaders to moderate the stand of his own people. The man Shaul chose to accompany him to Palestine was Shaike Dan: a fine soldier, a courageous and (what was most important in this case) loyal individual. Shaul flew directly from Paris to Lydda, but Dan was obliged to improvise a circuitous route: Sofia – Prague – Zurich – Geneva – Milan – Rome – Athens – Nicosia – Lydda. By chance he arrived at the same time as Pino Ginsburg, the Mossad treasurer. The three of them had no time for discussions. Everything was quick and rushed – a brief visit to the family, the kibbutz, and back to the Mossad office in Tel Aviv to hear the latest news. On the evening of 9th December, 1947, the Mapai secretariat met in the Histadrut (Federation of Labour) building in Tel Aviv. The first forum for discussing important matters, including national issues, was traditionally the Party. Since its establishment in 1930 Mapai had been the largest party in the country. It elected representatives to national and Histadrut institutions and decided what line they would adopt.

Ben-Gurion, who was chairman of the Jewish Agency Executive and *de facto* leader of the Yishuv on the eve of the establishment of the state, held this position by force of, and as emissary of, the Party. Thus, in this bitter debate about the *Pans*, Ben-Gurion repeatedly stated: "I shall not act against the decision of the Party."[41]

The Mapai secretariat meeting had been called to discuss "security questions". The War of Independence had just commenced. The Yishuv, which was familiar with long and bloody battles, was stunned by what had happened in the first days of December. Opening the meeting Zeev Isserson spoke of the daily toll of casualties but despite events in the country and the urgent necessity to react, the first item on the agenda was unauthorized immigration, which, as Isserson said, was "no less important than security".

Shaul Avigur enjoyed the respect of all the varied ideological groups that constituted Mapai. Despite the aura that surrounded him because of his close relations with the leadership of the labour movement, and his activity in the Hagana leadership, he was not a man of words. He rarely addressed official forums. He was often present on the sidelines, attentive and grave. When his advice was asked, he preferred to give it not from the platform but from a corner of the hall.

Even on this occasion, when a weighty matter hung in the balance, Shaul was not anxious to speak. He belonged to the labour movement, performed its bidding and was therefore answerable to the forum he was now attending, but it seemed to him that there was a disproportion between the importance of the subject and of the group that was to decide upon it. Seated in the long, narrow meeting room were Dovdevani, Neustadt, Isserson, Lubianiker and Yishai, all second-rank members of the labour movement; where was Golda? where was Ben-Gurion? Zeev Isserson, the chairman, urged Shaul to speak. To Shaul's enquiring look, he replied: 'Ben-Gurion is in Tel Aviv, he is busy with security problems and we are doing everything we can to get him to the meeting.'[42] Shaul was disappointed. He had flown back especially and it seemed as though all the important people were avoiding him. Shortly before the meeting he had seen Ben-Gurion, who seemed evasive. Shaul had almost begged for attention and reminded him that he was bringing the matter to the Party but Ben-Gurion had not reacted. And now he was not present, not coming. Since everyone was waiting for him to speak and Shaike Dan, sitting next to him, was nudging him, Shaul rose hesitantly. He briefly described the history of the *Pans* up to their arrival in Romania and the importance of rescuing the Jews. Suddenly, Ben-Gurion entered the room. There was a palpable tension, everyone anticpating a confrontation, but Shaul only spoke for a few moments as though finishing a recitation. He left Shaike Dan to complete the moving, vivid and persuasive story of the *Pans*. Shaike Dan was a young Palestinian fighter and pioneer. But, in addition to his toughness and courage, he was a born diplomat and speaker. This combination of qualities had enabled him to play an important part in the reorganization of the Zionist movement in Romania at the end of the Second World War. He had successfully concluded a deal with the Bulgarian government for the departure of the ships from Burgas, and explained vividly to the Party workers the Mossad's arguments in favour of the departure of the *Pans*, allowing himself a little poetic licence.

He told the meeting that the Jews were already assembled at the departure points and that the thousands waiting there, in hardship, at the height of the snowy Romanian winter, could expect only hunger, cold and even death. If the thousands of Jews who were already waiting to go were not allowed to board the *Pans*, the Romanians would go back on their agreement and suspend their discussion, and the gates of Eastern Europe would close forever. This would simply mean victory for the Yishuv's enemies, the greatest of whom were the Jewish Communists who were now waging a campaign of provocation against the Zionist movement. Such shameful abandonment of the Jews would be regarded by them as lasting proof that Zionism spelt disaster for the Jews. And finally, he pointed out, it would be impossible to maintain control at this critical juncture over 14,000 Jews, not including their friends and families. "These Jews will break out and go to the harbour. They will take the law into their own hands, board the ships and try to sail, and then there will be a real pogrom!"

When Dan had finished and all those present seemed stunned into silence, Shaul took stock of the situation and again rose to speak. This time he dealt with the political aspect of the matter: the Zionist Executive, he said, was not responsible for unauthorized immigration. This was a spontaneous phenomenon and the Palestinian emissaries could only direct it. If they had not mobilized for this project, it would have happened anyway. It would continue with or without the Yishuv – and preferably with it. "I am not a professional in this business, my father didn't do it and I hope that I myself won't have to do it for long," he explained. The responsibility was collective, and there should be no arguments about gain or personal empire-building. The acuteness of the problem can be glimpsed from an interjection by Ben-Gurion: when Shaul said, "I am happy that Ben-Gurion is present and sorry that Moshe (Sharett) is not here," Ben-Gurion interrupted him to say, "I am sorry that you are not in Washington." Shaul seemed to lose his fire. Once again, instead of attacking, he tried for a compromise; "We shall seek and find together a way to bring them in." His final remarks offered neither a solution nor a proposal.

When Ben-Gurion rose to speak, he was decisive, blunt and tough. It was a difficult and painful matter; he was going to strike at unauthorized immigration, the most cherished activity, on political and practical grounds. His speech was wide-ranging, dealing with the nature of unauthorized immigration, the relationship between the Mossad and the national institutions, relations with the U.S. and Britain, the constitutional significance of bringing the ships and the dangers of the voyage itself. His conclusion sounded cruel to whoever had been brought up in the traditions of the labour movement. Shaul Avigur rose agitatedly, claiming that Ben-Gurion had implied that unauthorized immigration had completed its task. Elchanan Yishai, a faithful follower of Ben-Gurion, asked his revered leader whether, in all seriousness, these two ships were endangering the fate of the Jewish people. The meeting continued for hours. Ostensibly it had the power to make a decision. If Shaul's views regarding the necessity of the immediate departure of the ships from Romania had been accepted, Ben-Gurion would have concurred. This was doubtless the fervent wish of the people present, all of whom had grown up in a movement that regarded action as crucial and scorned diplomacy. But Shaul Avigur was still walking the tightrope. He did not want a decision, for he had not decided for himself, and the meeting terminated without one.[43]

The participants dispersed with a heavy heart. Shaul decided to locate the members of the Jewish Agency Executive in Jerusalem and to persuade them individually, but the most important person was the one closest to himself, his brother-in-law, Moshe Sharett, then in the U.S.A. It may be assumed that he slept little that night, and towards dawn he and Dan were summoned urgently to Ben-Gurion.[44]

Ben-Gurion too, had not slept. He received Shaul and Dan on the second floor of his home in Keren Hakayemet Boulevard, in Tel Aviv. His face reflected the tension of the past few days – firstly the voting at the U.N., then the fighting, the organization of the defence of the Yishuv, and now, the problem of the *Pans*. So many matters of life and death – in the space of two weeks.

Shaul's face also betrayed signs of strain. Those who served under him knew that under emotional pressure his face seemed to swell and darken and his silences became even longer than usual.[45] Ben-Gurion, in a rare moment of personal confession, stood in front of Shaul, who was sitting hunched up, and told him that there was a tragic split in his soul. "I must object, because the difficult front is now in America. Moshe Sharett is at that front, facing the leaders of the world. If I do not help him to the best of my ability, I will be making him fight both in the front and the rear and I have no right to do that. If Moshe agrees to alter his position, I will immediately cancel my objections to the departure of the ships." With a weary gesture he turned to Shaul and said, "You and Shaike must go at once to America, speak with Moshe, explain and let him hear your views." He then returned to the main problem. He went over to a large map hanging from a bookshelf: "There is going to be a hard war," he said. "All the Arab countries will join in; we need arms, military advisers, money and above all, organization and a command structure." Ben-Gurion was drawn into a description of the problems of military organization. Shaul knew him well and realized that the discussion about the *Pans* was over. Silently he rose from his chair, patted Ben-Gurion on the shoulder and together with Shaike Dan went out into the cool Tel Aviv morning.

He did not speak as they left and Dan took the initiative. Their urgent trip home had been aimed at enabling the ships to sail, and they had to do everything possible. Ben-Gurion had suggested that they go to America at once, but how could they manage this? First of all, they needed visas, which were not easy to obtain. Dan contacted Reuven Zaslani (Shiloach) of the intelligence service of the Hagana, who had a finger in every pie. He was worried – to obtain visas for the U.S., they had to apply to the American Consulate which was in Jerusalem; the road to Jerusalem was dangerous because the Arabs controlled Sha'ar Hagai at the approach to the city.

In the atmosphere of friendship and cooperation prevailing in those days, the problem was solved within a few minutes. Reuven made a few telephone calls and within half an hour Chaim Weizmann's bullet-proof armoured car had appeared. The vehicle took the three of them straight to the American Consulate in Jerusalem. Dan and Shaul had their fingerprints taken and with the help of a few suitable hints they received the visas at once. Despite the speedy preparations Dan felt that Shaul was not happy about going to the U.S.; he was deterred by the idea of direct confrontation with his brother-in-law. One of the characteristics of the leadership of the Yishuv was the well-worn concept of the "vision". Above and beyond the somewhat bathetic image it evokes, and its popular usage in later years which eroded its meaning, it should be emphasized that without this concept it is impossible to explain the history of the establishment of the state. The "vision" soared above concrete and rational considerations and made it possible to defy logic which at times could easily prove that there was no point to the struggle and that the efforts invested in the Zionist endeavour were in vain. Vision, by its very nature, respects historical criteria. Thus, it is not by chance that members of the leadership, especially from the labour movement, took note of the historical significance of their activities and took great trouble to document them.[46]

This sensitivity to the judgment of history, which is a corollary of "vision", deterred Shaul from turning the affair of the *Pans* into a direct conflict between him and his beloved brother-in-law. He felt that this problem would be of decisive importance when the day came for historical reckoning. Shaul was convinced that he was right, that the sailing of the ships and the bringing of 15,000 people (the final number of passengers) to the shores of Israel were of supreme value and that the Zionist ideal would pay a heavy price if the ships did not sail. He felt that the diplomatic considerations were mistaken and contained the seeds of disaster. But he felt that it would be a grave offence if the argument focused on personalities, on Shaul and Moshe.

As they left the American Consulate in Jerusalem, Reuven Shiloach asked, "Well, are you flying to America?" Shaul, deep in thought and huddled in his long overcoat, blurted out, "To Golda!" Golda Meir, a tough, decisive woman, was head of the Political Department of the Jewish Agency in Jerusalem. She was a contemporary of Shaul Avigur and many times they had found themselves in agreement. They had much in common; they were not ideological standard-bearers, they did not write long articles for the labour movement daily, *Davar* and its other journals, and their positions in the labour movement made them more or less of equal rank. Shaul and Golda were people of action, they said what they felt and spoke directly and to the point.

With Golda, uncharacteristically, Shaul spoke at length; he was moved and gave expression to his pain and fear. It was only with Golda that he was able to show his innermost feelings about his predicament. She also spoke emotionally, and occasionally a tear was seen to glimmer in the corner of her eye. Golda's conclusion was apparently blunt and decisive and perhaps, somewhat harsh. Shaul's summing up: "Golda opposes," does not sufficiently express how much the conversation stunned him.[47] The extent to which it influenced him and the importance he attached to it can be seen from his proposed chapter headings to his planned book on the *Pans*; there is a special chapter entitled "Golda". Dan, who was present at the meeting, absolutely refused to describe the conversation. "I shall not say a single word about that conversation. It will go with me to the grave." Question: "Why do you refuse to speak about it?" Dan: "My friend, you are sitting with a man who considers himself a professor of what not to say. If I have regretted anything in my life, it is what I have said; I have never been sorry for what I have not said."[48]

It was getting dark when they left Golda's office. Reuven had

arranged some meetings for that evening and he begged Shaul and
Dan to stay the night in Jerusalem. He said it was dangerous to go back
down to Tel Aviv at that hour, but Shaul, very agitated, said that he
had to get to Tel Aviv at once. David Shaltiel, head of the Hagana
intelligence service, volunteered to drive them. It was a bold
undertaking to leave Jerusalem in the evening but the Arabs were
taken by surprise by this splendid vehicle speeding westwards and
they merely shouted and threw stones.[49]

On the way to Tel Aviv Shaul turned to Dan and said, "Go to
America and speak with Moshe." Dan was uncertain. He had
conducted the negotiations with the Bulgarian government; heavy
pressure was being exerted on them and someone should be there to
keep watch on events, to act as a counter-balance to the British, to
reassure and encourage them. Furthermore, Dan felt that if Shaul, his
superior, who was so close to Moshe, refused to go, it would be strange
and confusing for someone as young and junior as he to tackle the
highest political level of the Zionist leadership. The idea of flying to
America had not been a serious proposition from the start but had
served to cover the lack of certainty; Ben-Gurion was supposed to
think that Shaul was going, Shaul was supposed to think that Shaike
was going. When asked, they spoke about the proposed journey,[50] but
it was clear to everyone that nobody was going to America to speak
with Sharett. The use of this pretext reached absurdity when Sharett
himself, speaking on the telephone with Golda, asked that no one be
sent. The journey was superfluous, he declared, and added that in any
case he would be returning in a few days.[51]

At times, when improvisation was the prevailing method of action, it
was not customary to finalize operative decisions. Dan and Shaul had
not decided on a clear course of action. Shaul was staying on in Israel in
a desperate attempt to persuade Golda and Ben-Gurion while Dan
spoke about travelling but contemplated a number of options;
ostensibly he was going to the U.S., which was also what he told Shaul,
although the latter sensed that Dan wanted to return to Bulgaria. The
provisional decision was – Bulgaria; from there, if possible, Dan would
go to the U.S. In a discussion which Dan considered final, Shaul said,
"Try to get to America and persuade Moshe; if you can't reach him, try
to delay the departure of the ships, but if the situation there requires
other measures and you can't prevent them – you must do your
duty!"[52]

Dan, who knew Shaul well, was troubled. Shaul was usually

authoritative, spoke straight to the point and never flinched from giving clear, express orders. Now he seemed to be evading the issue, and the manner in which he did this was indicative of his predicament. It was not a question of shedding responsibility or trying to put the blame on others while preparing to justify himself, but resulted from a temporary inability to reach a decision. Shaul's operatives, who did not understand his dilemma, interpreted this as weakness. Pino Ginsburg, treasurer of the Mossad, approached Shaike Dan and suggested a way of resolving Shaul's indecision: "Let's go to Shaul and tell him that we, the Mossad operatives, have decided to take the responsibility out of his hands. We'll take the ships out and if we have to conceal the fact that Shaul was in on the secret, we'll conceal it." Shaike Dan had reservations about the idea but went along with Pino to the America Hotel on Yehuda Halevi Street in Tel Aviv where Shaul was staying. Pino, a meticulous man of German origin, with a relaxed and logical way of speaking, unfolded his plan. Shaul did not even wait to the end and turned on him angrily, "Absolutely not! If I am in on it, I'm in to the end."[53] In this atmosphere of indecision, Pino Ginsburg returned to Geneva. At Ben-Gurion's request, Shaul remained in Israel. Ben-Gurion, completely preoccupied with the deteriorating military situation, asked Shaul to leave the Mossad and handle the organization of the army. In their lengthy conversations, Ben-Gurion angrily dismissed the question of unauthorized immigration, but Shaul declared flatly, "until the *Pans* affair is settled, I am not abandoning it."[54] Meanwhile, Shaike Dan awaited new developments, but each passing day was proof that his waiting was pointless. Communications with Romania and the Mossad headquarters in Paris were difficult; the British were tapping the telephones and nothing could be done in Palestine. Ben-Gurion and Golda were backing Sharett, who was also encountering difficulties with telephone calls and cables. The initiative lay with the immigration operatives in Europe. They decided to establish firm communications between their various centres and to open up a direct channel of communication with Moshe Sharett in the U.S. and with Brodetzky and Goldmann in London, bypassing the intervening levels of the hierarchy.[55]

In Geneva, Pino Ginsburg reported on the impossibility of reaching a decision in Palestine and conveyed what Shaike Dan's report had told him about Shaul Avigur's attitude: "If there is no alternative – sail." Pino understood this to be a kind of sanctioning: "Let the vessels leave, black or white."[56] In other words, if the Jewish Agency authorized it, so much the better, and if not, the ships would sail on the responsibility of the people on the spot, without authorization! The problem was how long to wait for authorization. Moshe Auerbach in Romania was pressing to explore every avenue in the effort to gain approval. They worked in parallel and exchanged information. An agreement took shape between them to provoke a crisis that would provide a legitimate reason for ordering the ships to sail, as proposed by Shaul Avigur.

The crisis, as a dialectical point of departure, was a powerful tool in the hands of the labour movement in Palestine. An authoritative observer of Israeli politics has claimed that when Ben-Gurion as premier wanted to attain an objective and his colleagues were opposed, he would deliberately create a crisis. In the ensuing situation, his will prevailed.[57] The present crisis was prepared hesitantly. At first Moshe Auerbach tried the old method of raising an alarm. On 11th December 1947 he sent a telegram to Shaul Avigur in Israel, describing a most difficult situation: hundreds of families, candidates for immigration, had left their homes, in accordance with the plan drawn up before the postponement. The Romanian authorities had confiscated their homes and they could not return there. Heavy pressure was being exerted by the people themselves and by the authorities. The cable ended with a simple question: "What should we do?"[58] From Shaul Avigur's point of view, this cable was not very helpful. He had already pounded on all the doors and Shaike Dan had described the situation most persuasively and in the gloomiest terms – all to no avail.

NO WAY BACK

When this opening shot did not produce the desired reaction, Moshe Auerbach took a further, and this time decisive step, from which there was no way back. On 13th December he cabled to Shaul Avigur:

> Urgent, 13.12.1947
> Since we have been granted as of last night, permission to stay one more week in Constantsa, I have given orders, following your promise that the vessels should sail "black or white", to prepare the consignment for departure on the 21st of this month. I was forced to do this after it became clear from conversations yesterday with the great friend that further discussion would mean complete cancellation of the whole consignment. I request that Dan return at once.[59]

This cable created a new situation. The order had already been given; trains had been mobilized, the project was in motion and there was no way back. Moshe Auerbach had prepared a dubious alibi; he credited Shaul with a promise that the ships should depart with or without the express permission of the national leadership. This was a rather subjective interpretation of Shaul's remarks to Shaike Dan, which had undergone modifications during transmission through Pino Ginsburg to Moshe Auerbach. Venia Hadari, in Paris, warned his colleagues that their solution, based on what Shaul had said, was simplistic, transparent and unacceptable. A more persuasive argument was therefore produced: "The great friend" had given an ultimatum! This "great friend" was in fact both great and a friend. He was Bodnares, head of the Romanian secret services as well as deputy Prime Minister, and an enthusiastic advocate of unauthorized immigration. He had good reasons, namely the desire to get rid of the Jews, take over their homes, speed up the socialization of Romania by ensuring the departure of the middle class of businessmen and professionals and last but not least, undermine British imperialism. Moreover, Yosef Klarman and Moshe Auerbach had succeeded in establishing friendly relations with him. Shaul Avigur, who was shy and reticent, did not know Bodnares and had not come into contact with him. Moshe Auerbach knew with certainty that Shaul had no means of contacting Bodnares, checking his story or trying to persuade him to cancel the ultimatum. At that time all communications with the Romanian authorities were in Moshe's hands and he exploited them to the end.

Because of ties of friendship and the tendency, which became second nature, to maintain secrecy even when there was no operational justification, it is difficult to obtain a clear-cut answer to the question of whether Bodnares was in fact a party to the decision attributed to him, which served as the pretext for setting the operation in motion. A meeting apparently took place on 12th December between Auerbach and Bodnares, at which the latter may conceivably have asked why the sailings were being delayed. Such meetings took place frequently. However, this time the operational programme was disclosed in full and Moshe Auerbach took the initiative and gave the order to move. It is easy to imagine the tension that prevailed among the Mossad operatives in Constantsa, Bucharest, Sophia, Burgas, Istanbul, Prague, Geneva, Rome and Paris. One of the biggest operations in the annals of unauthorized immigration was about to commence and this time it was to be carried out by the rank-and-file, because the leaders were out of action. The leaders of the Yishuv and of American and British Jewry did not react at once. This inertia worried the operatives and the two principal partners in the decision, Moshe Auerbach and Venia Hadari were particularly troubled by Shaul Avigur's silence.

Two days after the first cable when the good news had spread through Romania, Moshe Auerbach cabled Shaul:

Immediate 15.12.47
The last date for the operation is the 21st of the month after which we will be unable to leave. I have decided to sail. Advise at once.[60]

This cable seemed to plead for a response. The decision had already been taken, the spring had been released. What was there to 'advise'? But it was now that they needed the guidance and authority of the head of the Mossad. Moshe Auerbach cabled Venia Hadari in Paris and Ehud Avriel in Prague, "Why is Shaul silent?"

Faced with the growing excitement among the Jewish community in Romania, they became apprehensive. Perhaps their decision had been too hasty? The ships were waiting to sail; up to this point they had been in control, but from now on they were helpless. What if the British decided to sink the vessels? The ships were not sailing with the backing of the national leadership but because of a secret plot devised by a few young hotheads. This time the Jews were really on their way to the trains and the doubts were sincere.

Once again consultations were held over international telephone lines. Venia in Paris, Ehud in Prague, Moshe in Constantsa and Pino in Geneva analysed the situation. The passengers were *en route*, the trains had to move, the ships would sail. So far, everything was ready, prepared and well coordinated. But afterwards? Should they fight? Should they force their way to the shores of Palestine? These were decisions for the highest national echelon. Only they could take the responsibility on such a decisive question. The agents could send the ships out, but no more than that. Ehud even proposed the revolutionary idea of sending them straight to Cyprus.

It is inherent in an established hierarchy that the senior leadership favours moderation, mitigating tension and aiming at compromise, while the younger and more enthusiastic people lower down the scale, whose criteria are more rigid and who tend to attach greater importance to operational aspects go for extremes, favour conflict, want to wield their power and abhor compromise.

The Mossad had been involved in many controversies on unauthorized immigration. Generally, the leaders of the Mossad tried as far as possible to avoid violent confrontations while the young operatives demanded uncompromising opposition to the British.[61] The organized Yishuv had been divided by similar controversies on the question of "restraint" and how to fight the British since the nineteen-thirties,[62] with the leadership almost always attempting to tone down the force of the conflict, while the rank-and-file pressed for action. And now, when the rank-and-file suddenly found themselves in the position of ultimate authority, they were affected by the dynamics of leadership.[63] Now they themselves advocated an idea to which they had always objected, and which was even more moderate than Shaul Avigur and even the leaders of the settlement would have wished – namely bringing the ships straight to the British internment camps in Cyprus.

Due to the difficulties of communication with Palestine and because of Shaul's continued silence, Ehud Avriel contacted Sharett in New York and informed him that the decision on the sailing had been taken and the ships were to leave. He proposed however that they should aim for Cyprus and requested that this be coordinated with the British.[64] Sharett was stunned by this information. He had been involved in politics for many years. Together with Weizmann, Ben-Gurion, Goldmann and Stephen Wise, he had contacts with world leaders. Successful negotiation called for patient, balanced judgment, cunning and finesse. Despite his deep-rooted connections with Palestine and the labour movement, he had, in the course of his activity, somewhat forfeited his direct contact with the young generation. Ehuv Avriel's outburst, his blunt declaration and radical proposal were sudden and confusing. Sharett's answer was ambiguous, and the call that followed from Pino Ginsburg in Geneva did not give Sharett time to review the matter. "What does the Jewish Agency Executive in Palestine think?" he asked Pino, as though expecting him to help reach a decision. Paul Shulman, who also contacted Sharett, suggested, on behalf of the Mossad operatives in Europe, that the ships declare themselves mutineers so that the whole matter would be forcibly taken out of the Mossad's hands.[65] Sharett, who was at a loss, said he would consider the matter and consult Ben-Gurion.[66] The spring however had already been released. The responsibility was theirs, and since the entire operation involved half-decisions and incomplete hints, the Mossad operatives in Europe decided that Sharett "was inclined to agree" that the ships should sail straight to Cyprus.[67] Thus it followed that he agreed to the actual sailing and that there was official support from the highest political level. Since the trains had not yet set out and were not due to move for another five days, Sharett's retroactive approval was regarded as an operational order from the Jewish Agency Executive that the *Pans* leave Romania.

It was in this spirit that Auerbach, on behalf of Pino Ginsburg, notified the Mossad headquarters in Israel that Sharett had agreed to the sailing of the two ships if their destination was Cyprus. The Mossad operatives, seeking retroactive sanction for their actions, based their decision on Sharett's authorization.[68] Ben-Gurion was informed immediately. He was stunned: How could this happen? Shaul Avigur was in Palestine and had promised not to act without authorization. Moshe Sharett had, only shortly before, reported to him on a meeting with Johnson, deputy head of the U.S. mission to the U.N., who had insisted, on behalf of Secretary of State Marshall, that the ships should not be permitted to sail. Sharett had promised him to do everything in his power to prevent this.[69]

Ben-Gurion knew Sharett well – they had worked together for many years. Sharett was not capable of insisting on Ben-Gurion's complete backing for his guarantee to the State Department on the one hand, while permitting the ships to sail, on the other. Shocked and worried, Ben-Gurion drafted a cable, informing Sharett that the Mossad operatives had reported that he (Sharett) had authorized the ships to sail for Cyprus. Ben-Gurion demanded that Sharett "cable immediately if this is correct."[70]

At this point there began a spate of feverish activity. Sharett contacted Ben-Gurion and informed him that the decision on the sailing was not his and that furthermore he objected to any sailings before 1st February 1948. Furthermore, he was strenuously opposed to sending the ships to Cyprus.[71] In a conversation with Venia Hadari in Paris, Sharett tried to halt the process, but Hadari explained that this was not possible. Sharett then, almost in desperation, tried to contact Nahum Goldmann in London, explain to him what had happened and ask his advice. At the same time he contacted Joseph Schwartz, the representative of the Joint Distribution Committee in Europe, but was again unable to find a solution. Powerless, he left the issue undecided.[72]

The next move was up to the people who had started the affair, the Mossad operatives in Europe. This crisis had revealed their true power. During all this feverish activity they had organized themselves. Moshe Pearlman flew to Turkey, Amos Manor coordinated activities in Bucharest. Shaike Dan left for Bulgaria, Yaakov Salomon drew up an operational map for train movements across Romania. As the pressure reached its height, the complex machinery began to function. It should be emphasized that the machinery was well prepared but that, in the special circumstances in which it had been constructed, ample room had been provided for mishaps. And these occurred in rapid succession. In some places the departure was not smooth. Some of the documents were invalid; there were more people trying to get away without permits than had been estimated; some of the local officials had not received proper instructions or had received contradictory orders. Some of the foreign crew members suddenly announced that they refused to sail. But these obstacles, any of which could have ruined the whole enterprise, were minor compared to the struggle these young operatives were forced to conduct with the whole Zionist leadership.

Brodetsky and Goldmann, the outstanding leaders of the Zionist movement, who were then resident in London, cabled Ben-Gurion to warn that "the results of the sailing would be catastrophic" and advised that a full meeting of the Zionist Executive be called to discuss the matter.[73] They strongly urged that the sailing be stopped at any price. Ben-Gurion summoned Avigur from Galilee and told him that his people in Europe were liable to cause a disaster of historic proportions through their rashness. He held Shaul directly responsible for the affair, and in harsh terms demanded that he resume control, put his people in Europe in their place and stem the growing wave of irresponsibility.

One can only guess at Shaul's dilemma. On the one hand, the devotion to duty of his operatives was the realization of his own philosophy and expectations. Moreover, they had every right to assume, since he had hinted at this clearly, that it was his wish that if there was no alternative, the ships should leave "black or white". He assumed that his agents had not staged a coup and had not decided to leave without agreement of some kind from an authorized source – in this case, from Moshe Sharett. On the other hand, Ben-Gurion was applying stifling pressure. At this critical moment he was burdening Shaul with a question of conscience: "Ships or a State". Shaul sent an urgent cable from Ben-Gurion's Tel Aviv office to Venia in Paris and Pino in Geneva: "What is Sharett's precise answer to the proposal to transport to Cyprus?"[74] In his heart of hearts, Shaul hoped that there was some kind of sanction for the decision to sail. For this reason, he hastened to Shaike Dan and said, "You have surrounded me with deceptions but I cannot be angry with you. You deceived me in a good cause."[75]

A cabled reply arrived from Moshe Auerbach. The question of backing was obfuscated but he stressed the human side of the operation with a somewhat exaggerated description of the disaster that would have befallen thousands of Jews if the decision had not been taken. He claimed in his letter that the Romanian government had begun to suspect that the list of emigrants included thousands of deserters from the Romanian army. In his cable he noted that this was correct and that if the authorities were given the opportunity, they would locate the deserters and thousands of young Jews would be court-martialled.

Once again Auerbach proposed to Shaul, as a compromise, not to impede the immediate departure of the ships. In return he promised to keep the ships at sea for as long as two weeks. He concluded his letter with a special request to Shaul: "Please believe that I acted under pressure of the situation without being influenced by anyone else."[76] Even more dramatic was Venia's cable from Paris, "Many of the emigrants are in immediate danger and I fear arrests and suicides,"[77] so that there was no going back.

Shaul had cited these same reasons in various forums in Palestine. He knew that the picture was somewhat exaggerated, mostly propaganda directed at the Zionist leadership and that the ships could have been held back in Romania. Auerbach's letter disturbed him. It did not explain clearly who had given the order. The nebulous authorization from Sharett evaporated when the latter finally succeeded in contacting Shaul Avigur and informed him bluntly that he was opposed to the decision to despatch the ships. Now that he had a clear answer on Sharett's position, when Ben-Gurion was furious and pressing him to leave the Mossad, when the cables from the Zionist Executive in New York and London were prophesying doom, when everything indicated that the matter was being discussed at the level of the President and the British Premier, Shaul had no alternative. He cabled Auerbach in Romania and Venia in Paris, "To sail now is a breach of the decision of the Executive" (of the Jewish Agency).[78]

However, it was of course too late. Auerbach had already planned the next steps and cabled to Shaul:

Urgent, 21.12.1947
To Arnon from Agami
We cannot hold up the sailing. It is no longer in our hands. Instructions have been issued to give no opposition;[79] great efforts will be made to bring the vessels to Famagusta and if needed, to sabotage the engines so that they cannot take them to Israel.[80] We will attempt to hold them *en route* if possible.[81] The rotters (the British) will be told that they left without permission and against the advice of the authorized bodies because they were ready and had left their jobs and homes in October.
Try to find a constructive solution perhaps keeping the people in Rice (code name for Cyprus) at our expense, etc.
Once again, understand that our decision is not based on our own interpretation or mere obstinacy. If I am destined to violate a decision of the Executive, the responsibility will not be ours. You should have stopped the action while the doctor (Moshe Sneh) was with us. Now the situation is forcing our hand.
There is food on the vessels for 15-17 days,water and fuel for 10 days.[82]

This cable reflects apprehension. The Mossad operatives in Europe understood that their crude attempt to claim that they were forced to sail by the Romanian authorities, or that they had understood from Avigur that there was a tacit agreement, and certainly their attempt to claim that the sailing had been approved by Shertok, had easily been refuted. Only now, when Weizmann in the U.S.A. and Goldmann in Great Britain were urgently and directly telephoning to the anonymous operatives throughout Europe, did they understand how great was the risk they had taken upon themselves. The tendency to despise "politicians" was valid as long as there was a separation of powers, and when there was an intermediary, Shaul Avigur, between the agents in the field and the Zionist leadership, who was accepted by both parties. But when Joseph Schwartz of the Joint Distribution Committee, Ben-Gurion, Chairman of the Jewish Agency Executive and Sharett, Foreign Minister of the Zionist movement, contacted these young people and quoted Truman and Attlee, Bevin and Marshall at them, their resolve weakened. They were told that they had committed a rash act that would harm the Zionist ideal on a historic scale; because of their foolish decision the work of decades of preparation for statehood would come to nothing, the dream of generations shattered. They had enabled the Americans to back out of their agreement to establish a Jewish State.

The pressure increased. But the decision could not now be revised. Streams of people were making their way throughout Romania to the railway stations. What was going to happen? On their initiative, aware of the heavy responsibility they bore, the agents issued an operational order to the commanders of the ships, the most moderate order ever issued by the Mossad – not to oppose the British, not to give them an excuse to damage the ships and not to give the vessels Hebrew names.[83] They were still highly apprehensive. Telephone calls were made around the world. Venia Hadari put himself at risk and tried to contact Shaul by telephone direct from Paris. For cover, he pretended to be a French official and spoke about a consignment of 15,000 tons. Shaul, surprised, heard his cry of distress, understood thoroughly but had no real answer.[84] Venia made another round of telephone calls, this time to New York. Two or three times a day he tried to reach Sharett. It was obvious that the line was being tapped. In New York, Zippora Sharett answered: "Moshe cannot speak. He is travelling between New York and Washington, and anyway, it is not a good idea for him to speak at the moment." Venia constantly called attention to the fact that the ships were to sail in another week, another six days, another five days, until finally on 22nd December, the trains departed. Then the operatives met to deal with the problems with which they were familiar, seeking solutions to the operative problems of unauthorized immigration.

Toward morning on the day of the ships' departure from Constantsa, the telephone rang in Venia's modest room. Yonit, his eighteen-month-old daughter, woke up startled and began to cry. Venia found it difficult to hear – it was Moshe Sharett from New York. "Is it possible to cancel the sailing?" "No", replied Venia. "The ships have left Constantsa. Now we have to find a way to act in accordance with the new circumstances." "What do you suggest?" asked Moshe. Yonit's wails disrupted the conversation. "Could you come here straight away?" Venia ventured to ask. "We will sit down and see what we can do." Sharett was apprehensive about leaving America at such a critical period and Venia felt he would be deserting the battlefield if he were to go there to Sharett. Therefore, he rapidly contacted the airlines, checked departure times, telephoned Shaul Avigur and then Sharett again. A few hours after his conversation with Sharett, he had arranged a meeting for the three of them – Sharett, Shaul Avigur and

Venia Hadari - at Geneva airport. The meeting at the airport restaurant lasted half an hour during which Moshe embraced his brother-in-law Shaul who had just arrived from Palestine, sent regards to friends and received the latest information on the progress of the war for Israel's independence. Venia had to press the two brothers-in-law and friends. "Your plane is waiting to take off," he said to Sharett, "let us finish the matter." Sharett was in a good mood. Venia felt that matters were working out. In the few hours that had elapsed between the last telephone call and the meeting, the ships had left Burgas and were on their way to the Bosphorus.

Sharett emphasized that there was tacit agreement on the part of the British to take command of the ships as soon as they emerged from the Straits into the Mediterranean, but this was based entirely on the assumption that the decision on the ships' departure had been taken without permission. The solutions had not resulted from formal negotiations but from a verbal understanding, without specific promises or guarantees. "This time", he said to Venia, with a half-serious threatening gesture, "you will do what I tell you, according to the letter of the law and even more important, according to the spirit. Firstly, the ships will not have Hebrew names, and it is absolutely forbidden to give them any official description, such as 'Hagana Ship'. When you encounter the British, you will take no provocative or defensive action and you will go where they order you, except back to the Black Sea. If you are interrogated, you will say officially that the Jewish Agency ordered you not to sail." However, as an experienced diplomat, Sharett advised caution since, on the other hand, it must not be stated that the ships had left because of pressure from the Romanian authorities. If such a conclusion had been suggested to Venia in different circumstances, such as the *Exodus* operation, when he had also been operations officer for the Mossad, he would have rejected outright the idea of surrendering to the British, of denying national sovereignty. But now he accepted the decision happily; it was as though a heavy weight had been lifted off him. While Moshe Sharett was hurrying to his plane, there was a telephone call from Moshe Pearlman in Istanbul: "The ships have passed safely through the Bosphorus."[85]

The hasty meeting at Geneva airport was late and superfluous. One of the characteristics of the *Pan* story was that the moments of crisis occurred after their significance had waned. An overall view of the subject suggests that the *Pan* operation was the high point of the unauthorized immigration project. But it occurred at a time when the focus had shifted from immigration to the War of Independence. This war, then rapidly escalating, threatened the actual physical survival of the country. After a long struggle against British rule, hesitations and second thoughts were now being voiced: could the British evacuation be slowed down, or even halted? Prof. Brodetsky, a member of the Jewish Agency Executive in London, spoke about "organized withdrawal", placing responsibility on the British and helping them keep order;[86] in other words, Zionist entreaty to Great Britain not to leave the country.

The situation raised many questions: Would the neighbouring Arab states join in the war? What would be the British position in the event of all-out hostilities? What would be the borders of the state? What would happen to Jerusalem? The Yishuv was faced with grave internal problems such as the establishment, training and equipping of an army, the organization of a proper civilian administration and above all, the imposition of sovereign authority. The question of authority was the most sensitive of all the problems which rose on the eve of the establishment of the state. History showed that the establishment of an independent state, after years of conflict, could lead to civil war between the different organizations that had fought for independence. The Yishuv might face a similar situation. The ideology, mentality and command of the Irgun Zvai Leumi were essentially different from those of Lechi. The fighting methods of these two underground organizations were in complete contrast to the Hagana's policy. The Irgun and Lechi organizations were defined as "seceders", "outsiders", in other words, they had seceded from the framework of national authority. It was common knowledge that the Irgun was nurturing a civilian periphery of supporters and a separate fund-raising organization, was conducting its own arms-purchasing activities in Europe and the U.S. and aspired to establish its own political structure with a view to controlling the emerging state. At the same time, clashes continued between these two military organizations, with casualties on both sides.[87]

All these crucial events were happening at the same time, all the participants were profoundly involved. Each organization sincerely believed that it held the key to national salvation, while the actions of the other organizations would lead to disaster – clearly, the state was not going to be handed to them as a gift, without considerable suffering and sacrifice. In these circumstances, the Mossad was gradually losing its prestige. Public opinion began to doubt the political and economic value of continued unauthorized immigration. On the day that the ships left Constantsa, *Ha'aretz*, the major Hebrew-language daily in Palestine, published an editorial, which said, "If we ask ourselves today to what extent and under what conditions it is worth continuing with unauthorized immigration, we do solely from Zionist considerations and we know that such questions are being asked by a large section of the public. Unauthorized immigration has fulfilled its main political purpose." The newspaper went on to claim that immigration had become routine and no longer made an impression on public opinion and that immigrants were being detained in Cyprus at the expense of the Jewish people just at the time when the Yishuv needed this money for equipment. The British Mandate was about to expire and then in any case immigration would flow freely. *Ha'aretz* ends magisterially: "The conclusion, we think, is obvious."[88]

A study of the newspaper headlines on the day the *Pans* sailed does not reveal high morale. The black-framed announcements of war casualties dampened any feelings of jubilation. There was a growing tendency to have reservations, and there were those who saw unauthorized immigration as a new kind of "secession", this time from the left wing of the Yishuv.[89] Even Golda Meir began to condemn and oppose the Mossad. In a conversation with Shaul Avigur she claimed that it was liable to split the community and that its activities bolstered the tendency of the activist left to operate from outside the framework of national sovereignty. "Golda attacked me furiously", Shaul recalled, "she was ready to tear me to pieces."[90]

It may be assumed that in the activist sections of the community – the United Kibbutz movement (Kibbutz Hameuchad), the Palmach striking force and even the leadership of the Hagana – the sailing was seen as good news. The people of Kfar Giladi, Auerbach's kibbutz, of Ramat Hakovesh, Pino's kibbutz, Ehud Avriel's comrades at Neot Mordechai and the people of Ramat Rachel, Venia's home, who had known many years of suffering, who had stood alone against hostile Arab villages – all certainly grasped the significance of the large number of immigrants who were on their way. Their reasons – exhaustion from constant guard duty at night and from endless skirmishes in which they were equipped with outdated weapons inferior to those of their leadership and of the general public.

In the small, intimate Yishuv everyone knew about the Arabs' violent objection to the establishment of the state and about the British objection to immigration. There was a clear feeling that the State

Department had been unfriendly towards Zionism since the time of the Balfour Declaration and that since the appointment of General Marshall as Secretary of State at the beginning of 1947, this attitude had become actively hostile.[91] Eliahu Elath, close adviser to Moshe Sharett in the U.S. described Marshall as "a callous man, without human feelings, vengeful and vigilant".[92] It was well known that Marshall strongly influenced Truman, who considered him "the greatest American of his generation".[93] When there were rumours that Marshall was strongly opposed to unauthorized immigration and considered it a provocation that could force America into a position of openly opposing the establishment of the state, public opinion in the country tended to support Sharett's attempts to prevent the continuation of immigration, at least until the beginning of February 1948.

The main opponents to immigration at that time were Weizmann and Ben-Gurion, Sharett and Golda Meir, Goldmann and Abba Hillel Silver, and behind them stood the majority of the community. Against them were ranged the members of the Kibbutz Hameuhad, the Hashomer Hatzair settlements and a handful of Mossad operatives in Europe. Even their revered leader, Shaul Avigur, was concerned about national sovereignty and was not willing to be party to a contravention of the Jewish Agency decision to hold up the departure of the ships. There was no overt confrontation between the two sides. The notion of opting out and of rebellion was totally alien to these young operatives; they restricted themselves, in the case of the *Pans*, to evasive tactics, to minor distortion of the facts in their reports and ostensible naiveté. But as soon as the order was given, and thousands of people had begun flocking through Romania, they suddenly felt that they had taken on a responsibility which was not theirs by right. Suddenly the dilemma arose – ships or state?

The courage, albeit rash, of these young people was somehow in tune with the sentiments of the national leaders, who had also been nurtured on daring, radical ideas. Although the implications were grave, these leaders in their heart of hearts seemed to be grateful that these young people had taken the decision and carried it out. Ben-Gurion, Moshe Sharett and even Golda followed the progress of the ships with apprehension but also with pride. On the morning of the sailing, Shaul Avigur sent a cable to the commanders of the operation. "Bon voyage and may you fulfil the verse: 'you have striven with God and men and have prevailed.' "[94] Was Shaul hinting that he was grateful to his beloved agents and adversaries for striving with him and winning?

CHAPTER SIX

Romanians and Bulgarians

FAREWELL TO ROMANIA

The feverish preparation for the sailing of the *Pans* coincided with the bustle of the Christmas season in Romania at the end of 1947; it was almost as if the planned voyage concerned the whole country and everyone was caught up in it. Mossad headquarters were located in the offices of the central communications building in Bucharest, to which four telephone lines – all that were at the disposal of the Romanian railways – were transferred.[1] Here were located the offices of the Mossad operatives, local Zionist leaders, representatives of the Romanian government, the railways, the Health and Interior Ministries. The Mossad, which worked around the clock, decided to launch the *Pans* operation in the morning of 22nd December. This calculation was based on a countdown according to which the ships were to pass through the Bosphorus on a Saturday night. The directives given by the railway management did not allow for possible breakdowns since, in fact, regular services throughout the country had been suspended for three days because of the *Pans* transport. On short notice, in some communities no more than twelve hours, the immigrants were summoned to an assembly point, where the local Mossad representative met them and processed, with the help of the local police, carriers of permits and their families, and eliminated aspiring stowaways.

At the assembly points trucks waited to transfer the immigrants to the nearest railway station. At this stage diversionary action began: false rumours were spread regarding boarding points, in order to deflect pressure from the stations that would be used. Each train consisted of fifty cars: forty-three for freight and seven for passengers.[2] The passenger cars were comfortable and heated and were designated hospital cars, where nursing mothers grouped. One car was reserved for the headquarters and command of the train and two others for passengers without proper documents.

According to the plan, passengers were to arrive in groups of forty-five, led by one of their number. They were to board the car booked for them and noted on a list that had been prepared in advance. This was the only way to keep to an orderly timetable. Reality, however, proved to be different. Already at the local collection points the Mossad operatives' illusion of determined young pioneer immigrants was shattered. What they did find were bewildered families who had assembled at the collection points in their villages and townships at a few hours' notice, leaving behind them the towns where their families had lived for generations and the only friends and relatives they had known. It seemed as if the whole village had come to see them off. In addition to the pangs of separation, they bore the burden of their heritage of wandering and hardship. The astonished Mossad operatives saw whole families laden with blankets, blackened pots and pans and even tubs and primus stoves. Some clutched Torah Scrolls and others precious religious texts. The more practical had brought goods with them to start businesses in Israel.

There was no way of arranging them in categories and lists. They formed their own groups: family, friends and occasionally Zionist movements and organizations, all boarding the trains together. The Mossad had to shrug its shoulders and put aside its lists in order not to incur any delays. The train commanders could only warn headquarters in Bucharest to expect some problems to arise during the boarding of the ships. Testifying to the assiduity of the Mossad are a meticulously detailed series of reports from the various trains, describing the command structure, change of guards every twenty-four hours in each car, maintenance of contact with the train command by means of flags by day and flashlights by night, schedules for stopping, sanitary problems, and water and food rationing. There is an impressive concern for sanitation, handled by teams of cleaners, and close communications with headquarters, via railway telegraph.

But all this planning was to no avail: no list could stop the passengers forming their own groups. In some cars over one hundred passengers huddled together. Such kinship or ideological groups were self-contained; they required no checking or orderlies. They brought along food and water supplies, took care of their own sanitation and apparently made it possible, by covering for each other, for people who had not passed the preliminary screening to join the group. Pressure of time before which the train commanders had bowed did not affect the Romanian officials. In accordance with the original agreement, the

Romanians shared in the screening of the immigrants and therefore insisted on taking part in the inspection, to check that only those who had been passed were on the train. It was also strictly forbidden to take foreign currency and articles of value out of the country. Long experience had taught the Jews to hoard their few possessions and never part from them, and the Romanian authorities suspected as much. The officials were therefore particularly anxious to stop the trains for a thorough inspection.

When the first train was stopped at Giurgiu, a crossing point on the Danube between Romania and Bulgaria, it seemed to bode no good for the trains to come. The train commanders, who were aware of the number of stowaways on board, realized that among them were people who, if caught, were liable for severe punishment, even death. There were hundreds of deserters from the Romanian army, some of whom still had their uniforms and even weapons. Some had escaped from the U.S.S.R. and were Soviet citizens; there were wanted criminals and professionals in reserved occupations who were expressly forbidden to leave.[3] A thorough search would discover them all, stop the journey and place the Mossad operatives in delicate situations and perhaps even cause the authorities to have second thoughts.

The Mossad leaders knew that they were "making history". They took pains to document their work, although there were severe constraints; the British authorities would have been pleased to confiscate documents and records of meetings about illegal immigration and operative decisions of the Mossad. Thus, together with the comparatively extensive documentation kept in the Mossad archives,[4] there are "blank pages" which could have condemned important parts of this story to oblivion. After the establishment of the State of Israel, much time and attention were devoted to filling in the gaps. Aliya Bet operatives were interviewed, missing papers were located and unpublicized incidents were reconstructed.[5] However, one key factor in the story of unauthorized immigration remains shrouded in mystery to this day: the use of ransom.

From what has been mentioned, it can be understood that from the beginning a price had been set for the general agreement, a special price for participating in the operation and a price for every separate activity, such as providing trains, policemen, passports, etc. The price was in hard currency and was arranged on commercial lines, including guarantees. The guarantors were not bankers or financiers but, quite simply, the immigration workers who guaranteed the operation with

their own persons. The additional price was to compensate for the
financial benefits that could accrue from a meticulous body search of
the 15,000 people who, it was supposed, were carrying their most
valued possessions; for most of them, this was the barest minimum but
it could add up and the Romanians were in no hurry.

As already stated, we do not have conclusive data on the amount of
the ransom, but the telephone conversation between Giurgiu and
Bucharest was short and effective. A few moments later, a message
reached the railway checkpoint and the inspection suddenly stopped.
It was almost possible to hear the sigh of relief that went up, releasing
all fears and apprehension. The inspection of the trains that followed
was cursory.

The subject of ransom is still consigned to the "blank pages" of
historical documentation, but it should nevertheless not be inferred
that we are dealing here with personal corruption and graft. The bulk
of the money was earmarked for political funds and the state Treasury.
For the war-ravaged economies of the Eastern European states,
foreign currency, in general circulation in the West, was a valuable
commodity.

The Danube was crossed by ferry. At Ruse on the Bulgarian side
they were warmly received by Bulgarian Jews, who provided hot
drinks for the weary travellers[6] and then, back to the trains – this time,
Bulgarian – taking them straight to the ships waiting at the port of
Burgas.

BULGARIAN IMMIGRATION

The long border between Romania and Bulgaria separated two
different Jewish communities. The dominant heritage of the Bulgarian
Jews was Sephardi, based on the culture of the Jews expelled from the
Iberian Peninsula during the Spanish Inquisition. This was closer to
the Jews of the Arab world than the East European traditions of the
Romanian Jews. Bulgaria's Jews had enjoyed full equality since its
establishment as an independent state in 1878, while at the Berlin
Conference of the same year there was bitter protest against the
discrimination and persecution suffered by the Jews of Romania. The
geographical proximity of the countries had not produced any real
links between the two Jewish communities. They did not even share
the *lingua franca* of the European (Ashkenazi) Jews, Yiddish; the
language of the Bulgarian Jews was Ladino. In some respects

Bulgarian Jewry was unique. The community was small; in 1943 it numbered 50,000, only one per cent of the total population.[7] Despite their high educational and social levels, Bulgarian Jews were not prominent in the economy or in politics, nor did they pursue a way of life that distinguished them from the society around them. Their position in society was comparatively relaxed, partly because their public activity was largely conducted within the Jewish community, which had developed extensive institutions and maintained a complex system of mutual aid, synagogues, communal services and even its own newspapers. The leadership of Bulgarian Jewry was in the hands of the dominant Zionist movement,[8] around which youth movements and political parties had developed and Zionist awareness had grown.

For a variety of reasons beyond the scope of this book, Bulgarian Jewry did not bear the brunt of the Holocaust that decimated the ranks of Europe's Jews. Representatives of the Rescue Committee from Palestine had already arrived by September 1944 while the Red Army was still in the process of conquering the country – Venia Pomerantz (Hadari), Aharon Ben Yosef, Yosef Klarman, and others who followed.[9] They found a community which had survived in body but had suffered expulsion and the loss of all their property. The new government was clearly Communist and sought to include the Jewish youth in the ranks of the revolution. As in Romania, it was the Jewish Communists, comprising a separate section of the Communist party,[10] who conspired most ardently against the Jewish community and the Zionist movement. This section was mainly concerned with the Jewish youth who were being called upon to join the ranks of Ramsa, the Communist youth organization, and join in the revolution.

This was a tempting proposition, an opportunity to become part of the glorious enterprise that was sweeping Eastern Europe, inspired by the U.S.S.R. At that time, Russia symbolized liberation, the mother of the Red Army, which had defeated the Nazi monster. The call to Jewish youth beckoned: "let us build a new world, egalitarian and just, in which man will be exalted." Some responded, joining the Bulgarian Ramsa movement and even holding key positions. However, in the confrontation with Zionism, Ramsa did not gain the upper hand. As one of the members was to explain later: "Although we were drawn to the new regime, the Zionist roots of Bulgarian Jewry were so deep and the attraction of immigration to Israel was so strong, that when the opportunity came, we had no hesitations."[11] Thus, after the establishment of the State of Israel, when the Jews of Bulgaria were free to leave, ninety per cent emigrated to Israel.[12]

Looking back at the story of the immigration of Bulgarian Jews, and the success story of their integration into Israeli society, it is easy to say that Zionism was bound to gain the upper hand over Communism, but this was not so obvious at the time. David Ben-Gurion, as chairman of the Jewish Agency Directorate, visited Bulgaria in December 1944 for an exhaustive journey on behalf of the Zionist movement, aided by the Bulgarian regime.[13] At one of the enthusiastic receptions that had been arranged in Sofia, Ben-Gurion said, "We have done some fine things in Palestine." Princeps, one of the heads of the Ivsektia (the Jewish Affairs Section of the Communist Party) interposed, "Hitler also did some fine things." Ben-Gurion was shocked by this reaction and it disturbed him for many years.[14] On his return home, he reported on his visit to the Fourth Zionist Congress and stated that the Jews of Bulgaria were in danger of spiritual degeneration.[15] The opportunity to acquire an education, study at university and obtain an influential position in the new political and economic system was a powerful temptation to the young people.

The first emissaries from Israel played an important role in this confrontation. Venia Hadari, Yosef Klarman and Aharon Ben Yosef succeeded in establishing contact with the emerging political leadership. In return for various unspecified favours, they were able to broadcast weekly for an hour on the state radio and they used this to rally the community to the idea of Zionism. Shaike Dan continued to negotiate with the leadership of the Communist Party on the one hand and the Jewish community on the other.

Among his other tasks he was asked to solve a problem that threatened to wreck the *Pan* project. The Romanian authorities had agreed to a once-only departure of the Jews from their country, on condition that the ships did not leave from a Romanian port, to avoid any appearance of cooperating with the Zionist movement.[16] The only alternative was to sail from Bulgaria. Shaike Dan's mission to persuade the Bulgarian authorities to permit the ships to sail from their country was extremely delicate. The constraints that influenced the Romanians applied equally to the Bulgarians, upon whom the British were exerting enormous pressure.[17]

The man with whom Shaike Dan was dealing was a central figure in Bulgaria. After exhaustive negotiations, in which the Russians were also involved, this man agreed to give the Mossad the port of Burgas, at which the *Pans* were due to arrive from Constantsa and where the unauthorized immigrants would embark. When the matter was decided, two representatives from the Bulgarian security service were appointed to implement the decision.

As long as the archives of the Eastern European countries are closed to free researchers, it will be impossible to ascertain what went on at these meetings and how the decisions were reached. Furthermore, for political reasons related to Israel's present contacts with these countries, former Mossad operatives are still reluctant to speak freely about a subject which is barely mentioned in the archives. Shaike Dan was prepared to say that the two representatives who worked with him – devotedly, he wished to emphasize – succeeded in their careers and became national figures; later, they were both removed, tried and sentenced to life imprisonment. One of them was later rehabilitated, and as to the fate of the other, Dan was not even prepared to offer a hint. There were two reasons for the decision to allow the passage of the Romanian immigrants through Bulgaria. One was simple and obvious; what was bad for the British was good for the Communists. The passage of the Jews and their immigration to Israel struck at the British imperialist interests, it would cause them to quarrel with the Arabs and the Americans, they would tie down troops and lose control, contributing to a general undermining of the West. But these reasons applied equally to the Romanians and they had refused. There was clearly a stronger motive, according to the Mossad operatives, and this was ransom.[18]

Once again we were left in the dark. Shaike Dan, who carried out the negotiations, made the financial arrangements, and personally guaranteed the agreement, refused to divulge any details. From the size of the ransom at the lower levels, which is partly known to us, we are able to infer that a sum was transferred directly to the Bulgarian leadership and used to fill the empty coffers of the Treasury.

The payment was for one thing – the passage of the trains to the ships. However, this agreement opened the way to negotiation about an additional goal: immigration of Bulgaria's Jews to Israel. Shaike Dan had dealt with the immigration of Jews from Eastern Europe for years. He travelled on behalf of the State of Israel on many occasions, to the most sensitive areas, negotiating with the most senior government officials in each country. He was a key figure and without doubt must be considered instrumental in the immigration of tens of thousands of Jews to Israel. Nonetheless, in summing up his activities, he regards the immigration of 420 young people from Bulgaria as "the dearest thing in my life".[19] In Ben-Gurion's diary entry of 8th August 1947, he wrote: "Isaiah Dan visited me and told me that he had a dream of bringing to Israel all the Jews of Bulgaria."[20] Ben-Gurion, who was unable to forget his visit to Bulgaria, suggested to Shaike that he send 10,000 pairs of shoes for the barefooted children in Bulgaria, and Shaike, who had only one idea in his head, replied, "Bring the feet to the shoes and not the shoes to the feet."[21]

In a rare moment of expansiveness, which contrasted with his stern image, Shaike described the story of the immigration of the group of young Bulgarians.

> I will now tell you something from the depths of my heart which you cannot find in any psychological, historical or political study. A man lives only once. I knew what it meant to parachute into Romania during the Second World War. I knew what was involved and I knew that I had little chance of remaining alive. There were different methods of jumping and I chose what was called 'blind dropping', where you jump in a place where there is no underground to back you up, nothing. I knew that, and I was prepared to do it in the belief that I would be able to rescue fellow Jews. The fact that we did not succeed during the war is another story. I volunteered for the jump to rescue Jews and joined Mossad Le'Aliya Bet to rescue Jews and bring them to Israel. As for the rest, you can analyse it, but it's not part of my world.[22]

These heartfelt words were spoken by a man of action. In most cases action took precedence over reason, judgement and planning, but it made possible the immigration of Jews to Israel, and for Dan that was what counted. There are numerous examples, from the parachute jump to unauthorized immigration and the modest room in the Foreign Ministry where Shaike Dan carried out his personal goal in the style of early Zionist pragmatists like Berl Katznelson: "In the beginning was the act."[23]

Shaike Dan's attempt to influence his two Bulgarian colleagues did not succeed at first. It was only in the last week of 1947, when the trains began to move in Romania, that he was able to make a breakthrough, and once again he gives an emotional description of the conversation:

> I said to him, "How can you see with your own eyes thousands of people travelling and then be so cruel as to prevent the Jews from here going too? How can that be?" I think that the walls and the

floor were crying, and not only I. He said to me: "What you can take aboard the ship tonight, you can have." And that is how four hundred and twenty young people came to make the journey.[24]

The verbal agreement was for two hundred people who would be located in one night, 27th December and collected between 28th and 30th December. In fact four hundred and twenty embarked and the operation was completed before the deadline.

The plan had doubtless been drawn up well before permission was granted, and all that was needed was the signal to act.

From the point of view of the young people, who received twenty-four hours' notice (and in some cases much less) with no previous warning, it seemed quite straightforward; they were all members of the Bulgarian pioneer youth movement. Roni Alshech explains:[25]

I was only a girl of seventeen and up to the day I left, there had been no concrete proposal to go to Israel, neither had it been thoroughly discussed at home, but as a member of Hashomer Hatzair the idea of immigration to Israel was a keystone of my thoughts and activity in the movement. I never had any doubt that one day I would go to Israel and I was sure I would go as part of a group, with all my peers in the movement. It was clear that in Israel I would go to a kibbutz and work in agriculture. The movement was the dominant force in my life; it represented everything correct and just and so, when one day at the end of December 1947 a member of the group came to my home and said, "Tomorrow, all our group is going to Israel, are you ready to come?" I did not hesitate. I went down to the street to look for my mother and told her. As was to be expected, she did not welcome the news. Even in those difficult days it seemed very impetuous and rushed. "Already, now? With whom? How?" and all the other questions that are so reasonable when a young daughter suddenly announces that she is leaving her home, her family and way of life to go on an unknown road to an unknown country. We compromised to the extent that my brother went with me to the leadership of the movement to get further details. We got there and they explained very simply: the whole senior group of Hashomer Hatzair in Bulgaria was going to Israel in two immigrant ships coming from Romania. Since there were a few places left, some of the younger group of which I was a member, were going with them, and since I was lucky and lived in Sofia, and was at home and the movement courier had found me – I was to take part in the journey . . .[26]

This simple story was, of course, just the tip of a complex structure that had been built slowly, by hard work, in pioneering groups, in conditions of secrecy and danger. One of those that helped was a young Jewish law student and member of Hashomer Hatzair – Moni Diga.[27]

Moni Diga, a senior member of the movement, was caught up in the pioneering enthusiasm of the young Zionists who were impatient to get to Israel. It was the comparatively comfortable situation of Bulgarian Jewry, the relaxed activity of the Zionist movement and the attitude of the authorities that made him fear that insufficient attention was being given to the immigration of Bulgarian Jews. Moni and some of his friends decided to take the initiative – they would establish an internal structure and offer it to the Mossad. Contact with the Mossad was difficult. In the suspicious regime of post-war Bulgaria, it was impossible to imagine that a local youngster could telephone or send letters abroad. Moni had to find a cover. The solution was similar to the one found by Zeev Shind in the U.S. He found an old businessman with a dormant import-export business, and in return for a small payment became a "partner". His office became a centre for timber exports and most of the business was with "Hamashbir" (in fact, a co-operative retail organisation) in Palestine. It was now possible to maintain a wide correspondence and there were good reasons for mutual visits and transferring money. Here, again, money was of critical importance. It allowed the youngsters to prove that they were serious and to establish contact with the decision-makers in Bulgaria. This contact became the infrastructure of the activities of the Mossad, led by Shaike Dan, whose channels of communication to the heads of the administration had been opened by a group of impatient youngsters. The formation of this infrastructure, although it necessitated contacts at the very highest level, took place in absolute secrecy. It was impossible to reconcile active membership of Hashomer Hatzair with the image of a big businessman, so it became necessary first of all to remove Moni Diga from the movement and to make sure that everyone knew about it. This the leadership decided to do and found satisfactory grounds – Moni Diga, one of the leaders of the movement, was found guilty of smoking . . . and growing a moustache. These points illustrated the negative qualities in the personality of a young man who was even interested in higher education and other decadent pursuits. The fact that by the time he was expelled he was already in business showed that whoever grows a moustache can degenerate into a businessman, and so his dealing in the export of timber was no surprise.

There were other picturesque and even absurd aspects of the activities of the youth movements in their drive for immigration. Only obstinacy and pluck can explain their posture in the face of the honoured leaders of the Bulgarian Zionist movement, the directors of the Joint Distribution Committee and even the Mossad emissaries. These youth movements were responsible for enlarging the number of immigrants for whom Shaike Dan had obtained authorization from two hundred to four hundred and twenty, for the personal outfitting of the immigrants and their special function on board ship and later in the Cyprus camps.

When a Communist regime reaches a decision, it is not likely to waver. When the Bulgarians agreed on two hundred people, it was seen as an achievement, but when the news reached the activists on the spot, they took a further initiative. Forty-eight hours before the sailing of the ships the green light was given; they were told to hurry and collect two hundred people. The two hundred places were divided up, as was customary procedure, among the pioneering youth movements on a proportional representation basis, with the intention of including the senior groups. Moni Diga and his friends translated the number and proposed that the movement double it and include their next senior groups. Caution was overruled by ardour: "We left Shaike to worry about what was involved."[28] On the same evening, the leaders of the youth movements were assembled and asked to draw up a list of two hundred immigrants and another list of two hundred reserves, but only one list was prepared which eventually contained four hundred and twenty names. At the same time a relay contact system, which had been arranged a long time in advance, was put into operation and the candidates were quickly located and prepared for immediate immigration.

It is doubtful whether those four or five young activists from the youth movements had given much thought to the ramifications of their decision but they succeeded. "The exercise" became evident only at the last moment and everyone – the Bulgarian authorities, the Zionist movement, the Mossad and the captains of the ships – was forced to accept a *fait accompli.* In return for an additional payment, authorization was given from above and the people were assembled in the Sofia football stadium. The short time available did not allow for any personal arrangements. In the bitter winter conditions of December 1947, there were many without proper shoes and adequate clothing. Among the candidates there were those who had not been able to obtain the most basic equipment. Many did not have blankets; at home they were used to sleeping with their brothers or sisters, wrapped in the same blankets. The paucity of equipment and lack of blankets drove the operatives to Joseph Schwartz, European director of the Joint, who was then in Bulgaria because of the sailing of the *Pans*. Schwartz, an American Jew whose function was to provide welfare assistance to European Jews after the Holocaust, was surprised when Moni Diga and his friends came to his hotel and urgently requested personal equipment for four hundred and twenty people. He asked them to wait while he checked who they were and how he could help them. But there was not time. It was a strange situation: Schwartz would not fulfil their request on the spot but he would order the manager of the Joint storehouse in Sofia to keep the store open for a short time during the evening. If their activities were legitimate they would be able to go and take what they needed and if they were illegal he would go later to the police. However, it was the youngsters who went to the police. Time was short and the group could not wait for them, so they went to the Sofia police, obtained a police van and loaded it with four hundred and twenty suits of clothes, hats, shoes and blankets. The van drove straight to the football stadium and in a few minutes the group had acquired a new appearance.

Many years after the event, the immigrants from Romania remembered meeting with the Bulgarians who looked like a special army unit, with their solidarity, their tradition of singing together (they were all youngsters of the same age) and their uniforms. The clothes taken from the Joint storehouse were new U.S. Army surplus fatigues, as were the shoes and hats. The uniformity of the khaki clothing, the equipment, the blankets and the knapsacks contrasted with the colourful clothing and belongings of the Romanians. They made identification easy and boosted morale. Their clothes were warm and comfortable, and they were with their friends from the pioneer movement and they were on their way to the land of their dreams.

CHAPTER SEVEN

To the Ships!

TROUBLE AT SEA

Romania and Bulgaria are on the shores of the Black Sea, a name the Mossad operatives considered most fitting. As Dov Magen put it: "Why do they call it the Black Sea? Firstly, because the sky is dark and lacks the blue of our sky; secondly because the water is murky. But the main reason is that this sea is a black prospect for ships and sailors. It can become stormy in a few minutes. In the Mediterranean a storm takes several hours to blow up and you have time to prepare for the change in the weather, but not in the Black Sea!"[1]

The difficulties of sailing the Black Sea were particularly onerous for the *Pans*. Their crews were not familiar with its waters and did not possess charts of the minefields left there from the war. The ships were very high in the water and the force of the strong winds made it difficult to navigate between the mines that were spotted by the lookouts on the bows. There was a serious problem with fueling and with the ambivalent attitude of the bordering states. The ships were being hunted and the British were seeking ways to delay and even damage them at sea.[2]

The difficulties of the voyage of the *Pan Crescent* from Venice to Constantsa were described by Dov Magen in his final report:

> After repairing the damage from the explosion in Venice we did not even try to conceal our activities. It was known that this was a ship handling illegal immigration. The British immediately operated against us and ordered the Italians not to supply us with fuel. The ship had engines of 4600 H.P. Daily fuel consumption at sea was approximately forty tons and there were around 230 tons of fuel on board. The Italians claimed that maritime law required every port to supply a ship with enough fuel to enable her to reach the next port and refuel. They suggested that we sail to Malta and refuel there. In view of this we were unable to obtain fuel. According to our calculations we had to reach Constantsa and there we would have

enough fuel for a further six hours (if the voyage went well). Generally ships do not sail in such conditions – it is against maritime law. However, when we have no alternative we do many things and we did this too. The sea was quiet for the whole voyage. The ship maintained a good speed and we reached the Dardanelles. Despite all our previous notifications, the agent there did not materialize and it emerged that he had lost his nerve and backed out. Instead, an English agent approached us and informed us that our agent had not arrived but he was ready to make all the necessary arrangements for our ships to pass into the Black Sea. I asked him his name and he gave me a name that sounded English. I told him I would make my own arrangements and I did not need an agent even though I knew they would take the dollars anyway but it was worth it not to get involved with the agent. We paid in dollars for the health inspection, etc. and passed without trouble through the Dardanelles and the Bosphorus.

In the Black Sea the weather was fair and our chances seemed good. In the evening we cabled our agent in Constantsa that we would reach the first buoy before the minefields about forty miles from Constantsa, at 7 a.m. We asked him to send us a pilot to bring us into port. This was fortunate, because at 3 a.m., four hours before the point we should have arrived at, the sea became rough before we were able to get to the shore. The ship was rolling badly and the bows rose seven metres out of the sea and took the force of the wind (because the ship was empty and high out of the water). I knew in my heart what to expect because I knew what was happening in the fuel tanks. When you take on fuel you never know the exact amount because you never get clean fuel and you do not know how much water is in it. When you measure how much fuel you have in your tanks you do not know how much water is mixed with it. Sometimes, in ninety tons of fuel there can be forty per cent water. Despite all this we reached the point as arranged and the engines did not let us down and we only had to wait for the pilot. As soon as we got to the point I realized that something was wrong. There were Russian ships circling about, one large Russian ship and two small vessels and none of them was going into Constantsa harbour. I saw that even the agents of these ships did not dare to come out to them. Up to 10 a.m. nobody came. We were very nervous because we did not know the minefields or how to sail into port. We knew one thing – we had reached the point of no return; we were unable to go to another port and we could not go back because we had no fuel and it was impossible to enter Constantsa. I began at once to send signals to all the coast guard stations: "Send pilot, no fuel!" I contacted everyone possible, but none of the stations answered except for a Russian agent at Constantsa who replied. "Pilot cannot get out because of storm, lifeboat cannot get out in such stormy sea, do what you can." I could only pray. I started sending signals to our people to take a boat and pay enough for her to come and tow us in because I had finished all the reserve fuel and it was a miracle that the ship was functioning. Everyone replied that no ship was prepared to come out in such a rough sea. There was a tug belonging to an Englishman that was for hire but it was hard to believe he would agree to tow an unauthorized immigrant ship. By now it was noon and signals were still being sent. I started to ask for one simple thing: to come in alone on my own responsibility but for someone to send me a chart of the minefields. I received this information from the Russian agent: at night the buoys of the minefields were illuminated for their whole length and breadth. He could not send a map but he informed me that between 12.00 and 2.00 p.m. a tug from the Russian navy was going into Constantsa. I should do my best to stay behind her and keep my direction. Beneath this message was the word "information", underlined. He was afraid that I would hold him responsible for sending me this message. I sent him my thanks but asked him to put me in touch with the tug. On this, he informed me that he knew where I was, the tug was short and sat deep in the water and had an engine powerful enought to tow a large ship. She went out to sea in storms and fell from wave to wave but did not lose speed. Our ship was very fast but was so high in the water and there was such a strong wind against her that most of our power went into resisting the force of the wind. When we had to enter the minefield, we had to go broadside to the waves and wind and the ship, instead of advancing with the bows forward, proceeded sideways to take advantage of her height. I explained to the people who were with me on board that it was forbidden to do this because we were in a minefield, but the tug did not take into consideration that we were following her and continued on her way at speed. She moved away from us and the waves hid her and we could not see any buoy. The wind and poor visibility misled us, but since we had entered the minefield there was no way back. I telephoned the engineer and said to him: "Do you want to hit a mine?" His reply was negative, so I told him to do everything in his power to make the engines work all out. He gave the engines all the reserve fuel and the ship did not let us down. To our good luck, after seven miles the tug reached the buoy, turned round on the spot and began to advance into the wind. Our immediate problem was how to turn the ship around. The tug turned inside a 50-metre radius; with our ship such a move would need a turning circle of half a mile.

If I were to lose the buoy I would go into the minefield opposite or the one on the other side. I decided to go in a little on each side and started the turn four hundred metres before the buoy and finished four hundred metres beyond it. However, after the turn the ship picked up speed and caught up with the tug. We were close to her and by the time she had managed the second turn and was advancing broadside to the waves we made up all the time we had lost and realized we could keep it up. After this adventure, which caused us quite a lot of anxiety, we succeeded in entering Constantsa.

A further problem was fuel. We knew we had none – we entered the harbour by a miracle. In port the ship needs much less fuel than at sea – four to five tons a day are enough. We started to invent ways for the pumps to draw fuel from the boilers. We pumped salt water through the tanks and it floated the fuel up higher and this allowed us to keep going for another six days. All this time we did not get any fuel right up to the bitter and crucial moment. I do not know if any of you understand what a dead ship means, a ship with no electricity, the pumps not working, not pumping sweet water or salt water, no toilets, the galley out of use, no heating, nothing at all. And then you can not only pray, you can cry. Every day I received news that the British had damaged two of our ships in Italy and were trying to catch us. I had to look after the ship in these conditions, but how could I look after her when she was in complete darkness? There was no electricity in Constantsa so how could I get electricity to the ship? The *Pan York* gave us a little fuel but afterwards we were again without. We went about the port full of fear – we guarded the ship but were afraid. The fuel arrived three weeks later and the results of this delay were very serious; there was no heating in the ship, everything was damp and the crew were falling sick. There were days when thirteen seamen became ill because of the cold. Our men held on by sheer will-power but the hired Italian seamen gradually dropped out and were taken to hospitals and private homes to recover.[3]

The difficulties of entering one ship, empty and with apparently valid papers, into Constantsa harbour showed what could be expected when two ships, fully laden with a human cargo of over fifteen thousand souls, sought to enter a port that was not prepared to receive them. The voyage from Constantsa in Romania to Burgas in Bulgaria began without passengers. During the three months the ships stayed in Constantsa, they were overhauled and fitted out to carry passengers, and were loaded with large quantities of fuel, provisions and water. When they weighed anchor, on Monday, 22nd December 1947, they were like well-oiled machines ready for action. But there were enormous obstacles in their path.

THE CREW

In the art, literature and especially poetry of pre-independence Israel there is a special place for the crews of the unauthorized immigrant ships. These consisted of the ships' escorts from Israel and the professional seamen, the foreigners. In his poem, dedicated to "The Italian Captain", Nathan Alterman wrote:

The work of our boys is wrapped in the secrecy of night.
Let us bless it as we do our daily bread.
See now from ship to shore
They carry their people on strong shoulders.
Here's to this cold, staunch night!
To this dangerous, backbreaking life!

Here's to the little boats, captain!
And to the others on the way!
To the boys who got the command
To steer their craft through the fog
At the right time, to the right place
Without compass or map.

About them a certain story will be told
By the waves and the open sky.
How they fought their people's Battle of Trafalgar
On a lonely boat cutting through the water.
The clouds float above. The wind holds firm.

The work is done, as the sky's overhead!
Let's drink to it, captain,
To our next meeting on the seas.

A day will come, and you'll sit in a corner of a tavern.
You'll sit, Granddad, with a bottle of Chianti,
And you'll smile, chewing your tobacco,
And say: Well, fellows, I'm an old man now.[4]

The voyage of the *Pans*, the climax of unauthorized immigration and possibly its curtain call, came after a long and difficult period of trial and error by the Mossad. They had worked with dozens of vessels of different sizes, with varying degrees of success. Gradually, through intensive screening and selection there had emerged a group of experienced seamen dedicated to the idea of immigration and prepared to accept the hardships that would accompany it. Over the years Palestinian naval officers joined the ranks, some of whom had earned their master's ticket.

However, there were not enough men to undertake the voyage of the *Pans*, despite all the skilled and qualified people ready to do so. Since the *Pans* were to sail from a *bona fide* port, with the authorization of the host country, the ships had to meet maritime standards based on international agreements. The ships carried a flag, worked for an approved agent and had a qualified crew. The Israeli "fleet" was unaccustomed to such large vessels; there were only a few who had tickets for small ships, and even then in junior positions. The Mossad did not have access to a sufficient number of Israeli naval officers authorized to take command of large passenger ships.

The immigration emissaries were generally able to recruit foreign crews for their needs. The stereotypical adventurous sailor was not in evidence here. At a time when Europe was seeking to restore normal life and governments were anxious to establish stable regimes, irregular activities like unauthorized immigration were dangerous occupations. In the traditional areas of unlawful activity at sea, such as smuggling or violence, the authorities were able to impose the conventional punishments, such as fines and imprisonment. But helping unauthorized immigration was a political misdemeanor and its ramifications more risky. The penalty could be the cancellation of professional qualifications. This the sailors feared more than imprisonment. Thus it was not surprising that at the end of 1947 it was difficult to recruit sailors, and in particular officers, to work on Mossad ships.

The solution as usual, was money. Ada Sereni, the Mossad coordinator in Italy, agreed to find a crew for the *Pan Crescent* and offered higher pay than was normal in Italy, and, more important, promised a bonus at a rate ranging from $500 for the captain to $150 for the seamen. Since this would apparently be a comparatively short voyage the bonus made it seem worthwhile. However after the attempt to blow up the ship at Venice, it became clear that a long Odyssey was in the offing. The Italian captain withdrew and many of the sailors threatened to leave the ship, until the "owner", Paul Shulman, promised to double their monthly pay.[5]

Due either to pressure or haste, no agreement on pay or work conditions had been drawn up and since most of the seamen had been employed on the ship from October 1947 to the end of the winter of 1948, the problem of their pay and rights became complicated. This was compounded by the solution that had been found for the crew of the *Pan York*. Hiring this crew had been entrusted to a reliable agent from Marseilles. Mindful of the disadvantages of working in unauthorized immigration, he approached a special group – Spanish sailors who were refugees from the Spanish Civil War. They had thrown in their lot with Republican Spain, had taken an active part in the war on the socialist side and were now homeless and jobless refugees. Many of them had already been cooperating with the Mossad for some time, and another thirty-nine were now recruited for the *Pan York* in jobs ranging from skipper to deckhand. This should have been a willing and even enthusiastic crew; however, the long time they spent on board ship – over six months and for some of them up to nine months – created tension and conflict with the Mossad representatives. This began when they discovered that one Italian seaman had been offered double pay, they threatened to strike for equal treatment[6] and the captain, Gad Hilb, was obliged to meet their demands.[7]

The Spaniards were further worried by the news reaching them from their families about financial hardship and persecution. They asked the Mossad to transfer part of their pay directly to their families in France, Central and South America. Tension reached a peak later, after the voyage was over, when the ships were anchored in Cyprus for over four months, from 1st January, 1948 until the establishment of the State of Israel. While they were stranded there the Spanish sailors began wondering where they would go next. In Spain they could only expect persecution. France did not want them and the British had cancelled their professional qualifications. In desperation they turned to the Mossad to help them, either to gain entry visas to the U.S. or France, or employment in the emerging Israeli shipping company.[8] The Mossad could not ignore these repeated requests. It had a moral obligation towards the sailors whose difficulties were genuine. In addition, they had a powerful hold on the Mossad who did not want international scandals and sailors' strikes which would make them appear as exploiters and reveal a new and unpleasant side to the immigration story. Furthermore there were grounds for fearing that the British would take advantage of the dispute and use it as an excuse to put their own crews aboard the ships and confiscate them.

The files of the ships and the Mossad correspondence show that a large proportion of the thousands of documents dealing with the *Pans* was devoted to the problems of foreign sailors. The Mossad took great pains to look after all the sailors on the ships and their families abroad. It provided them with a new place to settle and the necessary papers, sometimes forged.[9] All this had the expected results. The paean to the Italian captain composed by Nathan Alterman did not mitigate the difficulties, misunderstandings and even treachery, blackmail and sabotage committed by foreign seamen working for the Mossad. As their importance grew, their bargaining power increased. This was expressed not only in financial terms but also in their degree of willingness to work. The *Pans* operation, the most extensive, complex and prestigious in the entire immigration effort could not be left to the whim of a motley crew of hired sailors from all the ports of Europe.

Since the *Pans* could not be entrusted to a foreign crew, efforts were made to find professionals for key positions who would provide a solid core with higher motivation and dedication. In fact, there were two completely different crews for each ship, although this was not usually apparent because of the division of responsibilities. The engineers, oilers and stokers were almost all foreign while the radio operators were all Israeli.[10] Friction occurred mainly at the command level.

Here, too, there was ostensibly clear division of authority, according to the traditions of unauthorized immigration procedure. The commander of the ship, generally a member of the Hagana, was in charge of contact with the Mossad, the welfare of his passengers, confronting the British in case of trouble, and decisions concerning the destination of the ship. The captain, who was a hired professional, generally Italian or Greek, took orders from the commander as to the destination of the voyage, but in everything connected with the routine running of the ship and command over its crew, he had complete control. With the *Pans*, the differences among the crew began in the U.S. when some of its members who had been recruited there to sail the ships to Europe, asked to remain on the job. At the time of the voyage from Constantsa, there were four Jewish crew members from the U.S. on each of the ships. Following the Mossad code, they were called Sam, since they came from the land of Uncle Sam. They held volunteer status, although, as one of the Mossad treasurers pointed out, "payments to volunteers were usually higher than that of the Spanish sailors".[11] Some of the Americans had taken part in previous operations, including the voyage of the *Chaim Arlozoroff* and the *Exodus*.[12] Since they were qualified seamen as well as Zionists, volunteers and with experience in immigration operations, they were fitting candidates for positions at the the top of the command structure on the ships. Meeting their Israeli counterparts highlighted their greater experience and skill. Nevertheless, the Mossad preferred the small coterie of young Israelis, all from the same age group, who had gone through youth movement, Kibbutz and Palmach together. The tradition of the pre-state Israel labour movement had cultivated a myth about the building of the country in which these young people had a key part, creating something out of nothing by virtue of sheer faith and tenacity. Far greater importance was attached to these qualities than to professional expertise, planning and reason. Veterans of the Hagana, leaders of the Histadrut labour federation and, of course, Shaul Avigur, head of the Mossad, could prove from personal experience that it was these people, inexperienced but bold and loyal to each other, fired with a sense of purpose, who had produced the revolutionary structures of the Yishuv and brought it to national independence.[13]

The Kibbutz and the Moshav, the Federation of Labour and the Sick Fund, the Hagana and Palmach were not founded by engineers and planners and based on fixed standards of management and budgeting. On the contrary, attempts to establish projects based on long-range planning had all failed. The idea of unauthorized immigration and the structure of the Mossad were the result of trial and error over fifteen years. The successes and failures were related not to the professional ability of the people but to their personal fortitude.

It was not by chance that most of the Mossad emissaries came from the ranks of the Hagana. They were mainly between twenty and thirty years old, members of pioneering movements and kibbutzim. They all had ideological ties to the labour movement in Palestine, and as

Hagana members they understood the security aspect of immigration. This meant bringing as many Jews as possible into the country, and being prepared to defend them, if necessary resorting to the use of force against British attempts to block immigration. Their youth was also a function of the nature of the work: long periods of isolation, secrecy, a high degree of mobility, personal danger and anonymity were not suited to the family man but rather to the unattached kibbutznik. The kibbutz would always be there to receive him back again, and his agricultural work was taken care of by his fellow members in his absence.

Command of the entire operation was placed in the hands of Yossi Harel, who was twenty-eight years old. Yossi was neither a qualified naval officer nor an expert in management and organization and had no professional qualifications relating to the complex problems of transporting masses of immigrants from country to country. Moreover, he did not know Romania or the problems of the Romanian Jews and it seemed that he had no common language with the thousands of people he was supposed to be in charge of and who were about to entrust their fate to him. On the other hand this young man had a surprising long history for his age in which he had revealed the required qualities – tenacity, loyalty and faith. He had joined the Hagana in 1936 and had been active in different areas. After the war Yossi had worked in unauthorized immigration and before the *Pans* he had commanded the *Exodus*. He also had some political background to help him to overcome the problems of moving thousands of people across countries, oceans and obstacles, both expected and unexpected. In 1945 he became the personal bodyguard of Chaim Weizmann, the president of the Zionist movement. Weizmann quickly discovered that he was not just a strongman and bodyguard who also acted as a driver. Yossi became the president's adjutant and was put in charge of communications between the head of the Zionist movement and the Hagana staff. The affection and friendship between the two was circumscribed; Weizmann did not involve his young adjutant in the difficult problems of the leadership of the Zionist movement and Yossi did not tell Weizmann about his activities in the Hagana and Aliya Bet. When Yossi was called to work in unauthorized immigration Weizmann must have guessed what was happening and acquiesced, but nothing more. When the *Exodus* operation was over, Shaul Avigur offered Yossi Harel the command of the *Pans*. However, Yossi had already been appointed aide to Yaakov Dori, then Chief of Staff of the

Hagana, which was preparing for the possible eventuality of war. Once again there was pressure and personal appeal and only at the end of November, less than a month before the ships were due to sail, Harel was released from his position and left for Europe.

Yossi's meeting with Shaul Avigur took place in a cafe in Prague. Mossad activists often recall Shaul's cafe meetings.[14] The choice of cafe was arbitrary, but it was always near the centre of town; it had to be unobtrusive and the table was always in a far corner. When the waitress came Shaul ordered tea for everyone. If somebody had just arrived after a long journey (from Palestine, for example) straight to the meeting, Shaul would ask him if he would like a cake. Yossi recalled the phrasing of the question: "You don't want a cake, do you?" Yossi, of course, declined.[15] Admiration turned to emulation. The personal frugality of the emissaries was out of all proportion to the enormous sums of money they were handling, sometimes tens of thousands of dollars in cash carried in suitcases for which they could not always obtain receipts. But they would save where they could, beginning with Shaul Avigur's glasses of tea.

At this meeting with Yossi, Shaul seemed worried. This was hardly news; the weight of his responsibilities, the tensions, and his solitary nature, as well as the difference in age between him and his subordinates gave him the appearance of a stern, harsh man. This time he was more expansive in his conversation and revealed his problems. He did not refer to the difficulties with ministers and governments which made the *Pans* a problem and endangered the very establishment of the State of Israel. Shaul was worried about the unavoidable encounter between the *Pans* and the British navy. No solutions were found at that meeting; Yossi restricted himself to pinpointing the main difficulties, agreeing on the principal lines of action and obtaining Shaul's promise to recruit the best possible people for the operation. Shaul was able to make this promise – most of the crew had already been recruited and some of them had taken part in preparing the ships.

This meeting in Prague was also attended by Yaakov Salomon, commander of the "operations section" and in charge of the operation's organization in Romania; Shaike Dan, the paratrooper and soldier, who was the Mossad's political contact, particularly in Bulgaria; and Pino Ginsburg, Mossad treasurer, whose duties included mediation, advice and command. They discussed the crew at their disposal and the quality of the people at length and Yossi received a very favourable impression – no operation in the history of the Yishuv had been so well manned.

At this stage, at the end of the Mossad's activities, a good crew meant a stable and experienced one, and Yossi decided to divide it so that each ship would have a complete Israeli core, which included the commander, captain, navigator, signals officers and a few professionals, generally from among the Americans. This core, consisting of Mossad workers and Palmach members, could easily absorb the foreign, professional crew. The multi-purpose group wa s a guarantee of high professional standards, and more important, first-class manpower. However, there were many areas of tension. The division of labour between the foreign skipper and the Israeli captain was not clear; occasionally there was tension between the captain, a Palmach man, and the ship commander, a Mossad man and between the ship commanders and the commander of the operation, who was aboard one of the ships. Ike Aharonowitz, who was appointed captain of the *Pan Crescent*, was twenty-four years old and by the standards of those days had a long maritime background and was considered to be an experienced naval officer. He had been at sea since his youth, had served in the Royal Navy during the war and afterwards joined the naval department of the Palmach, and like Yossi Harel, had been on the *Exodus*. He joined the *Pan Crescent* on 26th December 1947, just before she sailed. The ship was already in Bulgaria and passengers were embarking when he took command.

A generation after the affair, his hair grey at the temples, Ike is still the *enfant terrible* of Israeli shipping. His seniority and charisma have not altered his lifelong contrariness; and he still continues to rise in the maritime world and then come down to earth with a bump because of a serious disagreement with the establishment. A twenty-four-year-old activist, bold, inclined to take risks and believing in the supreme importance of "smashing the British blockade" for the purpose of achieving Jewish independence, he assembled the ship's crew which he had seen for the first time in his life less than an hour before, and advised the Italian skipper to take his pay and go.

Yossi Harel vetoed this. He liked this wiry, wild young man but thought it would be a good thing if the old Italian skipper remained. The skipper's last entry in the log book reads: "I hand over command and remain as an observing officer on the ship until I am returned home."[16] His journey home took another six months . . .

The conflict concealed the ideological differences, both individual and collective, between the *Mossad* operatives, who had made all the preparations for immigration up to the actual voyage, and the Israeli crew on the ships who were from the Palmach. The Israelis sent out by the Palmach staff nicknamed the Mossad operatives "Shooshoo", which seemed to express the feelings of awe as well as the dark side of the Mossad work, the subterfuge and intrigue which were the antithesis of the open pride and comradeship of the Palmach way of life. Ike Aharonowitz and Gad Hilb, who was captain of the *Pan York*, were part of a group in Israel whose contacts with their superiors were relaxed and friendly. Yigal Allon, commander of the Palmach, was their contemporary, lived with them, and together they developed an activist viewpoint that scorned the circumlocutions of diplomacy in favour of personal example, persistence and fighting to the end.

The Palmach felt that the political leadership of the Yishuv and the Zionist movement was too hesitant and that it needed stimulation from below, and so it was they who pressed for bold and decisive action. Ike Aharonowitz brought this feeling with him to the *Pan Crescent*. He considered Yossi Harel, from the Hagana – a few years his senior but not yet thirty himself – a representative of the other side, an establishment man, with obligations to a heavy-handed system.[17] Ike's loyalty was to the Palmach and Yossi's – according to Ike – was to the Zionist leadership; friction between the circumspection of the latter and the bold activism of the former was likely to be felt on the ships. For their voyage into the unknown, a varied crew had been deliberately chosen: the *Pan Crescent* was commanded by Dov Magen (Barchik) and the *Pan York* by Nissan Levitan. Both had been with the ships for months and had been responsible for fitting and preparing them. While the Italian skipper on the *Pan Crescent* was purely an observer, there were good relations and close cooperation on the *Pan York* between the captain and the Spanish Republican skipper, Estaban Hernandora, who served as first mate. Hernandora, who became "infected" by Zionism, continued to serve for many years in "Zim" and was known as Captain Steve.

There were thirty Americans and Israelis; men from the Palmach, the Mossad, the Gideons and sailors such as Grisha Sheinkman from kibbutz Kfar Giladi. Ostensibly they all belonged to the same movement, had the same loyalties and were subject to the same command. In fact, they represented a wide ideological spectrum. In such a broad cross-section there were necessarily tensions but there was one shared goal – national independence and social revolution in

Israel. They were also alike in age and their labour movement
background.

Conflicting ideas about how statehood would be achieved were rife
in Palestine, but on the high seas they were moderated by the common
purpose the crew felt in their responsibility for the lives of thousands
of Jewish refugees.

ON THEIR WAY

No immigration operation had been planned with as much care and
expense as the voyage of the *Pans*. One critical planning problem was
that of passing through the Bosphorus. The plans called for the ships
to reach the Straits on Saturday evening, 27th December, 1947.
Everyone knew that the British were putting pressure on the Turkish
government to arrest the ships in the Straits and prevent them from
sailing into the Mediterranean.[18] The Turkish government hesitated,
but since the matter had been raised in general terms it was able to
avoid taking a stand. It was clear that the problem would arise in
earnest when the ships approached the Straits and stopped at the
entrance for inspection. It was then that the heaviest possible pressure
would be brought to bear on the Turks and it was doubtful whether
they could withstand the British demands. The Mossad had assumed
from the beginning that the Bosphorus could be used to block the ships
and attempted to overcome this difficulty by a fairly simple method. It
was the Christmas season – Boxing Day, in fact – and the British
Consul in Istanbul would surely be pleased to drink to that. Moshe
Pearlman was despatched to Istanbul and Jon Kimche to Ankara.
They were both British journalists, Jewish and Zionist sympathizers,
charming and urbane conversationalists who would not find it
difficult, in the foreign isolation of Turkey, to get their hosts to drink a
great deal. By the time the consul in Istanbul returned to work on the
Monday, he would have been neutralized as would be the British
diplomatic representative in Ankara, and the Turks would be released
from pressure.[19] A healthy bribe[20] ensured an "easy" Turkish watch in
the control system on the Straits on Saturday evening, so that the
report to Ankara on the approach of the ships and the nature of their
cargo would be garbled and the ships would pass through unhindered.

With the time pressing on Saturday evening, with a drunken British
consul in Istanbul and a bribed Turkish watch, the timing had to be
precise. The countdown had been carefully planned from the

departure of the first train from the furthest Romanian station. The task of gathering 15,000 people and boarding them on the ships had been detailed on thousands of pages of notes and precise timetables.

It was different in execution. The broad outline of the programme was carried out according to plan but because of its complexity and the different factors involved there were breakdowns. Some of them were in the organization of the convoy – delays at the Romanian control points, heavy snowfall and people attempting to get on without proper papers. As a result of the cold, three children died on the trains which had to stop in order to bury them in the frozen fields along the way.[21] This sad accident, which was familiar to the Mossad people from previous voyages, was highlighted in a particularly bitter way when a baby was born on the last train, which arrived just as the ship was ready to sail. The birth took place a few hours before the train arrived, but when the passengers were about to get off and board the ship, the baby was found to be dead. The orderlies whose duty it was to get people on board did not show sufficient sensitivity and rushed the passengers along, including the frantic mother. She became hysterical and refused to leave her dead baby. It is not difficult to imagine the distress with 15,000 people waiting to depart for the Promised Land, the screams of the grief-stricken mother from the shed on the quayside and the confusion of the commanders worried about keeping to the timetable. Shaike Dan took the initiative. Despite pressure of time, he asked Yossi Hamburger to delay the sailing, contacted the local rabbi, located a small wooden coffin and calmed the mother as the members of the Burgas Jewish burial society took the dead baby and promised to bury it according to Jewish law.[22]

The delay began before this sad outburst. As already mentioned, the plan to organize each carriage into a group of forty-five passengers with a leader was completely ignored by the thousands who thronged the trains in their own configurations. It is easy to picture thousands of people, tired and hungry from the long journey, weak from cold and travelling in cattle trucks, facing two enormous ships in a primitive port and creating a confusion that was impossible to unravel. Yet in spite of this, one important principle still applied. A team of orderlies went to the station before the port and stopped every train that came in. Passengers were told to leave the train, have a drink of water and relieve themselves and were warned that this was the last chance for several hours. Everyone rushed to the ruins around the station and scurried back to the trains. This time they did not bother to look for members of their families or return to the same car, assuming that the journey was over and they would be joining their loved ones anyway. But they were wrong. The trains moved from there straight to the ships. The track ran along the dockside, beside the water, three metres from the gangways. The long train stopped beside the two ships, with half the cars designated for one ship and the other half for the ship behind it. The people leaving the train were pushed onto a narrow wooden raft that was laid between the track and the gangway.

At this point they were met by orderlies who had been told to be extremely strict. One group of orderlies kept the crowd moving, not giving them time to search for relatives, even children who had been separated from their parents or husbands from wives. The strictness of the orderlies was helped by the terrain; one side was blocked by the train and the other by the ship. The few people who tried to escape from the flow of people from the carriages to the ships fell into the cold, filthy water. There was no possibility of standing against the tide of people scrambling from the trains to the ship – even those who had not found their relatives had no choice – and the embarkation proceeded quickly and smoothly. When there was an organic group to be embarked, its leader recorded the names of his group until their number reached forty-five, received an identity disc with the names of his people and then went on up the gangway. In the case of a mixed group that had come together on the train by chance, the counting and listing of names was improvised and based on intuition. They selected a member of the group who looked like a natural leader or simply like a sensible person and gave him the disc with the names of forty-five people in the group which he had chanced to join.

The third group consisted of the strictest orderlies and its task was to solve problems of excess baggage. Although the instructions were to bring one piece of baggage, people arrived fully loaded with food for several days, tools, pots and pans, blankets and even washtubs. As they were starting the steep ascent to the ship up the shaky gangway, the orderlies advised the immigrants to tie their extra baggage to their knapsacks on their backs and even provided string for this purpose on the trains. The passengers liked this suggestion and tied their belongings to their backs in great humps. The "excess baggage group" rubbed their hands with pleasure at the terrifying sight of the long snake of people, stooped under the burdens bound to their backs. In one of the corners on the way up, when the immigrant on the twisting ladder was hidden from the one in front of him, they waited with long, sharp knives and when, with a final effort, he grasped the gangway, they rapidly cut the string that they had just given him and threw huge piles of parcels on the raft in the water. The immigrant was concerned with what was before him and did not have time to complain before he came to the group waiting for him on the deck which directed him to his place in the hold.[23]

The intensive pace of the embarkation process left the immigrants bewildered. Many years later some of them noted with astonishment that they did not remember getting to the ship or boarding her. A few were able to say that because of the short distance from the train to the high ship, they could not see her. The first place they remembered was the gigantic dormitory to which the orderlies had directed them. The unattractive sight of thousands of narrow cots became in time one of the images that was to stay with the immigrants all their lives.[24] On the first day, when eight thousand people had embarked in eight hours, every immigrant was taken to his cot. The orderlies, like concerned parents, stood by each immigrant, took his possessions and his coat from him and only after he had got onto his fifty centimetres of cot were his possessions returned to him, so that he would not try to take up some of the adjacent cot. Then a curfew was called. Whoever had gone to his cot was forbidden to leave it until the whole dormitory was full. At the same time the group leaders were asked to make an updated list of their group on a form that had been prepared in advance, and on which they had to write the names of their people, their age, state of health and special problems. Another form explained the plan of the ship, daily routine and standing orders. Loudspeakers explained in Romanian, Yiddish and Hebrew the importance of keeping to their places and groups and in pre-arranged order told the group leaders to go to assembly points and receive water and biscuits. The feeling that there was somebody to take care of matters helped to calm down the people and to maintain this improvised structure of groups throughout the voyage.

On the second day it was impossible to sustain the rapid pace of embarkation. The orderlies were exhausted and some of them had to spend a large part of their time dealing with the personal problems of a few individuals among the thousands that were crammed in the hold. Furthermore, only six thousand places had been prepared in each ship and it now emerged that nearly fifteen thousand people had come from Romania. Then there was the sudden addition of four hundred and twenty young people the Bulgarians had permitted to leave. At this stage the ship commanders were on the point of giving up. The trains continued to arrive and discharge their cargo into the two ships. The people swarmed up and only the loudspeakers told them to go to the dormitories in the hold. The system that had worked so well on the first day, now collapsed. The teams that had directed the people to the dormitories had broken up. Only a few people obeyed the request to go below, because there was little temptation to meander down dark corridors with the smell of overcrowding and the dull echo of thousands of people.

The information from below was that all the cots had been taken so there was no need to hurry down to the darkness and crowding. A bottleneck quickly developed on deck, preventing further embarkation. Yaakov Salomon, who was in charge of the railway operation, was worried and wondered whether there had been an error of judgement and started to suggest that the last trains should be stopped. Shaike Dan, who was standing next to him, rejected this idea with a slap. "But where are we going to put them?" asked Salomon. "Hang them from the mast but they are coming along," he declared.[25]

It is difficult to move people who are clinging to each other after an exhausting journey and as they were collapsing on deck it required superhuman strength to get them up and persuade them to move and make room. This superhuman strength was found just at the right moment. Suddenly it began to rain heavily and everyone began to go down hurriedly and in disorder. Since the dormitories between decks appeared full, the immigrants, wet and exhausted, made their way down to the lower dormitory, deep in the hold. Almost no cots had been prepared there so some sort of space was available for several hundred people.

The last trains arrived followed by the Bulgarian youths. With their American G.I. overalls and hats they looked like the cheerful finale to a special kind of carnival. It was a huge body of people – women and old men, teenagers and babies, city people and villagers, distinguished professors and escaped criminals –all bringing long memories of exile and looking ahead at an unknown road, together on two banana boats under the leadership of young Jews from Palestine. Shaike Dan, who had worked in Jewish immigration all his life, sometimes in very special conditions, and who can be considered a key figure in the immigration of hundreds of thousands of people to Israel, describes with great emotion the moment when the anchors were weighed: "I have had many moving experiences but the singing of the Jewish national anthem 'Hatikva' by 15,000 people on the deck and below – I have never heard anything like it since."[25]

It should be remembered that Shaike Dan's personal situation at that moment was not pleasant. He joined in the singing with an additional personal prayer, because he was sailing only as far as the coast of Varna. From there a boat came to take him, carrying the director of the passport department of the Bulgarian secret service who had been supervising the operation. Dan was a hostage and the prosaic reason for this was money. As mentioned earlier, the Mossad request to the Bulgarians for permission to use the port of Burgas had to come wrapped in cash. As far as we have been able to ascertain, $50,000 was the price for agreeing to the transit of Jews from Romania and a further $25,000 for agreeing to let the Bulgarian youths go. Pino Ginsburg, the Mossad treasurer, did not want to pay until he knew the Bulgarians had carried out their part of the bargain. They had then demanded a further payment for other Bulgarian youths in addition to the $75,000. Their demands for the money were firm and they informed Shaike Dan that if the money was not paid to them at once they would not allow the ships to sail. He did not want to give the ship commanders further grounds for worry, it was impossible to obtain such a large sum at once and it was out of the question to delay the ships, so he offered himself as security. The Bulgarians agreed unwillingly. Only after Pino Ginsburg had paid the full amount to the Bulgarian representative in Switzerland was Shaike "released" from this unpleasant captivity.

The Mossad operatives had to be both sensitive and hard: sensitive to Jewish suffering and hopes and hard in the many cases when they had to make cruel decisions to overcome an unexpected obstacle. Shaike Dan needed a full measure of these contradictory qualities at this time. A few days earlier he had been in Tel Aviv and at his frequent meetings with Ben-Gurion and Golda had learned of the gravity of the situation. He had read the cables from Sharett and Goldmann and was familiar with the British and American positions. He had participated in the final, hasty decisions and the trial negotiations with the British – but was aware of the lack of clarity or agreement. The ships were sailing and they presented a terrible danger. They could create a storm that might sweep away the idea of a Jewish state and perhaps even the ships themselves. He had needed a great degree of hardness to be party to the decision to sail. This obduracy was however tempered by sensitivity to the situation of the Jews in Romania, their plight and their yearnings. Dan, now acting as a Zionist hostage in the hands of the Communists, sat in the small Bulgarian boat and looked towards the ships. They were moving. He could not describe his feelings. It was the greatest moment in his lfe but his joy at seeing the ships sailing was too closely mingled with heavyhearted misgivings.

CHAPTER EIGHT

Black Sea, Blue Sea

"Like the echo of a lost ship in the fog"
(Yisrael Efrat, *Words and Silence*)

MINEFIELD

At 10.30 in the morning of 27th December, 1947, the flags of the emerging state were raised, anchors were weighed and the *Pan York* and *Pan Crescent* set sail. Looking back, the immigrants remembered the excitement and elation as the flags waved at the tops of the tall masts and the voices of 15,000 passengers, packed into the four levels of the hold and on the deck, rose in song.[1] The commanders remembered their fears. The destination was Palestine, but no one could say with certainty where the ships would actually end up, after running an obstacle course beginning with the mine-infested waters along the Bulgarian coast and ending perhaps in armed confrontation with the British, as had been the fate of the *Exodus*. The first problem the commander of the ships, Yossi Harel, had to face was that of the minefield along the coast, and it was a curious one. The *Pans* were not the first ships in the port of Burgas. Since the end of the war a broad channel had been cleared stretching from Burgas to Varna on the route to the Romanian coast: it was considered clear, although occasionally a powerful mine would surface.

The conditions in the channel demanded cautious navigation, alertness and constant attention. The Russian pilot who had been engaged to navigate through the cleared channel insisted on departure at dawn. When the loading delayed the ships he suggested postponing the sailing until Sunday morning. A simple calculation proved that if the ships left at 10.30 a.m. they would reach the most sensitive section of the minefield at night. A bitter argument broke out between Yossi Harel and the pilot. Yossi's concern was to get to the Bosphorus as quickly as possible and certainly no later than Sunday evening, in case the watch was changed, the ships held up, the British Consul returned to work and diplomatic action was taken which could detain the ships in the Black Sea. At the height of the argument a strong easterly wind blew up from the minefields in the direction of the cleared channel but Yossi was adamant. The pilot, a good Russian and a loyal Communist, accepted the order to sail, boarded the *Pan Crescent* and with a bottle of vodka to strengthen his heart and constantly crossing himself to strengthen his soul, gave the signal and the ships got under way. The passengers were not involved in the argument and knew nothing about it. Only thirty of the Bulgarians were called to the bridge on each of the ships and given large flashlights. The *Pan York* sailed just behind the *Pan Crescent*, keeping in her wake. For fourteen tense hours, the Bulgarians acted as lookouts and kept a watch for unknown objects in the water. Yossi Harel, who had sailed on the *Exodus* and served in sensitive positions in Israeli espionage remembered those hours as a nightmare. He later described it: "The night voyage was nerve-racking. All around, the sea was black. The wind was terrible and the small flashlights were probing for mines. You kept on moving and didn't know . . . just one mine . . . when we reached the lighthouse, opposite Romania, I breathed easy: we had cleared the minefields."[2] Although the passengers had no idea they were crossing a dangerous minefield, few of them slept. Some of them went to look for relatives they had been separated from during the various stages of the journey, some went to inspect the ship and some could not get used to their cramped sleeping quarters; some found the large hold oppressive, packed as it was with hundreds of people; some were cold, thirsty or needed the toilets and everyone wanted some exercise after they had almost frozen on the train journey through the snowy Romanian December.

The curiosity, boredom and especially disquiet had been taken into account in planning the operation. The experienced operatives knew that the immigrants down in the hold of the ship were frightened, insecure and curious about what was going on around them and that tensions could easily arise among themselves and between them and the crew. There were passengers who, out of nervousness or boredom might play dangerous pranks or even sabotage the water and supplies installations. Aboard the *Pans* the main dangers were the blocking of the passageways, inability to reach the toilets and loss of central control over the people. There was also the fear of damage to the huge fans which supplied oxygen to the compartments in the hold. For this reason, a detailed schedule had been planned to regulate access to the deck and to classify the various cabins for food, recreation, water and cultural activities. Particular attention was paid to two subjects: health and religion.

FROM ASPIRINS TO TORAH SCROLLS

The Mossad workers had become very sensitive to the problems of health involved in immigration operations. These young people, mostly from kibbutzim in Israel, were used to normal living arrangements with regular meals and a system of developed institutions for mutual aid even in times of difficulty; with the survivors of the Holocaust they encountered behaviour they had not known before. Signs of the physical suffering they had endured were evident on their bodies while their mental anguish was expressed in hysterical outbursts and bouts of deep apathy and withdrawal. Tragedy and death had struck during the various voyages.[3] The young operatives were helpless in the face of such problems and the only solution they could propose was a comprehensive health service. The immigrants on the *Pans* were not, in the main, concentration camp survivors and during the Holocaust had suffered less than the Jews in other European countries; however, the very nature of their grouping in whole families was of medical importance. Among the immigrants there were the aged, infants, the sick and the handicapped. There were a large number of pregnant women aboard and births were expected on the voyage.

Medical care, which had always been given priority by the Mossad, reached its peak in this operation. At the time the ships were being purchased and fitted out in the U.S., advanced medical equipment and drugs, including costly antibiotics, were acquired. The operative section in Bucharest devoted considerable time to medical planning and engaged forty-eight doctors and eighty nurses in Romania who were given preference in the various selection processes and some of whom helped organize medical service aboard the ships. The Romanian authorities were not happy about the intention to take so many doctors at once and vetoed the immigration of a Dr. Ashkenazi, who was a famous brain surgeon. The Mossad used their ingenuity and persuasiveness, some forgery and, of course, a little bribery to secure the release of the medical team which was divided evenly between the two ships. On each ship a special area was designated as the hospital, next to which was a kind of operating theatre with the best equipment, a delivery room, and isolation wards for people with infectious diseases. Altogether there were eighty hospital beds on each ship. Each dormitory was provided with a small surgery with first-aid equipment and a doctor and nurse, on twenty-four hour duty. Since the voyage itself lasted only five days, the weather was mild, the supply of food and water was sufficient and the ventilation system in the holds functioned, there were no special difficulties as far as health was concerned. The principal call on the doctors was to deal with the delicate problem of severe stomach complaints among passengers who confessed their suffering might be due to the fact that they had ingested their valuables. Rather than give up their possessions they had exchanged them for diamonds or even money which they then wrapped and swallowed. Once they had passed all the customs examinations and were in safe hands, they begged the doctors to relieve them of their precious hoard.[4]

A scene of more pleasant activity was the delivery room. The loudspeakers turned this into a kind of competition between the ships. The labour pains of some of the women were accompanied by the shouts of thousands of people in the holds who shared in this exciting experience.[5] *Pan York* was the winner, with three babies – only two were born on the *Pan Crescent*. None of the mothers could have given birth in finer conditions or with better medical attention from so many doctors and nurses and with so many well-wishers.

Despite differences between regions and organizations, the Jews of Romania maintained a fairly traditional religious life-style.[6] Even the hardships of the war had not destroyed Jewish institutions and in spite of great difficulties, plots, and changes of leadership, there were districts of Romania where communal life had continued uninter-rupted.[7] Thus, large sections of the immigrants took for granted that on Jewish ships, carrying Jews to the Land of Israel, Jewish rituals and customs, including prayer and dietary laws, would be scrupulously adhered to.

The Mossad workers had, before the *Pans* operation, come into contact mainly with members of pioneering movements who were generally non-religious or with concentration camp survivors who had been forced to abandon their religious observance. There was a distinct difference in the mentality of a young Jewish farmer from the Valley of Jezreel and a Jew from a small town in Eastern Europe. The patience and consideration with which the emissaries dealt with the immigrants' family and health problems did not apply in questions of property or religion. The ship commanders could see nothing wrong in cutting the string holding together the immigrants' miserable belongings and throwing them into the water. They had the traditional socialist scorn for the "petit bourgeois" mentality with its regard for personal property.[8] They could not understand the reason for carrying worn-out and broken possessions such a long way. They had no experience of the kind of life where objects sometimes had an importance far greater than their apparent value. The founders of the Palestinian labour movement, who had tried to create a new man as the antithesis of the Diaspora Jew, considered the desire to accumulate and to preserve property as a sign of the wretchedness of Diaspora life, while cooperation and the renunciation of personal possessions were seen as a symbol of Zionist renewal.[9]

This also accounted for the hostile attitude to religion. The descriptions of small-town Jewish life by writers such as Mendele Mocher Sforim fostered an image of religious obscurantism combined with laziness, fatalism and squalor.[10] This was all part and parcel of Jewish life in the Diaspora and the Israeli attitude demanded a complete break with these primitive symbols of religion which, in the spirit of the times, they saw as "the opium of the people". The founders of the socialist movement in Palestine, such as Berl Katznelson and David Ben-Gurion and most of their contemporaries came from traditional Jewish homes and their immigration to Palestine represented a deep and decisive change, a clean break with religion. Dov Magen, commander of the *Pan York*, came from a religious home and had spent a few years studying at a Yeshiva (rabbinical seminary). But the socialist Hashomer Hatzair movement, immigration, and life on kibbutz had removed him completely from his traditions and led him to reject the "old order". His mission in unauthorized immigration also embraced the need to "change" the Jewish immigrants. However, these age-old traditions could not be routed in a few days. Dov Magen understood that he could not introduce a secular life style to thousands of people all at once; space was provided for a synagogue but it was in the stern of the ship between huge piles of equipment.

On Saturday morning, just before the sailing, while the commanders and crew were dealing with last-minute problems, hurriedly boarding the people who had come on the last train, trying to calm the hysterical mother of the still-born child, arguing with the Russian pilot who was afraid of mines, and maintaining continuous contact with Tel Aviv,

Paris, Geneva, Bucharest, Sofia and Istanbul, there was a stream of worshippers to the improvised synagogue in the stern for Sabbath prayers. The heavy rain, which had earlier relieved the congestion on deck and driven the last immigrants down into the crowded hold below, did not prevent a reverse flow from the hold to the synagogue. Many of the immigrants took out their finest clothes which made a striking contrast to their earlier bedraggled appearance after the long railway journey. Wearing their prayer shawls and carrying their prayer-books they made their way to the packed stern; the "synagogue" quickly filled up and most of the people could not find any room. The emotional moment of departure allayed their dissatisfaction and with patience and understanding they agreed to the suggestion, made over the loudspeakers, to return to their dormitories and pray there. Almost miraculously there was somebody in every dormitory who had brought a Scroll of the Law with him from home and in dozens of praying groups the singing of "Hatikva", which accompanied the weighing of the anchor, was mingled with the liturgy.

This first setback on the morning of departure aroused misgivings among the religious immigrants. Activists from the ultra-Orthodox Poale Agudat Yisrael movement, which had some 1,500 members on the ships,[11] set up a committee which went to inspect the religious arrangements aboard and the situation they discovered was very grave. For example, there was no ritual bath (mikva) for the women. It is doubtful whether any of the organizers had thought of this problem but for the Orthodox the mikva was of extreme importance. The laws of family purity were strict and the penalty for their violation was, as prescribed by the Law, excommunication. Even more serious was the question of kashrut (dietary laws). The Orthodox were ready to accept that the use of loudspeakers on the Sabbath was an operational necessity or a simple oversight due to the excitement and were already prepared to forgive the mishap over the synagogue; as the time for the midday meal drew near they discovered to their great distress that the preparation and cooking of food on the Sabbath was in full swing. Their amazement turned into shock when one of the rabbis on the hastily convened committee found that the canned meat being used in the midday meal was not kosher.

The two sides, the ship commanders and the Orthodox activists, were surprised at the magnitude of the misunderstanding between them. The Orthodox had not realized how "lax" those in charge of taking Jews to the Holy Land would be; for some of them this was their first encounter with the secular attitude of the young people who were the backbone of the Hagana, Palmach and the unauthorized immigration effort. The ship commanders, who in their hearts must have expected the immigrants to be unquestioning in their gratitude, were surprised by the strength of the opposition from the members of the *ad hoc* committee for religious affairs.

Dov Magen, commander of the *Pan York*, at first tried to shrug off these problems: it was an underground operation, there was a state of emergency, it was a short voyage, they should hold their counsel for a few days even though all the facilities did not comply with religious law. This did not pacify the Orthodox and their spokesmen reacted angrily. "In conditions which were much harder, we observed all the Laws and even the anti-Semitic Romanians understood that there were things we could not forgo – on a Jewish ship sailing to the Land of Israel, we will not give way." When the argument became heated and Magen saw that the religious issue was not a trivial matter and that if he could not find a solution to the main problems to the satisfaction of the Orthodox, there would be passive mutiny aboard, he sought help from the Jewish Law. Instead of a brief discussion, he assembled the rabbis on the ship, and the Orthodox committee, and began hairsplitting negotiations with them following the method he had learnt in Yeshiva.

As for the ritual bath, Dov said, it was impossible to rectify what had been wrongly done, for this reason: according to Jewish Law, collected water was needed, in other words, rain water, and since it had not been collected up to then, and the water aboard the ship was unsuitable, there was no possibility of making a ritual bath as required. On the other hand, as for the synagogue, he promised to enlarge the deck area allocated to it, to try to remove the equipment and also to stop playing music over the loudspeakers during prayers and do his best not to use the loudspeakers on the Sabbath.

The main difficulties centred around the kitchen and discussions on this subject were protracted. At first the rabbis wanted to throw the non-kosher food into the sea and to absolutely forbid cooking on the Sabbath. Once again Dov cited Jewish law and claimed it was forbidden to do this because it was a matter of saving life, and this, as they knew, took precedence over everything. We cannot know, Dov said, how long we shall be at sea – it may be weeks – and the supply of food is limited. Are you prepared to accept the responsibility for feeding fifteen thousand people after throwing a large part of the food into the sea? To the question why non-kosher food was bought at all there was a simple answer – it was not possible to buy kosher food in the required quantities in Europe so they bought what was available.

It is doubtful whether the Orthodox committee were convinced but there was no alternative. The rabbis, who had witnessed famine and war, did not insist on throwing the food away but demanded the right to sort out the food stores into kosher and non-kosher, to begin by eating kosher food and then the non-kosher food as a supplement for whoever wanted it. The commander agreed unwillingly and also had to accept supervisers in the galleys, appointed by the rabbis to oversee the implementation of this agreement.

A further difficulty was the question of cooking on the Sabbath. One Sabbath had already passed and no-one could say with certainty how many more would be spent at sea. The rabbis demanded a total prohibition against cooking on the Sabbath. Dov was stubborn and once again cited the argument of saving lives – there were many sick people aboard who, if they did not receive cooked food, were in danger of dying. This claim was rather weak. During the negotiations everyone had got to know the ship and the relatively healthy appearance of the passengers. The hospitals were not full, and the general atmosphere was calm and relaxed but for some reason Dov Magen was stubborn. This was not a religious ship, he emphasized, and it was permissible to cook on the Sabbath; whoever did not want to eat cooked food was not obliged to do so but it was not right for the Orthodox Jews to dictate the life style of the secular passengers. When the Orthodox committee understood that his obstinacy stemmed from a deep opposition rather than from the difficulties of implementing the religious requirements, they accepted his former justification – the saving of life – and conceded.

They finally agreed to circulate a notice to the effect that the galley was preparing cooked food and whoever wished to eat it on grounds of health – the saving of life – was free to do so. The argument over this question, which for two or three days had become a struggle, now concentrated on how to make kosher the utensils used for cooking on the Sabbath. The rabbis wanted to do this on Saturday evening, after the Sabbath, by boiling them, but Dov Magen, who was strongly opposed to the religious leadership developing aboard the ship, objected on the grounds that there was no spare water and electricity to waste on making utensils kosher. This time the rabbis got the better of him and said they did not need to boil water especially – it would be sufficient if the tea, which was made at the end of the Sabbath, could be prepared with clean water and then additional food could be prepared in the same containers. Once it had started, this conflict continued and the Orthodox committee came almost every day with demands for alterations or to insist on rules that had already been settled and Dov tried to argue and to oppose them until a compromise was reached. This was also the case with the lighting of Sabbath candles. Dov absolutely forbade this – the ship was made of wood and thousands of candles on the bunks and in the passageways could start a fire that would destroy the ship. Once again there was an argument but this time Dov decided that two women from each dormitory would light candles, representing all the passengers. The rabbis were obliged to agree to this and publicized it throughout the ship. However, when the Sabbath was approaching and the ships were at anchor off Cyprus, thousands of lights were burning in the dormitories. A Jewish wife who had blessed the Sabbath candles all her life would not trust a deputy to welcome the Sabbath on her behalf . . .

Perhaps it should be stated that there was a profound misunderstanding in the whole matter of religion; as each side went its own way, the friction at each point of contact illustrated the strong and differing beliefs of the two parties. This is best exemplified by the story of the wedding that was celebrated on the *Pan York*. One of the young girls discovered that she was pregnant and she and her boyfriend hastened to the rabbis and asked them to arrange a wedding ceremony. The rabbis refused: they had to establish their identity, and whether they were free to marry, and see to all the other matters involved in preparing for marriage. In desperation they turned to the commander, who went back to the rabbis and once again there was an argument as Dov Magen sought to invoke religious law: if they did not marry at once, there would be a mishap. But the rabbis stood their ground. To crown the argument, Dov Magen announced that he would marry them himself since, according to Jewish religious Law, it was permissible to marry a couple in the presence of two witnesses and without a rabbi. Dov Magen, donning his best clothes and a hat, put up a wedding canopy for the couple and arranged the Seven Benedictions; somebody gave the groom a ring, someone else found some bottles of drink and the whole dormitory celebrated this unusual wedding ceremony performed by the commander of the ship.

CHOCOLATE!

The absorption process aboard the ships was brief. The crossing of the dangerous minefield coincided with the first arrangements for accommodating the passengers and they were too preoccupied to worry about how a drunken Russian pilot was steering two American banana boats loaded with passengers through a narrow, winding channel between thousands of mines. Apart from the commanders and a few dozen young Bulgarians who were keeping an anxious lookout nobody knew about the problem. On the following morning, Sunday, the sea was quiet. Life aboard ship slipped into a fairly relaxed routine. The many improvisations that were used to get the people together were slotted into the pre-arranged system and the groupings that had been organized in haste and to a great extent inflexibly became established rules. The people saw that their ability to survive in the cavernous darkness of the dormitories and their only chance to get food and water and fresh air on deck was conditional on their willingness to keep to the framework of the groups in which they were placed. Since the arrangements on board seemed more or less acceptable and everyone had found a bunk or a patch of floor to lie on, the group leaders were called to a briefing at the side of the dormitory. Most of them were from the group that had undergone a crash course in Romania. They were familiar with necessary routine and a daily schedule was easily prepared.

The main problem was eating arrangements. Dozens of tons of tinned meat and fish, large stores of tomato juice, rice, semolina and forty tons of biscuits had been purchased and stored on the ships for a voyage lasting fourteen days. However, the existence of such large stores of food did not guarantee regular supply. The provision of food was planned round a full twenty-four-hour cycle, during which each group had a set time for receiving water, hot food once a day and two additional meals. It was impossible to call these meals breakfast or supper because groups whose turn for the hot meal was set in the morning had their breakfast in the evening. Each group sent a member to fill up buckets with water and another member took the food for his group.

Experience from previous ships had taught that the fight for survival in conditions of extreme hunger produced a tendency to hoard food and led to petty but sad incidents of cheating, stealing and even raiding the food stores. For this reason each group leader was given an

Exodus, 1947, in the French magazine *Franc-Tireur*

identity disc which he handed to whoever went to collect the food. The people distributing the food had orders to give the appropriate quantity for each group only to the person with this disc. In the various stages of preparing and distributing the food, dozens of orderlies were involved – these came mainly from the immigrants themselves and most of them had gone through a special training programme. These orderlies guarded the food stores, recorded the quantities taken out, supervised the distribution points, briefed the galley staff, distributed water, checked identity discs and prevented the unauthorized movement of people from the dormitories to the deck and between dormitories.

Control was supposed to be strict but in retrospect the supervision of living arrangements on the ships appears harsh and insensitive. Group leaders and orderlies were instructed to maintain a command structure while paying attention to the basic needs of the thousands of people under their command, but keeping close control over everything aboard. This question of control over people revealed a slightly covert aspect of the Israeli mission. These restless, active young people who had left their kibbutz or abandoned their studies at the Hebrew University on Mt. Scopus were motivated by the desire to help the hundreds of thousands of Jews who had lost their way in the ruins of Europe and who wanted to rebuild their lives. There were Mossad operatives whose main drive was to strengthen the Yishuv in preparation for the approaching national independence and others wanted to help the survivors who found it difficult to re-establish themselves in their former homes. They operated in extremely difficult conditions and sometimes endangered their own lives in obtaining the unauthorised passage of Jews to Mandatory Palestine and yet, beyond the sense of their mission, their attitude to their tasks betrayed a considerable degree of alienation, mistrust and even scorn.

The self-assurance of these Palestine-born young people, speaking Hebrew, their newly revived language, serving in the Palmach and perhaps having taken part in one of the night operations under General Orde Wingate, their British mentor, was a powerful contrast to what they saw as the wretchedness of the Jewish refugees, bowed, ragged and intimidated, who seemed to have no higher purpose than personal survival. It is doubtful whether any of the emissaries analysed his feelings but the great amount of attention that was given to preparing almost a thousand identity discs[12] for food, water and drugs and the strict instructions that were given to the food-store guards revealed serious fears based on the discouraging experience of several previous incidents. The story of the *Pan* immigrants was different. They did not appear to be terrified or sickly, many of them were well-dressed, they all behaved properly and there were no attempts to break into the stores. For the ship commanders, this was a pleasant surprise.[13]

There were provisions for fourteen days and breakdowns in supplies, spoilage and "disappearances" of various quantities had been taken into account. The unprecedented number of immigrants necessitated special attention to foodstuffs which were considered luxuries on other ships; women were allocated a substantial quantity of powdered eggs, children received a chocolate ration (and there were those who had their first taste of chocolate for many years)[14] and for the sick there was a special store of what was then called delicacies. According to the final report there were sixteen tons of tinned pears and peaches aboard the two ships.

The smooth voyage, the good order and the short time at sea, combined with the careful allocation of food produced surpluses which fed the ships' crews for many months. After the voyage, the meals that the crews prepared on the ships were known as "orgies" and the Hagana emissaries in Cyprus tried very hard to get invited to them.[15] Regarding the detailed food arrangements, the Bulgarians were specially favoured. These cheerful youngsters in their striking uniforms were immediately put in charge of important areas of responsibility. The ship commanders found it easy to use them for every task and they accepted everything they were asked to do as an organized group, making their own internal arrangements. They did not have bunks in the dormitories and they did not eat according to the pre-arranged schedule of mealtimes. However, they were compensated for this. Instead of bunks they found themselves places in the lifeboats where they made themselves nests to sleep using life jackets for mattresses and coils of rope for pillows. To their delight they found emergency rations that had been hidden in the lifeboats. These especially high-quality rations included dried fruits and chocolate which many of them had never eaten before.[16]

Preparations had also been made for "cultural events." There were reasons for this. Firstly, it was thought that idleness would lead to trouble and it was important to keep the people busy so that they would not become bored and restive.[17] Secondly, there was the question of education and this too was an expression of the emissaries' feeling of superiority. The voyage to the Land of Israel was to be utilized to reshape the Diaspora Jew and turn him into an Israeli. Members of the Hagana and the Palmach, with the heritage of the Labour movement behind them, were familiar with the seminars[18] that were frequently held by the various movements, at which the founders addressed the younger generation or members of their party about the building of the country, generally along their own ideological lines.[19] There were also special seminars for leaders of youth movements, new kibbutz members, Histadrut activists and of course for potential emissaries. A graduate of such a seminar was well equipped with material which he was supposed to transmit to the people among whom he was working. A top emissary from the kibbutz or the Palmach who had sat at the feet of the Fathers of the Movement, such as Berl Katznelson, Yitzhak Tabenkin or Meir Ya'ari, and had set out with their blessing, would have wanted to give the good news to the less fortunate who were just setting foot on the soil of the Promised Land. The new immigrant who had not been in the youth movement was liable to become a victim of Diaspora elements and end up running a snack bar in downtown Tel Aviv.

The ship on its way to the Land of Israel represented an important opportunity to refashion the new immigrants in the right way. For the emissaries all this was even more important because of the times the immigrants had been obliged to fight at sea and defend their ship against British destroyers. In any event "culture" was supposed to perform an important function during the voyage. However, there were several difficulties. The ships were large and the passengers were divided into separate dormitories so there was no chance of gathering everyone together for lectures. Another difficulty was political. This was the first time that a Mossad ship had carried organized groups of Revisionists, Poale Agudat Yisrael and the whole internal spectrum of the Labour movement from radical left Hashomer Hatzair and Poale Zion to the more moderate Dror and Gordonia.[20] Although the Mossad was a distinct product of the Labour movement, it was officially part of the Hagana which, in turn, belonged also to sections of the "civilian" Yishuv. Furthermore, Yosef Klarman, the representative of the Revisionist movement, took an active part in the political activity in Romania and was an important partner in the negotiations over the *Pans*. This broke the ideological and organizational monopoly of the Labour movement in immigration.[21] In addition, the state was about to emerge and ways of cooperation between the movements had to be found, so it was understandable that the urge to educate the immigrants had rather diminished – in such a situation, what were they to be educated for? The educational tradition of the various training programmes constantly called for immigrants to go to the Land of Israel to live a life of equality on kibbutz, but this was an integral part of the Labour element in Zionism and it was not possible to focus educational activity on the kibbutz. The demographic structure of the *Pan* immigrants, consisting of whole families with old people, children and infants, was unlike the preparatory groups that the emissaries were used to, and they had no real potential for kibbutz life. In view of these difficulties it was decided not to create unnecessary tensions and to cancel the "educational" lectures and settle for songs from the Land of Israel that were played over the loudspeaker system.

Each ship had dozens of records of songs about ploughs and vineyards, the greening of the Jezreel Valley and the building of Tel Aviv. But even this cultural activity, which was very poor by the emissaries' standards, did not operate properly. The loudspeaker system had been tested many times and used by the building crews on the ships at Constantsa, but it only worked for part of the voyage – on both the ships it broke down shortly after sailing. From time to time one of the Gideons managed to get it to work for a few moments and this was used by the crew to make hasty announcements which were barely audible in the dormitories in the hold; but usually the loudspeakers were silent.

Despite this, and the absence of an effective "cultural" programme, the ship throbbed with activity. Children quickly became friends, a rubber ball was discovered and they found a space to play among the crowds of people. The parents came down from their narrow bunks and got to know their neighbours in the dormitory and soon, a kind of seating arrangement evolved. Knapsacks became tables for chess players and their kibbitzers, and for poker games. The youngsters managed to get up on deck to follow the emissaries whom they admired so much. Here and there a tentative conversation would start up between a Romanian girl and Bulgarian boy, she speaking Yiddish and he Ladino: they would both turn to someone who looked like an Israeli and who, to their chagrin, spoke only Hebrew.[22]

On the *Pan York*, where the foreign crew was Spanish, things were better organized. The Bulgarian girl found a common language with the Romanian boy through the expatriate Spanish sailor who understood her Ladino, and by using the French he had picked up in

Marseilles could transmit what she said to the boy from Romania where French was the main foreign language taught in school.[23]

These fumbling attempts at conversation were all centred on one topic – what was going to happen when they met the British?

FROM BLOCKADE TO BLOCKADE

According to the convention of Istanbul, the Black Sea was out-of-bounds to British warships. The refugee ships were free to sail between the minefields to the Straits separating the Black Sea from the Mediterranean, but it was obvious that the British were waiting beyond the Straits and a clash was anticipated. This was one of the elements of unauthorized immigration and, occasionally, political advantage could be gained from it. This time the Mossad's concern was whether contact between the ships and the British waiting for them would be avoided, because of the degree of British pressure aimed at stopping the ships passing into the Mediterranean. The British government was not happy about a confrontation in full view of the world press and photographers who would show the whole world disturbing pictures of British soldiers capturing rusty old ships packed with persecuted Jewish refugees.

For this reason the Mossad had made thorough preparations to facilitate the passage of the ships through the Straits. This included a large financial investment in the commander of the watch which was to be on duty at the head of the Bosphorus on Saturday afternoon. The experienced operatives took the possibility of holdups into account, like the delay in leaving Burgas and so, for an additional consideration, the duty time of the watch was extended until Sunday. The two journalists, Jon Kimche and Moshe Pearlman, were sent to Ankara and Istanbul respectively, in addition to Akiva Levinsky of the Hebrew-language daily *Ha'aretz* who was then based in Istanbul.

Moshe Pearlman was a young Jew, born and educated in England, who had become a Zionist. At this time he was a roving reporter for a new American weekly. As an American journalist with a British passport he had several advantages. The British and American embassies were open to him, it was easy for him to establish relations with Turkish officials, he could make overseas telephone calls freely and at no cost or effort since his stay and expenses were covered by his newspaper. His mission had a double purpose. First, he was to be the Mossad contact man. In those days the chances of making an overseas telephone call from Istanbul were poor: there was a long waiting list and delays of several days, but an American journalist had priority and an immediate line. Moshe took a hotel room overlooking the Bosphorus in order to be able to report on future events. His second objective fell within his professional activity. One of the most important aims of unauthorized immigration was to arouse world opinion to the plight of the Jewish refugees and to illustrate how the British were behaving. As an objective reporter, Moshe Pearlman installed himself at one of the navigation crossroads. If the ships were to be arrested here by the Turks (and only the Turks were able to do this in the area of the Straits) he would cable the U.S.A. and stir up public opinion and the Administration about the plight of the thousands of people trapped on the ships.

The young journalist was spared both these activities, but before he knew this, he had had to establish contact with his colleagues in Istanbul to get them to prepare favourable stories. To do this he refrained from appearing an interested party and concealed his Jewish identity and his position. Thanks to his pleasant personality he got to know all the local journalists, one of whom, the editor of a well-known Turkish paper, even invited him to lunch on Sunday, 28th December, 1947.

Moshe accepted the invitation. According to his calculations the meal was due to take place the day after the passage of the ships through the Straits. If something were to go wrong it would be a good idea to talk to the editor of an influential newspaper. When the departure from Burgas was delayed the timetable was disrupted. On Sunday morning Moshe could see the ships in the Black Sea from his window. He could even see the boat taking the Turkish pilot to the convoy which then continued on its way through the Bosphorus. Just at this critical moment his Turkish host knocked on his door and Moshe, tense and excited, had to leave with him. His host drove him on a tour of the busy streets of Istanbul until they came to a luxurious restaurant in an old ship on the bank of the Straits. As they sat down at their table by a huge window, the ships reached the centre of the Straits and stopped a hundred metres from Moshe Pearlman's table.

His host did not notice the agitation on Pearlman's face because he, too, was watching what was taking place. "Something interesting is happening", he said, "these are Jewish refugee ships and the British want us to stop them and return them to the Black Sea." Close by the entrance to the restaurant there was a group of journalists. The editor asked one of them to find out why the ship had stopped. In the meantime a delicious meal had been ordered, but Moshe's heart was elsewhere. He had the impression that the ships were stopping too long for a routine health inspection. He could not eat anything and could not even play the part of a straightforward journalist. The morsels of food he had forced himself to eat stuck in his throat when the journalist reported to the editor that there were problems and that he thought they had discovered an arms store on the ship. Suddenly black smoke poured from the funnel of the *Pan York*. The group of Turkish officials were seen descending from the ship to their boat in great confusion. "It was the longest moment in my life," recalled Moshe Pearlman, and then the ship gave a long blast on its horn and started to move towards the Sea of Marmara. Pearlman turned to his lavish meal with gusto.[24]

If these were the feelings of an observer with a tasty meal in front of him, the anxiety of the ship commanders can be imagined. The pretext used for preventing the ships from passing through was that of inadequate sanitary conditions, a plausible allegation against banana boats loaded with people in difficult circumstances. The pilots who boarded the ships as they entered Turkish territorial waters were given very clear hints, which included gold coins, to suggest to the sanitary inspection unit which was due to come aboard in the Bosphorus, that they would prefer a good lunch to a thorough inspection.[25] When the ships stopped in the Straits, the inspection units on both ships were regaled with a magnificent meal consisting of several courses which were interspersed with fountain pens, cigarette lighters and even watches. The meal continued and with it the time allocated for inspection. The inspectors and pilots returned to their boats cheerful and satisfied. The signal was given and the ships sailed, but the tension did not relax. One blockade was behind them but difficulties increased from blockade to blockade. The ships were now sailing across the calm Sea of Marmara on a quiet night. Towards morning they were to pass through the Dardanelles, the gateway to the Mediterranean, and Yossi Harel heard on the BBC news broadcast that the Eastern Mediterranean Fleet was going out on exercises. It was clear that these Royal Navy manoeuvres were connected with the voyage of the *Pans*.

During the night the tension on board the ships reached its peak. The cranes on deck were lowered and pointed sideways, the Panamanian flags on the main masts were checked and the young uniformed Bulgarians became grave as their good humour gave way to deadly seriousness and they stood tensely on deck in readiness for the passage through the final Straits.

ENCOUNTER WITH THE BRITISH

The one certainty in Yossi Harel's mind was the encounter with the British as they left the Sea of Marmara. Everything else was unknown. Grave as the danger of the anticipated clash with the British seemed, the commanders felt a sense of relief. Yossi was happy. "That's it. Now they cannot stop us. They could have blocked the entrance to the Bosphorus or stopped us in the Sea of Marmara, but once we've passed the Dardanelles they can't return us to the Black Sea." Once the Straits were behind them, it was impossible to repeat what had happened to the *Exodus* – return of the immigrants to their country of origin. The British now had a problem. At the entrance to the Mediterranean there were two ships carrying fifteen thousand Jews with nowhere to return to.[26]

The British did have a problem but this was, to an even greater extent, a problem for the Jews on the ships. The exhilaration felt by Yossi and his friends vanished when a few minutes after they left the Straits, at three o'clock in the morning, two black shapes without lights suddenly loomed on the horizon, moving quickly towards them.

Each ship could feel the violent movement produced by the threatening manoeuvre of the destroyers as they provocatively circled the ships, and cut dangerously close across the bows of the heavy banana boats with their foamy white wakes. The crew were prepared. From their positions on the bridge and on deck they watched the naval dance with astonishment and fear. The rising dawn did not relieve their feelings. On the horizon there were more warships bearing down on the course the ships were taking. In the morning they could count a complete British flotilla of two cruisers and four destroyers filling the narrow space of the Aegean Sea.[27]

The tension could be felt in the hold and everyone was silent with anxiety. The thousands of people sat down below on their bunks and received second, third and even fourth-hand reports on what was happening, which became more exaggerated at each telling; they did not know what would become of them. No clear statement had been issued about the anticipated encounter, even though everyone expected it. The organized daily routine, the prepared announcements, meeting of group leaders – these had all ignored the problem.

And now it seemed that the thousands of passengers preferred to entrust their fate to these young Israelis. They had organized the whole journey and, it must be said, the organization worked very well so they certainly would know how to steer the two ships into position to face the best of the Royal Navy.[28]

Moni Dagan, one of the Bulgarian youth leaders, was expecting a real battle. From his "station" on deck he proudly watched his friends who, like him, were sure that their great moment had arrived and they would be called to fight for their Jewish honour and their right to their country against the overbearing and arrogant British representatives of imperialism and repression.[29] The background of the socialist youth movement and the feeling of power reinforced by the uniforms of his Bulgarian friends gave him strength: "Just let them come, those villains, those capitalist oppressors and we'll show them."[30] This was surely how the Romanian youths must have felt, but they were a minority among the thousands that had been gathered throughout the country in family groups. Old people and children, from Transylvania and Bukovina, some of them sole survivors of the Holocaust, looked fearfully at the British destroyers, their guns ready for battle. They prayed silently that their captains would rise to the occasion. They appeared confident but it was impossible to consider a real confrontation – the banana boats were so miserable compared with the gleaming polished menace of the ships of the Royal Navy. A whole range of thoughts and possibilities crossed the minds of Yosse, Ike, Gad Hilb, Dov Magen and Nissan Levitan. Their instructions were not absolutely clear. In unauthorized immigration, the commander in the field had wide powers. Local conditions dictated behaviour and decisions, and in the history of immigration there had been different decisions, some of them contrary to the operations orders agreed upon in advance.[31] If Ike Aharonowitz had been in charge, the decision would have been different from the one finally taken by Yossi Harel.

Ike had worked with Yossi on the *Exodus*; they were of the same age, the same movement, they had served on the same mission in the same organization, under the same command and inspired by the same leaders and yet they represented absolute opposites. Ike's struggle against the establishment for an extreme and uncompromising ideology was already evident at the time of the *Exodus*. Ike was a young captain who had served in The Second World War and was a member of the naval company of the Palmach; he wanted to fight the British who were blockading the ship. He saw the mission of immigration as a war and wanted to act accordingly. If sacrifices were necessary, they would be made, if only they could break the British naval blockade on Mandatory Palestine. Ike's commander on the *Exodus* had also been Yossi Harel. Yossi was only two or three years older than Ike but was politically more advanced. He had worked closely with Chaim Weizmann and Shaul Avigur as well as the Hagana leadership and at the time of the battle of the *Exodus* he had chosen not to endanger the ship; after a struggle in which he saw that the British were going to prevent the ship reaching land and might even sink her, he had given in.[32] Many years later Ike thought this was a mistake and that the ship could have continued and broken through to the coast and the British would not have sunk her, but even more important: "even if they had sunk her, the ship was a weapon. The immigrants were warriors. Immigration was the theatre of war between us and the British. The sea was the battleground. We should have fought and were entitled to fight, to kill and, yes, to be killed."

It is doubtful whether Yossi Harel was pleased to learn that Ike was the captain of one of the ships under his command. He did not object outright to his appointment but had expressed his hesitations to Shaul Avigur. Shaul was also uncertain. He trusted Yossi and had confidence in his judgment and perhaps for this reason he had been inclined to choose Ike for his daring, uncompromising readiness to fight. Shortly after his return from the *Exodus*, when he was in the Palyam (Palmach naval unit), Ike had been summoned to Shaul Avigur in Paris. In the conversation, in which Venia Hadari also took part, there was no real discussion. Shaul, as usual, spoke little: over a glass of tea he offered Ike the command of a ship in one of the largest immigration operations. Before Ike could react Venia Hadari ordered: "Fly to Prague today and then go on to Romania."[33]

As former captain of the *Exodus* he could anticipate problems. False documents had been arranged for him but they did not help. He tried unsuccessfully for many weeks to get away and enter Romania. He sometimes felt he was not receiving sufficient assistance, and the thought occurred to him that perhaps there were people who would be happy if he did not get to Constantsa in time.[34] In Constantsa, Yossi Harel was in no hurry to get rid of the old Italian captain of the *Pan Crescent* since Ike had not yet arrived. These ships were about to sail to Burgas, in Bulgaria, and Ike was still absent. On the very last day, when the ships were being loaded, this energetic baby-faced young man turned up aboard ship. At this last moment there were more important matters than an ideological discussion between the commander of the operation and the captain of one of the ships. Yossi was occupied with difficult last-minute problems and Ike carried out a hasty tour of his ship, got to know his crew superficially and had an unpleasant discussion with the Italian captain who, to Ike's displeasure, was ordered to continued the voyage without any real function.[35]

He also met, fleetingly, Geda Shochet, Micha Peri and his colleague, Gad Hilb, captain of the *Pan York*. "Fine fellows," he said to himself, "real comrades-at-arms." Like him, they were from the Palmach, they saw immigration as a battle ground where they could fight openly and bravely. Ike would have dearly wanted their mission to be to fight until they smashed the crude British arrogance that harried the Jews on their way to the Land of Israel and immigration could be carried out in the light of day and not as befits thieves in the night. As the ships advanced into the Mediterranean towards their encounter with the British destroyers, he was like a tightly drawn arrow ready to be released.

Yossi, however, thought differently. For many years he had been involved with the political aspects of organizing the Mossad. His attitude was far more complex and he had discussed it at length with Shaul Avigur, even before the *Exodus* affair, to clarify the problem. The decisive conversation took place in Milan after the explosion on the *Pan Crescent* in Venice. Drinking innumerable glasses of tea in a small cafe with Shaul Avigur, rejecting repeated offers of cakes from the waiter, Yossi Harel had explained his position.

On every ship which I have commanded (he told Shaul), there have been casualties. People were killed resisting the British. If you insist, we will fight this time too, but understand that the price will be very high. The ships are not sailing in secrecy and the British will not find them simply by chance – they will meet us in strength. With 7,500 people on each ship there will be at least 2,000 people on deck during the battle who have no idea what sea combat means and it will be impossible to control them. To stop the British from boarding the ships, we shall have to open up the cranes and lower them to the sides and place barbed wire between them. This will make it difficult for the English sailors to jump on deck, as they did with the *Exodus*, but if the British ships, which are higher than the *Pans*, decide to remove them by striking them with their bows, these cranes, which weigh over a ton each, will fall on to the crowded decks and dozens of people will be killed.

Shaul listened in silence and Yossi continued to press him. "I want a clear directive. If we are ordered to resist, we shall do so, but I want a decision now." Shaul, who had never balked at difficult decisions, maintained his silence. He bore the weight of responsibility of a man who remembered the *Patria*, when over two hundred immigrants drowned after the Hagana had given the order to scuttle her.[36]

This was not the first discussion about the nature of resistance. Shortly before, in Shaul's room at the Metropole Hotel in Paris, he had had a conversation with Venia Hadari which lasted the whole night. Shaul, uncharacteristically, had spoken of his difficulties. The commanders and crew on the ships were from the Palyam and both their traditions and the orders they had received from their commander, Yigal Allon, called for resistance. The Palmach and the Mossad were subject to the leadership of the Hagana which was tied to the decisions of the heads of the Jewish Agency, led by Ben-Gurion. Their demands were to moderate the struggle.

In normal circumstances, when there are contradictory expectations, the final decision is in the hands of the person in charge of the operation. Shaul, who could already see the light of the emerging state at the end of the tunnel, spoke about the ethical problem and the political implications. As for the latter, the importance of the *Pans* lay in the actual voyage of such a large number of people into the Mediterranean despite the so-called British victory in the *Exodus* affair when the immigrants were returned to Germany. Ethically, this was not a question of an organized group that had undergone some kind of military training but of families, with women and children.

Venia Hadari was sure what the decision would be and that Yossi Harel would be instructed accordingly, but instead Shaul preferred to listen to Yossi's proposal and the reasons for it. Yossi, not realizing that Shaul had already decided, was drawn into a heated argument about a previous order from Shaul, when he had been Yossi's superior on board the *Knesset Yisrael*, to resist in every possible way.[37] There were hundreds of children aboard the *Knesset Yisrael* and when the British had used tear gas it had caused havoc. There were eleven newborn infants aboard the ship and the panic was terrible. Why did these babies have to fight for a Jewish state when there was peace and quiet in Palestine? If we are to fight a frontal war to the death with women and children we should do it also in Tel Aviv and the kibbutzim. If a day-old infant, the child of a survivor of the Holocaust, was to be a soldier, the kindergarten at Ramat Hakovesh should also go to war. Yossi raised his voice when he said: "I did not agree to scuttle the *Exodus* even though Ike was prepared to do so, because we had not reached a situation of war to the death."

Shaul continued to sip his tea in silence and finally rose, shook Yossi's hand and said, "Look after the people and good luck" – and then left. Yossi thought he had persuaded him. Shaul was already convinced but was in a hurry to fetch Ike and give him the command of one of the ships. Yossi was right but so was Ike; it was good that Ike be there, ready for battle and it was good that Yossi be in command to try to restrain him.

ROYAL NAVY FLOTILLA

The Royal Navy H.Q. in the Eastern Mediterranean, based at Malta, had known about the two ships for months. They had trailed them on their voyage from Marseilles and Venice to Constantsa and had received copies of the hundreds of reports and cables about them during the long months from the time they had been "purchased" until their departure from Burgas. Like the Mossad staff and the Hagana and Palmach commanders aboard the banana boats, the British command was very tense. Shortly after the ships left Burgas a signal was received at the naval command and all available ships in the Eastern Mediterranean were ordered to the mouth of the Dardanelles.[38] The objective was to surround each banana boat, fully laden with Jews, with three destroyers and a cruiser, keeping two frigates in the vicinity.[39] According to the cables, it appears that, despite the time and attention given to the problem of the ships, no clear decision had been taken about how to deal with them.[40]

The commanders of the British warships had been warned that the ships had left, and although they pressed the Admiralty for firm directives, their orders remained unclear. They were simply told to provide a close escort and direct the ships in convoy through the Aegean Islands led by the destroyer commanded by the most senior officer out of those who had managed to reach the Dardanelles in time.[41]

Copies of the signals between the Mediterranean Fleet H.Q. and the ships were sent immediately to the Ministry of War in London, the Foreign Office and also to the British embassies and representatives in Ankara, Washington, Jerusalem and Nicosia. Commanders of R.N. fleets and bases around the Mediterranean were kept informed and they were all witnesses to the feeling of helplessness, and even panic, that seized the captains of the ships surrounding the unauthorized immigrants. The possibilities of finding a solution to the problem of fifteen thousand Jewish refugees sailing in the Aegean Sea on their way to Palestine were limited. There is no documentary evidence, but it appears that there were those who wanted to sink the ships together with all their passengers. The captain of the destroyer which steamed towards the *Pan York* without lights in the pre-dawn darkness did not seek a direct collision, but he had certainly reckoned on the possibility of the frightened Jewish captain suddenly turning his high ship towards one of the reefs in the winding channel through the Aegean. The destroyer continued these dangerous manoeuvres for over an hour as dawn was breaking, charging and pointing its raked prow at the soft hull of the crowded *Pan*. Another possibility suggested by British signals was that they were trying to provoke the commanders into committing a rash act which would contravene maritime law.

Information obtained by the British Mediterranean command suggested the construction of special defensive installations on the ships,[42] weapons in the possession of trained soldiers[43] and, of course, Soviet agents.[44] One item of intelligence spread by the British was that the ships were equipped with torpedoes and that when they were in the Black Sea they had undergone a training programme including instruction in how to ram destroyers.[45] Thus it was very probable that the "pirates" aboard the ships would open fire on the British destroyers, which was what the British wanted. The provocative manoeuvres around the ships were intended to incite the Jews to use their weapons so that the British could attack and force them to surrender. If this were to happen, there would be no repetition of the *Exodus* affair. The Mossad commanders would be shown in full view of the world as violent lawbreakers, exploiting the plight of the Jews to further the interests of a small and irresponsible minority of the Jews living in Palestine.

Many of the signals between the British flotilla charging towards the ships and the Mediterranean H.Q. dealt enthusiastically with these ideas and even discussed the most suitable location for this type of battle.[46] It would certainly be short. The ships were particularly high in the water and, for this reason, the cruisers, which were even higher, had been brought in. They would be assisted by the destroyers which would block the channel between the islands and, after a suitable bombardment, which would not have to be too sparing because the Jews had opened fire first, the destroyers would ram the ships. The warships would come close and, in an operation which involved spraying the passengers with tear gas, the obstinate pride of the Israeli command on the ships would be broken. It was likely that the immigrant ships would be severely damaged, so means of rescue were to be prepared to prove to all Great Britain's enemies, who were swayed by Zionist propaganda, that it was the British who were concerned for the good of the Jews and were the ones to save these unfortunate people from drowning in the icy waters off the Turkish coast.

This was the bizarre fantasy of the thousands of British officers and seamen who sensed the full measure of humiliation such an encounter would bring on them. They had been at sea for months, armed with the best equipment, with all the trappings of the Royal Navy, chasing shadows. And when, occasionally, these shadows became substance, they were nothing more than miserable, defenceless ships, loaded with suffering and persecuted people. The whole world scorned these heroes of the Royal Navy, hunting frightened, helpless people with their mighty warships. The *Exodus* incident was the depth of their humiliation and now they hoped the *Pans* affair would enable them to improve their image and prove they were not savages.

British tactics against the *Pans* were different. As soon as they had left the Dardanelles, they realized that this time the Zionists were being careful not to provide the slightest pretext for violence. Even in the face of the provocation from the destroyer threatening the *Pan York*, the captain, Gad Hilb, was not drawn into reacting. With patience and a degree of ingenuousness he slowed down his ship and, following international procedure, signalled to the destroyer that it had no navigation lights and was sailing without due care. At first the destroyer ignored these signals and continued to threaten the *Pan York* but suddenly stopped these manoeuvres when it realized they were not going to provoke the captain into action. He continued to signal and point out the destroyer's irregular method of navigation. At this stage the sun rose and illuminated the smooth, calm sea, dangerously full of ships. The threatening destroyer took up a position in front of the *Pan York*, a second destroyer manoeuvred itself between it and the *Pan*

Crescent, and a third moved in behind the *Pan Crescent*. At the sides, and at various distances, sailed the cruisers and the frigates so that without explicit orders a long, regular convoy formed. The range of possibilities was now reduced still further. They could not return to the Black Sea; there was no way the refugees could be sent back to their homes and no country in the world would take them in. There was no longer the threat of a violent clash at sea, but the British were not prepared to allow the ships to reach Haifa and let the passengers disembark. In fact, there was only one possibility and events themselves led irrevocably in that direction – Cyprus.

The dramatic encounter with the British had a somewhat artificial air. The confused signals which indicated a naval confrontation had been sent after Zionist leaders had proposed that the ships submit voluntarily to the British and the immigrants sail directly to the detention camps in Cyprus. Such a proposal had been made by Sharett and thoroughly understood by the British Embassy in Washington. No real negotiations had taken place; at chance meetings in Washington and New York arranged by "friends" in the State Department and "knowledgeable sources" in the Zionist Executive in New York, the British were told that the immigrants would not offer any resistance and would agree to go to Cyprus. The British were of course very interested. It was a solution acceptable to everyone: the Jews would leave and sail for Palestine but agree not to actually arrive there for the time being. However, there was no definite conclusion. Sharett knew his control over the situation was limited and so did the British. Furthermore, they were not happy about legitimizing a scheme that would rapidly fill Cyprus with tens of thousands of Jewish refugees.

Everyone realized that the outcome of the events at sea was unpredictable. At the stage when the ships were passing from the Black Sea into the Mediterranean, anything was still possible. The orders that Venia Hadari had transmitted to Yossi Harel were to sail to Haifa. The British fleet was determined to prevent this. The ships met at the exit from the Sea of Marmara prepared for any eventuality, probing each other suspiciously. Their formation into a long, bizarre convoy, weaving between the islands of the Aegean was, initially, uncoordinated and unplanned. Slowly the tension eased. Yossi Harel gave his orders quietly; no resistance was to be shown – there was no chance and, at this stage, no need. The convoy sailed towards its destination in a southerly direction.

The British were surprised; they were escorting two large, stable and well-ordered ships. There were no signs of rebellion or hysteria on deck. The command was obviously professional and obedient to all the laws of navigation. Tension only mounted again during the afternoon when the sky clouded over, the strong wind raised large waves and a storm blew up. The leading destroyer changed direction and began sailing west, leaving the short, fast route to the south. The *Pan York* started to slow down and once again the tension mounted. Gad Hilb reported to Yossi Harel: "There is a diversion – they're changing course." They had to make an important, even decisive choice before clear instructions were received from the Mossad; whether to follow the British directives and if so, where to, or whether to continue on their way south, to the Land of Israel, whatever the cost.

Suddenly, the voice of the British flotilla commander broke into the radio receiver: without any words of introduction he announced that because of the storm and the approaching night he proposed taking the longer course. This necessitated a long diversion to the west. His courteous tone and attitude were as though from a different world. At once the tension eased and his "proposal" was accepted immediately. From that time a working relationship was established between the *Pans* and the flotilla, which was a great advantage for the tight convoy moving through the Straits in the storm.

At the same time that contact had been made with the British, a signal arrived for Yossi Harel. It had been dictated directly by Ben-Gurion, Chairman of the Jewish Agency Directorate and read:

If the enemy proposes that you go straight to Cyprus, you must reply before agreeing: "We are sailing to the Land of Israel which was promised by God to Israel and reaffirmed by the United Nations, but if you intend to interrupt our journey, we shall go to Cyprus, in the certainty that we shall soon reach our liberated country. Give us the course to Cyprus and we shall follow you."[47]

This signal was sent when the ships were still in the Sea of Marmara, before meeting the British flotilla, but the Mossad's special communications centre in Italy had not been able to transmit it to the ships. The report of the Gideons, the communications group on the *Pans*, states that the reception of orders from the Mossad in Europe was poor because, as part of the preparations to repel an attack by the British ships, the fourteen cranes on the decks had been draped with barbed wire. The tall array of wire caused constant interference for the antennas of the radio sets so that the careful preparations for battle narrowed the chances of avoiding it. Only when they moved into more open sea was it occasionally possible to receive and transmit. On Tuesday, long after it had been agreed to submit to the British without fighting, this was confirmed to the ships.[48] The signal came at the last moment and was the result of an improvised agreement between people in the field; namely a British officer and Yechezkel Sachar, who took the agreement to Ben-Gurion just at the time of the meeting between the ships and the Royal Navy.[49] Looking back one is tempted to ask hypothetical questions about what would have happened if . . . because nothing had been arranged definitely. On the contrary, the doubts before the voyage about submitting to the British were forgotten. Pino Ginsburg's plan to sail the ships as though on the initiative of the immigrants themselves was not accepted; the last instructions from the Jewish Agency, which Moshe Auerbach could have given to Yossi Harel on the day before the voyage, were negative; there was no agreement with the British and plans for the voyage to Cyprus were cancelled.[50] Despite the failure to reach an agreement Sharett again insisted that there would be no opposition;[51] in other words, no fight with the British at sea. What, therefore, were Yossi Harel's orders? To sail to Palestine. And what would happen when the British prevented this? On the one hand, Sharett's request not to resist and on the other, the Mossad tradition not to surrender. Ben-Gurion's signal, arriving at the last moment, denied the Palmach crew members their freedom of choice which, presumably, would have been unanimously to use force to prevent the British taking control of the ships. Ike Aharonowitz was disappointed – in his opinion the order was shameful and even more important than that, harmful to the national interest. Yossi Harel was pleased because lives had been saved. Yossi knew his people. He assembled the commanders of the *Pan York* and called for a parallel meeting on the *Pan Crescent*. In his report he stated: "everyone thought we should obey and not rebel."[52] This shows there were some who thought openly about the possibility of rebellion. This strong wording was directed against the Mossad and the Jewish Agency directorate and it meant rebellion against their decision to submit to the British. Yossi was able to get the commanders of the operation to agree by means of compromise. The men of the Palmach gave up the idea of rebellion and agreed to follow orders but were not prepared to surrender and break their long tradition. The compromise, which was rather simplistic, went like this: "We will not oppose the British but will have no part in the surrender; we were not recruited to hand Jews over to the British." Ike Aharonowitz added some pragmatic reasons;

> If we land the ships ourselves we will endanger our legal status; if the British board the ships without us taking an active part in it, we will be able to claim them back because there is nothing illegal about this voyage, but if we bring them to port, we will be seen as carrying unauthorized immigrants and for that we will be liable to lose our personal certificates and even more important, the ships themselves.

No-one was happy with this compromise but it was doubtful whether anyone genuinely wanted to fight a naval war. The sun rose on the last day of 1947 after a long sad discussion.

The leading destroyer signalled to the *Pan York* to stop and the whole convoy slowed to a halt. *HMS Mauritius*, the flagship of the improvised British flotilla, approached the *Pan York*. Yossi Harel, together with Gad Hilb, Nissan Levitan, Captain Steve, the Spanish skipper, and a group of Israelis and Americans, were standing on the bridge looking at the gleaming British warships and the sailors in their battle fatigues and steel helmets crowded round the gunsights in their firing positions. The tension was palpable as the *Mauritius* stopped at a distance of 100 metres and asked for the names of the ships on the regular international radio frequency.

This simple question was baffling. "Please wait," replied Yossi Harel and tried to reach the communications office of the Mossad in Palestine and once again speak directly to Ben-Gurion and ask about the names of the ships. The question of names symbolised the whole problem of the *Pans*. Since the end of the war, all Mossad ships had been given significant names, such as *Tel-Hai* (a Galilee stronghold), *Hachayal Ha'ivri* (The Hebrew Soldier), *Hama'apil Ha'almoni* (The Unknown Immigrant) and *Shivat Zion* (Return to Zion). Other ships had been named after founders of the labour movement, such as *Berl Katznelson, Eliahu Golomb* and *Chaim Arlozoroff* or heroes of the Hagana: *Chana Senesh* and *Bracha Fuld*. Much attention was given to the Hagana, the military organization of which the Mossad was an extension for the implementation of immigration. The Hagana was commemorated in the ships *Palmach, Gesher Haziv* and the *Hagana*. Each of the Mossad ships carried the name *Hagana* in addition to the name of the ship; therefore, during the early discussion on the *Pans*, the Mossad had been requested to keep up the appearance that the ships were not connected with them, or, of course, the Hagana, but were the result of local initiative.[53] In view of the world-wide political conflict raging over the *Pans*, this permitted broader options for manoeuvre. The sensitive Palmach members were given a different reason. It was worth preventing an internal argument, because organizations outside the labour movement were involved in these ships and among the immigrants there were groups outside the framework of the Hagana. In a short while the State would be established and the Hagana would belong to the whole nation; it was pointless to create a dispute that would disrupt the harmony aboard the *Pans* and make it more difficult later on to promote the name and the idea of the Hagana.

The temporary names given to the ships had been *Chaver* (Comrade) for the *Pan Crescent* and *Achot* (Sister) for the *Pan York*. Since the ships were similar and had been handled by the same Mossad people, a degree of confusion was created. Messages for *Achot* reached the *Chaver* and vice versa. Even the nickname "Chevreman", given to the *Chaver*, did not help. This confusion had operational implications. In their report, the Gideons, the communications and signals section, pointed out that coded messages transmitted on the special frequency of one ship did not arrive because they had been sent on the other ship's frequency, and *vice versa*.[54] Eventually, when it was a matter for both the ships together, the simple nickname "the Big Ones" was used, and when it was necessary to refer to one of them only, they reverted to the original names, *Pan York* and *Pan Crescent*. However, at this stage, the voyage was intended to have publicity value and names were urgently required as well as slogans and prepared releases. At the beginning of the operation, when the trains started to move in Romania, Shaul Avigur had asked Venia Hadari to obtain from Moshe Sharett "the version of a broadcast in Hebrew and English to be transmitted by Agami to the world and the U.N. on the subject of the voyage". Shaul reiterated that this was absolutely necessary and that it had to be given to the commanders of the ships,[55] taking great care over the exact wording of the text. Sharett, who was considered an expert at drafting texts, had the previous day issued a direct order to Agami in Romania not to give official names to the ships and repeated that they should be in no hurry to leave.[56] In these circumstances there was no point in asking him to provide names or even the wording of a declaration to the world and the U.N.

The degree of attention given to the choice of names is surprising.

Cables flew from Romania, where the ship commanders were located, to Venia Hadari in Paris, to Sharett in Washington and to Ben-Gurion in Tel Aviv. At the last minute, when the confrontation with the British was about to take place, Shaul Avigur cabled the Mossad office in Israel and once again prompted them diplomatically: "Should you decide to give names to the vessels, please consult Amitai and Ben-Kedem. My proposals are: (a) *Kibbutz Galuyot* (Ingathering of the Exiles); (b) *Netzach Yisrael* (Perpetuity of Israel)."[57] Venia Hadari notified the ships, where there were signs of impatience, that they would receive instructions regarding the names from Arnon.[58]

The captain of the *Mauritius* must have looked at the two lumbering ships in amazement. For hours now he had maintained continuous and orderly contact with them during the passage between the islands and now they were delaying the answer to such a simple question. Had they refused to answer, it would have been understandable; had they answered defiantly, he could have accepted it, but his amazement grew when they answered all his other questions quickly and satisfactorily. For example, he was told without hesitation how many immigrants there were on each ship, how many of them were women and children and about the mechanical and sanitary conditions of the ships. A long time elapsed before they gave the names of the ships. It was a rather curious answer: *Pan York* and *Pan Crescent*, which he could see on their bows for himself.

Just before midnight, as the year was drawing to an end, a cable arrived with Ben-Gurion's version: "The names of the big ones: *Kibbutz Galuyot* and *Atzma'ut*."[59] But by this time there were already British soldiers aboard the ships and a British command was taking them to Cyprus. Yossi Harel, who was rather disappointed, asked whether it was possible to add "Hagana Ships" but received no reaction to this.[60] When a negative reply came two days later, it was no longer important.

The names were, of course, only the tip of the iceberg as far as the whole problem facing the ship commanders was concerned. After an hour's conversation on the international naval frequency, in which standard information on numbers and names was exchanged, the captain of the *Mauritius*, following naval procedure, requested the commander of the *Pan York* to move to a special frequency for the purpose of exchanging signals with the commander of the flotilla, who held the rank of admiral. Meanwhile the *Mauritius* changed course to the south, followed by the rest of the convoy. The admiral's first signal was short and to the point: "This is the admiral on the bridge of the *Mauritius*. I understand you have received orders from the Jewish Agency for your two ships to sail to Cyprus if I ask you to do so. Is this correct?" The answer was, "Wait". Yossi contacted the *Pan Crescent*. On the bridge, where the commanders were also listening to the admiral, a kind of staff meeting took place. The last order they had received was: "You have to go to wherever the rotters tell you, except back to the Black Sea."[61] There was no serious argument about this and in half an hour Yossi confirmed to the admiral: "We have received orders to follow you to Cyprus."

The admiral must have uttered a sigh of relief when, on receiving the agreement of the *Pans*, he gave the order: "Change course for Famagusta." Trained in a strict tradition, Yossi consulted with his friends regarding an official announcement. This was the largest operation in the history of immigration and should be remembered as such, but unfortunately there were no clear instructions, no noble and moving declarations. This was the time for negotiations where certain advantages could be obtained and it was wrong to miss it by agreeing so easily to follow the British and surrender unconditionally. There were other problems; the immigrants themselves should be involved in deciding where to sail and it was not known for certain how they would react, because no real contact had been made between them and the heads of the operation. What would happen to the crew, both Jewish and gentile, to the emissaries from Israel who were being sought by the British (Yossi himself was a wanted man as commander of the *Exodus*)? They could be arrested for engaging in illegal activities.

With no prepared version, with no experience in bargaining, Yossi replied to the admiral with a gravity that combined the bold dedication of the *Exodus* with the present need for negotiation:

> The Hagana commander of the *Pan Crescent* to the admiral aboard *HMS Mauritius*: our destination is the Land of Israel, we have the responsibility for sixteen thousand Jews on their way to the country that was promised them. We promised to bring them to the Land of Israel and we cannot deceive them and take them to Cyprus ourselves. But the order of the Jewish Agency will be carried out and we will not use force to oppose the crew that takes over command of our ships.

The second part of the message set out various conditions:

> We shall do all this, but in return you must permit us to continue to

keep control over the passengers and to be responsible for the daily routine aboard ship. And most important, since we have no arms, you must not interfere with what happens aboard. There will be no searches and the immigrants will be allowed to disembark in Cyprus with their possessions. The final condition is that the crew will be treated in the same way as the rest of the immigrants – they will not be arrested or discriminated against. They can return at once to their own countries according to their wishes.

This time the delay in answering was at the British end. The British agreed, with pleasure, to the proposal of the commanders that they should continue to be in charge of the immigrants. They also agreed to the second proposal: experience had taught them that it was better to allow the people to disembark with their possessions and not to hold searches or confiscate personal property on board. A refugee does not abandon his bags – he keeps them by him not because they are of great value but because they contain his roots, to be planted in his new country. These roots consist of family pictures, an object from his home, a souvenir of his village.[62] The rule "if you want to move an immigrant, move his knapsack" was known both to the immigration operatives and the British. The problem was with the crew. The orders were to arrest the crew members, both the Mossad group and the foreign seamen.[63] The British authorities were clearly angry with the people who had entangled them in the business of unauthorized immigration and blackened their reputation throughout the world. Urgent cables were sent from *HMS Mauritius* to Malta and Cairo. At first the replies were negative: the crew members were to be arrested. After an hour or two the admiral signalled the *Pan York*:

I agree to your proposal regarding the continuation of Hagana command on board the ships as far as Cyprus and I promise that the immigrants will not be detained aboard the ships, there will be no search and they will disembark with their possessions and only then will a search take place. Please stop your ships, and take aboard the crew that will sail them to Cyprus.

Yossi quickly replied. "We will not stop and we will not allow your crew aboard until we receive your written guarantee for the well-being of the foreign seamen." To strengthen his words, he announced a change of course – straight to Haifa! The admiral took the hint. He sent another urgent message to Cairo about the foreign crew, and then gave the reply: "we agree not to arrest the crew but to return them immediately to their countries of origin." The British knew very well that the crew of the *Pan York* consisted almost entirely of refugees from Republican Spain. Some of them had fought against Franco for many years and sending them Spain would be tantamount to a death sentence.

The answer was negative. "We have a moral responsibility towards them", Yossi declared.

The wheels of the British bureaucracy turned slowly: from the flotilla to Cairo, from Cairo to Malta and from Malta to the War Office in London where a group of top officials were assembled who discussed the question of the *Pans* with members of the Cabinet. Sir Alan Cunningham, the British High Commissioner in Palestine, was also involved in these moves. His urgent cable stated: "If fifteen thousand people come to Haifa now it will create a grave security and political situation."[64]

At this stage contact again ceased between the *Pans* and the British. The commander of the flotilla was at a loss. An agreement had almost been reached which would have resolved this difficult and perplexing affair, but it had run foul and now there was no way he could acquit himself honourably. It was a fight that was lost from the beginning, in which the certain victory of an armed British flotilla over two crowded Jewish ships was guaranteed to bring defeat and shame to the British admiral and his thousands of officers and sailors who would be guilty of the deaths of dozens, and perhaps even thousands, of Jewish refugees by drowning.

After four hours of negotiations with his superiors, and despite the fact that he had not received authorization for his actions, he decided to take the responsibility upon himself. Almost in supplication he contacted Yossi on the *Pan York* and made his proposal: "In order not to interfere with our agreement, I give you my personal word for the safety of the crew. They will not be discriminated against or identified by us. If you accept my word, this will be the most fortunate solution." The British admiral's proposal was a kind of deal. He did not have the power to rescind the instructions from his superiors to arrest the crew members and so he promised his Jewish counterpart not to make efforts to identify them. The Hagana commanders and the foreign seamen would have to mingle with the immigrants and disembark unidentified.

This promise was, however, incomplete since it did not cover the problems that would arise later, the question of who would look after the ships and how the foreign crew would leave Cyprus afterwards, but Yossi was relieved because he too wanted the negotiations to end in agreement. He knew that an officer with the rank of admiral would be the senior British representative in Cyprus and would have the power to control events there. He therefore replied: "The promise of a British admiral is sufficient for me."

It was also agreed that radio contact between the *Pans* and the Mossad could continue, on the condition that communications would be clear and not in code. One more delicate problem remained. The Palmach members were unhappy with the negotiations and the agreement and complained bitterly to Yossi: "British soldiers with steel helmets and clubs will board Hagana ships – the same ones that we saw at home beating our people at Ramat Hakovesh and Givat Chaim and who trampled on our national life." Yossi was aware of this delicate point and wanted to avoid a confrontation aboard the ships between British soldiers and the Palmach; at the last moment he asked the admiral if the soldiers could come aboard without clubs and steel helmets. He promised there would be no opposition. "I suggest we forget what has happened in the past and begin a new year. We want to see your men without their usual steel helmets and clubs – they will not need them."

The admiral apparently hesitated. There were thousands of people on the ships whose behaviour could not be predicted. But since he had put his prestige in the balance, rescinded orders and reached an ageement, he was amenable to this too. It was unthinkable that his men should board the ships without any protection so he agreed with Yossi that his crew would carry revolvers for personal protection although, as the admiral was quick to add, "I know they will not have to use them."[65]

The *Pan York* and *Pan Crescent* were now less than two sailing days from Haifa. When the ships stopped they turned into the wind. The British wanted to board as soon as possible but Yossi stopped them, because he had to explain the new situation to his people. The senior Palmach commanders had been involved in the negotiations for hours and there had been bitter arguments. The men of the Palyam, led by Ike Aharonowitz, begged and pleaded to be allowed to go on to Palestine, to fight against the British; they spoke of defeatism and treachery and of their promise to the immigrants. Yossi understood them, in his heart of hearts he was on their side, but his orders were not to resist. Now that everything was finalized, he told his comrades to elicit the support of the immigrants for what had been decided. While some of the girls were preparing enormous national flags, the communications section activated the public address system. The absolute silence in the hold of the ships made it possible for the feeble loudspeakers to convey the commanders' message:

> Following a decision of the Jewish Agency we have agreed to hand over the ships to a British crew who will take them to Cyprus. The British have promised to behave decently and courteously and we expect you to carry out their orders which you will receive through us. The Hagana promises to take every single one of you to the Land of Israel.

The passengers in the hold, who had been watching the British flotilla circling them for hours, were confused. Many of them, especially from the pioneering youth movements, the Revisionist group and of course the Bulgarian youth, expressed their disappointment by shouting and arguing, but the vast majority of the immigrants who, throughout the whole journey had felt themselves in safe hands, silenced their objections. They were helped by an intensive information operation carried out by the political leadership of the various immigrants' groups. Together with emissaries, they went from dormitory to dormitory and explained the decision which they too had accepted with difficulty.

Following the agreement, the British boarded at 2:30 pm. The cable that was sent to Palestine a few minutes later reported briefly:

> At 1430 this sad and beautiful naval spectacle took place. As the *Achot* and the *Chaver* were facing into the wind, a British ship drew alongside and transferred the boarding parties in boats: the whole area was surrounded by British destroyers. The parties went up to the bridge to sail the vessels themselves. Our command is still continuing and relations are very correct, exactly as you wished.[66]

The final sentence, with its bitterness, expressed their feeling of emptiness and exhaustion. With a strange kind of elation, still remembered by the commanders of the ships, they stood on the bridge, sang "Hatikva" and saluted the national flags that were flying at the masts. Since they were obliged to keep the Panamanian flag, they had run up flags "of a size never seen before."[67] The British parties, who had just climbed very cautiously on deck, were amazed by the order, the silence and the dignity of the parade. They marched up to the bridge, stood at attention and saluted the flag and the anthem in a premature gesture of recognition.

Nissan Levitan handed over the *Pan York* to a British captain from *HMS Mauritius* and Dov Magen handed over the *Pan Crescent* to a captain who had come aboard from *HMS Phoebe*. "The ships are at your disposal to sail to Cyprus", Yossi Harel said. The British were still surprised and kept looking around them suspiciously; they requested that Yossi's crew continue to sail the ships. Yossi refused, and the old crew members patiently explained the controls to their replacements. This encounter between wanted Jewish pirates and their hunters was affecting for both sides. The British, divested of their tools of oppression, steel helmets and clubs, were polite and attentive. The Jews, surprisingly well organized, with relatively clean ships, logbooks and documents in order, with professional expertise, responded with similar behaviour. Suspicion turned into curiosity and politeness into mutual understanding.

After eighteen hours of sailing, on the morning of the first day of the new year, the ships reached the port of Famagusta.

CHAPTER NINE

Cyprus

CABLES

31.12.1947
2100 hours
Immediate
To Israel
Ben Yehuda (Shaul Avigur)
Agami (Moshe Auerbach, Bucharest)
From Amnon (Yossi Harel)
Today at 1500 hours, after 4 hours negotiations, units of the fleet
boarded the vessels.
Internal command on each ship and on both ships continues as per the
agreement between the admiral and ourselves.
We continue to operate the radio without code. With your agreement.
Send all cables to Ben Yehuda. I request this.
Tomorrow at 0800 we reach Famagusta.[1]

31.12.1947
2315 hours
To the Big Ones (*Pan York* and *Pan Crescent*)
From Arnon (Mossad Headquarters in Israel)
1. Your names are Kibbutz Galuyot and Atzmaut.
2. Crew with official papers to remain aboard.
3. To our greatest immigration enterprise. You have broken the locks.
   With you on the island. In the final exile. With hope and joy we will
   await you at the open gate. Be brave.[2]

Captain Reynolds, the young Royal Marines officer who led the
boarding party on the *Pan Crescent*, looked around him suspiciously.
With him on the bridge there were two young men who gave only their
first names which were obviously false, and a terrified old man who
quickly identified himself as an Italian skipper and disclaimed any part
in sailing the ship. The younger of the two Israelis was baby-faced and

looked familar to Reynolds; he was the dominant one of the group. Firmly and even distantly, he asked the British officer to sign a letter which he had already drawn up: "At 1500 hours, at 34°06´ north and 31°22´ east, a British crew headed by Captain Reynolds from *HMS Phoebe* boarded and took command of the ship."[3] The British officer's first inclination was to reject the instant demand of this unkempt Jew standing defiantly before him but he kept in mind the admiral's orders – do not create a confrontation, agree to technical requests and get the ships safely to Cyprus. Moderating the wording, Captain Reynolds grudgingly signed the document which constituted an admission that the British had seized the ships, on the high seas, outside the territorial waters of any country, and with no legal justification in international maritime law. When he returned the document to the maddening young man, the latter saluted by raising his hand to his curly head. The British officer furiously returned the salute and then Ike, with ironic pomp, officially ordered his subordinates on deck and in the engine rooms to give way to the British. Captain Reynolds was momentarily startled. His men were not technically able to take control of this huge banana boat. Ike made a courteous gesture. "Very well", he said, "We will continue to operate the ship and sail it, but not to Cyprus. If you want to get it to Cyprus, at least the helmsman must be from your crew." A similar exchange was taking place on the *Pan York*. Gad Hilb, the captain, asked Esteban Hernandorna, the Spanish "Captain Steve", to stand by the wheel, to give instrutions to the befuddled British officer, but not to operate it himself. From this point onwards, relations with the British were satisfactory. The Israeli crews remained in command of the ships and organized their daily routine. The British did not interfere in this area: their only task was to navigate. Tension began to ease. They were surprised at the order and discipline and found themselves surrounded by young men and women who were in turn amazed by the politeness and respect they received from the British whom the Jewish refugees had imagined to be cruel oppressors.[4]

While the tension between the British and the crews and immigrants began to ease, it increased among the Israeli commanders. Contact with Shaul Avigur and with Venia Hadari in Paris was cut off, contact with Moshe Auerbach in Romania was irregular and the replies from Israel, in non-coded cables, were unreliable. The many questions that arose in the course of the encounter with the British ships did not receive immediate, clear replies. Yossi Harel had to decide for himself, time after time, the most important questions. The British were sailing the ships to Cyprus – in a little while they would arrive. What was to happen to the ships, the emissaries and the foreign crew members? Who was to supervise the disembarkation and how was it to be carried out. What was to be done with the supplies of food aboard the ships? The few orders that did arrive were confused and indicated an unawareness of the situation. For example, the cable that finally authorized the Hebrew names for the ships stated that crew members with official papers should remain aboard; the people in Israel should have known that none of the crew had official papers.[5]

As for the vital question of whether they were allowed to put up a sign "Hagana Ship",[6] the affirmative answer they had been hoping for came when the disembarkation was nearly completed and photographs of the names *Kibbutz Galuyot* and *Atzma'ut* had been taken without the superscription "Hagana".[7]

The responsibility for these questions fell on Yossi Harel. Previous instructions did not relate to the present situation and there were no updated ones. Yossi saw his task as taking the people from Romania to the Land of Israel. Since, on the orders of his superiors, they were being diverted to Cyprus, and the British were in charge of this, his mission was completed. Judged by his standards, which were to transport the passengers safely, to prove to the British that unauthorized immigration would continue and to show that the spirit of the Jews would not be broken, the task had been successfully accomplished.

Since their job was finished, Yossi proposed that the Israeli crew and the hired seamen should mix with the immigrants and disembark at Cyprus, where the Hagana escape network would remove them for further missions in the future. In this, Yossi was vehemently opposed by many of the Palmach members, and particularly Ike Aharonowitz. He had urged breaking through to Israel, even by force, and was furious about surrendering to the British. Now he demanded that at least they keep the ships – "They are ours!" he threw at Yossi. "How can we look after them?", asked Yossi. "The crew will look after them", was Ike's rejoinder. Yossi remained calm and asked how this could be done; not only would they lose the ships, but also expose the crew members to danger. Ike was agitated but not unreasonable, "We'll insist on a letter, signed by the admiral, guaranteeing the safety of the crew even if they remain aboard their ships; we'll make him sign and even use the immigrants to help us. When we get to Cyprus we'll tell him that if he doesn't allow us to keep the ships, we'll stop the ventilation in the hold and cut off the water and make him give in."

Yossi Harel hesitated. It was not his duty to fight over the ships after the completion of the operation. It was a legal matter and there were financial and even political considerations outside the scope of his authority. His decision was based on the publicity the operation was receiving. The B.B.C. was announcing the seizure of the ships at the beginning of each news bulletin, emphasizing the fact that they had been captured on the high seas. The British newspaper editorials that were quoted pointed out that this was an exceptional act, raising legal as well as ethical problems.[8] The fact that British warships had surrounded two ships flying the Panamanian flag on the high seas, boarded them and sailed them to Cyprus in an arbitrary manner resulted in complex high-level discussions and an exchange of letters lasting over two months between the High Commissioner on the island, the Minister of Transport and the Admiralty.[9] The confusion and embarrassment of the British were far greater than that of the Israeli commander who did not have to apologize to the media for helping to take Jews to their own country. For this reason, Yossi decided to accept Ike's forceful proposals and turned his attention to keeping the ships. However, there was still much exhausting work to be done and many important problems to solve.

CABLE
    1.1.1948
    1030 hours
    To Arnon
    Reached Famagusta 0730 hours. At 1015 hours beginning to disembark the immigrants. Send replies to yesterday's questions. The questions:
    The crew have no papers, should the foreigners appear without papers?
    Is it certain that the vessels will move to Haifa?
    Disembarkation has started. We demand immediate reply.[10]

The question asked in previous cables would be asked again and there were no official answers. In the meantime, part of the foreign crew, especially the Spaniards aboard the *Pan York*, began to mix with the immigrants. They were afraid that the agreement reached at sea with the admiral would require that they be returned to their country, to the mercy of the Franco regime. Meanwhile, some of the Palmach people were showing distinct signs of impatience and wanted to leave the ships quickly.

There was a feeling among the crew that the whole command structure was about to collapse. The huge ships threatened to block Famagusta harbour, so they were anchored outside it, and obsolete rafts were enlisted to go back and forth between the ships and the quay, slowly removing the immigrants. The slow pace, the low morale and the suspiciousness of the British lined up on the quay moved Yossi to decide to accept the responsibility for actions outside the actual mission for which he had been recruited.

He stopped the disembarkation and asked for the admiral. The admiral had accompanied the ships all the way and had received a continuous report on what was happening on them, and he boarded the *Pan York* without apprehension. Once again he promised that no harm would come to the crew. Yossi allowed the hired skippers to participate in this section of the negotiations and they asked for this agreement to be approved by the Governor and civil administration of Cyprus. The admiral agreed immediately and appointed an officer with the rank of colonel to procure notification and authorization that the crew members would not be arrested and that they would even be issued documents allowing them to remain on the ships. These documents would name the people as they wished without their having to identify themselves. This officer was also obliged to accept a letter of protest from Yossi about the seizing of the ships on the high seas, and to provide a report on the situation in the camps in Cyprus before the passengers went to them. Finally, Yossi demanded that the ships enter the harbour and unload the passengers at the quay-side. The admiral's patience in going aboard these illegal immigrant ships illustrates how wary the British were of being drawn into violent confrontation even in Cyprus.

Another day passed. The admiral had to put pressure on the Famagusta harbour authorities until they reluctantly agreed, since it blocked the port and put a stop to all activity, to allow one ship to draw up to the quay.[11] On Friday, 2nd January, 1948, disembarkation from the *Pan York* was speeded up while the *Pan Crescent* lay at anchor outside and two rafts took off the sick passengers and some of those crowded on the deck. The British intelligence officer, who was sent to follow what was happening, reported with some amazement:

Congestion on the two ships is still very great; the sailors and

Refugees, finally released from Cyprus, make their way aboard the
S.S. *Atzmauth* for their second journey to Israel

soldiers (British) do not leave the deck area assigned to them except to go to the engine rooms and certain key points on deck. The Jews are in very high spirits and very much want to get off the ships. They are cheerful and smiling and there is no sign of hostility towards our soldiers, from the airborne division of the Royal Artillery, who are supervising the disembarkation and behaving with customary tact and attentiveness and this time, to our great pleasure, without any special need for restraint. The passenger quay looks like a normal peacetime quay except, perhaps, for a strange smell easily identifiable and unforgettable, coming from this immigrant ship as from all previous ones. The Jews disembarking from the ships are handed over to units of the British military command in Cyprus and taken from the port to the camps where they and their baggage are searched by details of soldiers and military police.[12]

The tone of admiration for the order aboard the ships and the organization and discipline of the immigrants in this officer's report can also be found in the reports of the ships' commanders. The galleys were working up to the last moment and before disembarking each group received a meal, a hot drink and emergency rations which were to last them another twenty-four hours. In fact these rations soon created a problem; they were from Palestine and specially packed for the Hagana. In the course of the searches outside the port they were confiscated out of fear that they contained arms and explosives. When the ship commanders found out that the packages were being confiscated, they stopped issuing them to the disembarking passengers rather than have them taken by the British. This caused an uproar on deck. The first group not to receive emergency rations refused to disembark. Dov Magen's explanations did not help. When he told them that the British were confiscating the packages, they said they were prepared to eat all their rations on the spot. The argument held up the disembarkation and in his report Dov Magen reached this conclusion: "If you give an immigrant nothing, he will not complain, but as soon as you give something to one and not to the other, the complaints begin."[13]

This unpleasantness was cleared up when a representative of the Joint Distribution Committee in Cyprus was called and agreed that all the remaining food would be turned over to the Joint which would then distribute it in the camps. However, renewed tension was aroused by the news that thorough searches were taking place and that professional interrogation units consisting of British officers had been set up in the camps to check each group of immigrants.

By this stage the Mossad had achieved a great deal in the field of operations and organization, not only concerning purchasing ships and moving people. Its emissaries from the Hagana, Palmach and Palyam had found a way to smuggle radio sets into the camps in Cyprus and a special channel was fixed connecting them and the ships anchored in Famagusta. The chosen wavelength was written on a scrap of paper and given to Yossi Harel by an Israeli girl who rushed up to him on the quay and, to his surprise, embraced him with unexpected ardour; Yossi only realized what was happening when he felt the girl pressing a note into his hand. Very quickly a secret link between the camp and the ships was established, by means of which they learnt about the searches and the confiscation of the food; and then, suddenly, a more serious piece of information was received. Three members of the Israeli crew, including Geda Shochet, had been taken for interrogation.

This was a clear breach of the agreement and a disturbing sign of what could be expected from then on. The coded report from the camp said that they had found Geda's service paybook in his bag proving he had been a pilot in the R.A.F. The report added that the prisoners had been beaten and were being interrogated harshly and that the passengers' possessions were being examined with a fine comb. Documents, books and even personal photographs were being confiscated. The people were questioned as though they were Soviet spies.

Disembarkation ceased. The admiral rushed to the ships and was received coldly by Yossi Harel. "You do not keep your promises," Yossi accused him. The admiral felt how strong the anger was on the ships and hurriedly summoned the port commander. Their whispered conversation was overheard by the people standing nearby. The port commander pointed out in bafflement how quickly news about what was happening in the camps reached the blockaded and guarded ships. The admiral stopped him: "The most important thing is to carry on with the operation." A dispatch rider on a motorbike was sent with a written order to the interrogators to release the prisoners immediately. The admiral showed the written order to Yossi but he was not satisfied until he had received notification on the communications network that they had in fact been released. The admiral received similar notification at the same time and could not understand how these young refugee ship commanders could maintain regular communications with a transit camp in the middle of the island.

Disembarkation was resumed but at a slower pace. The people were tired and in no hurry to leave the ships which had become more roomy since the beginning of the disembarkation. The crew did not push them too hard. Information transmitted from the camp proved that the British were trying to get round the agreement with the admiral and were making efforts to identify "negative elements" who would help them demonstrate to the world that the immigrants were nothing more than pirates.

The British were, in fact, working to this end but the ship commanders incorrectly assessed the direction they were working in. The British were looking for Communist agents while the commanders thought they were after arms and explosives which were thought to have been given to members of Etzel and Lechi. The British were hunting for members of extreme left-wing organizations and the heads of the operation thought they wanted leaders of the extreme right-wing organization, in this case Betar and the Revisionist Party.

Tension reached a peak when the ships' commanders decided to search the immigrants themselves. When it was learnt that the British were searching the camps thoroughly, Dov Magen was secretly told that the Revisionists aboard the ships had firearms – a sub-machine gun and six revolvers. After a hasty consultation the commanders announced on the public address system that they knew about these firearms and if they were not handed over at once, passengers would leave the ships without baggage.

This threat went unheeded and the weapons were not handed over. The thought that they would be caught by the British terrified the commanders. In such a case, they would be in breach of their promise and all agreements would be cancelled: the British would arrest the commanders, confiscate the ships and treat the immigrants like prisoners. Gravest of all, it would cause serious damage to the Zionist cause and be a victory for the British who would be able to prove that they were dealing with armed groups of Jews who were hiding behind innocent children and old people.

No arms had been found by the appointed hour and it was unthinkable to hold an organized search among the thousands of immigrants, so the commanders used methods based on relations between political parties in the Yishuv at the time of their violent clashes with each other. Dov Magen forewarned the representatives of the "loyal" groups on his ship and gave them the task of holding the searches. During the night of 1st and 2nd January, politically-based committees were selected and a plan of action secretly decided upon. A curfew was imposed in the dormitories and a thorough search of the immigrants' possessions and even bodies was carried out. Eventually, only one revolver was found. The remainder – if there were any – were presumably thrown into the sea.[14]

In retrospect, this was an unimportant event, occurring at the end of the voyage, but it reflected the atmosphere of the time, the relationships between the parties and the fact that the voyage of the *Pans* was not in fact influenced by political factors, contrary to the accepted view that the whole Zionist effort in Palestine and the Diaspora, including the underground movements, had political coloration.

While this preventive search, striking a discordant note at the end of the voyage, was aimed at discovering weapons and avoiding difficulties in contact with the British interrogation units, the British themselves were looking for communist agents. This task was given to the British secret service in Palestine. On 31st December, 1947, at 1:00 p.m., whilst he was getting ready to enjoy New Year celebrations, Captain Linklater was called to the telephone. In a conversation with Middle East Headquarters, he was ordered to organize a team immediately and leave with it on a special flight to Cyprus. Captain Linklater, commander of section 299 of the P.S.S. (Palestine Secret Service), called five of his colleagues. They were an excellent intelligence group; they all spoke Hebrew, some of them knew Yiddish, one knew Romanian and two Russian. For six days, in 24-hour shifts, he sat with his colleagues and checked the enormous human cargo leaving the ships. Due to the priority that had been granted to this operation by the British H.Q., additional teams had been recruited to help him, and British officers' wives were used for body searches on the female immigrants.   At the end of six days of interrogation, after he had taken nearly all the documents, personal photographs and diaries from the immigrants and filled ten large crates with these papers, Captain Linklater flew to Fayid where he prepared a special detailed report. He had been able to confiscate, by cunning, all the papers of the *Pan York* and the list of sailors on the ship; he had exposed Geda Shochet and discovered the crew members who had been on the *Exodus*. He produced an accurate report on the selection of passengers in Romania, how they were transported, life aboard ship, the structure of the ships and how they operated, and the relations between immigrants and the crew. He had important information about Romania, in particular about the Jewish community, and also about that country's relations with the U.S.S.R. But to his great disappointment he was unable to catch any Communist spies. In an interim report, before disembarkation was completed, he wrote:

(A) If there are any large Communist guerrilla groups among the Russian speakers in this shipment, either they are still aboard the ships or else they have come unarmed and without documents.
(B) The movement, planning and administration of the final evacuation from Burgas was carried out skilfully and thoroughly at short notice.
(C) The Communist government in Romania, under supervision from Moscow, wanted to evacuate this shipment of Jews at all costs and reached an agreement with Bulgaria to use a Bulgarian port for this purpose after a delay at Constantsa which was due, apparently, to British protests.[15]

This long and detailed interim report betrays great disappointment at not finding Soviet agents or organized Communist underground groups, but it suggests that this was not significant. Captain Linklater was sorry to have missed a perfect opportunity to expose the threat the Jews represented, pretending to be persecuted while they were sworn enemies of the West, now at the height of the Cold War.

He was aware that he now had to produce proof for the assumption, already leaked by the British Foreign Office, that documents had been seized showing the ships to be full of Soviet agents. With typical British caution and by means of fairly broad hints, the military and civilian administration spread information about dangerous discoveries. For example, the British High Commissioner in Palestine sent a cable classified as "secret" to the Colonial Office, copies of which were simultaneously circulated to twenty-six different offices in London and Washington, on the discovery of an immigrant's briefcase decorated inside with pictures of Stalin. "Although this may not prove anything in itself", said Sir Alan Cunningham, "it should be realized that there are other facts . . ."[16]

These leaks made the Jewish Agency representatives in the U.S. fear that the British would turn every innocent document into incriminating evidence and they found themselves in an uncomfortable defensive position. In the hysterical atmosphere of the Cold War, great significance could be attached to the *Newsweek* story that active members of the Communist Party had been found among the immigrants. The article claimed that subversive literature had been seized in the immigrants' possession, such as *The Fundamentals of Marxist-Leninist Philosophy*, as well as Soviet citations for taking part in the battle for Hungary in 1944, Red Army pay books and, most serious of all, permits from the Soviet Secret Police (NKVD) for residence in certain areas and warning against leaving these areas, but none was stamped with permission to leave and certainly not to Palestine.[17]

Once again, as at other crisis points in this story, all the efforts of the Jews were pitted against the might of the British. At the climax of unauthorized immigration they stood facing each other, their weapons this time a publicity campaign. But new circumstances had created a new situation. The joint decision to transfer the ships to Cyprus was the apex of unauthorized immigration so that at a point when conflict had been avoided, the immigrants had not been returned to their country of origin and it was clear that, before long, in another month or another year they would all get to Palestine, the publicity campaign was too late and, indeed, superfluous. The emerging state and the war already being fought there overshadowed all other events. Concern now was to get people away from Cyprus as quickly as possible and to look after the ships.

Disembarkation continued for three days. The Joint accepted responsibility for the housing, clothing and food for the immigrants in the camps. The Hagana emissaries began to set up a training system for the young immigrants. Jewish Agency people, in conjunction with leaders of the immigrants, started information programmes and Hebrew tuition. Youngsters who qualified for Youth Immigration (Aliyat Noar) were screened so that they could be sent at once to Palestine.

Aboard the ships Gad Hilb and Ike Aharonowitz tried to form a crew to guard and maintain the ships. They were expecting legal problems because the Panamanian Government, which had given way to British pressure, had withdrawn its official registration of the ships and ordered its flag to be removed.[18] There were also technical questions: faults had been discovered, the special equipment for transporting the thousands of passengers had to be dismantled and the ships prepared to conform to international regulations in order to continue to operate. There were also problems with fuel, food for the crew and positioning the ships, since no harbour in Cyprus could accommodate them. The escorts, Palmach men, whose mission was drawing to a close, felt tired and drained. Yossi Harel conveyed this in a special cable to the Palmach H.Q.

CABLES
2.1.1948
1555 hours
To Hativa (Palmach HQ)
From Amnon
We maintained the honour of the Hativa in the difficult circumstances we were in. We did not take the ships into exile ourselves. The British respect us for this. They are amazed by the good organization and perfect order in which the people disembark, in organized groups with leaders and orderlies. The gang sat all morning on the bridge and they all watched the disembarkation and sang: "The servant has done his job, the servant can go."[19]

2.1.1948
To Amnon
From Arnon
". . . the gang: every institution is following your actions with pride and appreciates your work and as you had the privilege of taking them from exile you will have the privilege of bringing them redeemed to Israel. Servant, servant, there is still work for you . . ."[20]

The feeling that "the servant has done his work" needed wider horizons. This was the greatest immigration enterprise and perhaps the largest planned operation in the history of the Yishuv. Although it had ended safely, there was a feeling of anticlimax. The Israeli crew members who were completing their missions began to abandon the exhausting work of disembarkation. As the ships unloaded, more and more young Palmach men gathered on the bridge. They watched the immigrants busy with their own problems and wondering about the unknown path they were to take. One of the Israelis began a song but it did not catch on; it was as though they were looking for the right tune to relieve their tension. And then, as though by order, as the *Pan Crescent* was finishing unloading and her bridge was crowded with crew members from the *Pan York* which had already finished, the last doctor to remain in sick bay appeared and asked for "the boss". The Palmach men, amused by something, asked in broken Yiddish what the matter was. The doctor sought somebody in a position of authority from the noisy crowd of young men before him. They all looked the same and there was no time because he also wanted to leave and so, by means of Yiddish, a little Romanian and much gesticulation, he explained that one of the female immigrants had inserted a wad of dollars irretrievably into her rectum and was now in great pain.

An uproar of mirth burst out on the bridge. A lovely problem! Typical of the Diaspora Jew, thought these cocky youths fostered by the pioneering youth movements, to smuggle money and debase himself! They all jumped from the bridge and rushed to leer at the discomfited woman. The Gideon in the signals room wanted his friends in Palestine and the Mossad to share the joke and sent an urgent message:

CABLE
    12.1.1948
    To Arnon
    From Atzmaut
    Disaster has struck. Prepare hooks. Woman stuffed herself with
    360 "Stephens" three days can't get them out. Help! Treasurers,
    get ready.

The treasurers were known for their tireless pursuit of funds to finance Mossad activities, but in this case there was no need for them to get ready. A specialist was brought in, and in the process of removing the dollars they were torn beyond further use. Such were the distractions in the last hours of the *Pans* operation.

From then on there was another meaning to the message "there is still work for the servant". After a temporary list of crew members for the two ships had been drawn up, all the others disembarked carrying bags like the immigrants. Captain Linklater's team knew that the last ones to leave were the leaders of the illegal immigration, which had kept them awake at nights and made them a laughing stock in the eyes of the whole world. They were aware of the admiral's order not to arrest them. In fury they saw their prey walk past them but their hands were tied. Captain Linklater's restraint was put to the test when the Jewish sailor from America, Theodore Rosenfeld, passed by him with a triumphant grin on his face. He had met this sailor in the *Exodus* affair and also on the *Chaim Arlozoroff*; when he searched his bag there were even photographs of those ships and yet he was neither afraid nor apologetic, and showed no hostility. He was sure of himself – he had

challenged the British Empire three times and had won.²¹ Captain
Linklater swore that very soon he would find a way round the
admiral's promise and arrest these men.²²

The Hagana was also aware of the danger that its men in the camps
would be discovered, caught and arrested by the British. They had
constructed a tunnel in the camp which led beyond the fence and, by
means of complicated arrangements including a diversionary
operation by the Palyam, an Israeli fishing boat *Nesher* and local
Cypriots, they had begun to remove Palmach members from the
camps.²³ In this way some of the prominent leaders of the immigrants
were smuggled out, as well as people urgently needed in the defence of
the Yishuv in its battle for survival and ultimate independence.

Heads of the Mossad in Europe extracted every advantage from the
success of the breakthrough. Since the British had weakened but still
refused to permit immigration to Israel, ten more immigrant ships
were sent. Their instructions were to sail to Israel and not to resist the
British by force. Six of the ships were seized and the passengers
transferred to Cyprus and only two of them, which arrived two days
after the establishment of the State of Israel, made the journey
unhindered. However, there were only six thousand immigrants on
board all ten of them, less than on one of the *Pans*.

The Hagana commanders in Palestine were completely taken up
with the War of Independence. The Palmach platoon commanders,
who had served as escorts and Gideons, ship commanders and sailors,
were now battalion commanders and staff officers, taking part in bitter
blocking actions and bloody attempts to burst through besieged
Jerusalem and the Negev. Leaders of the Yishuv were making
supreme efforts to find sources of arms and money and to organize civil
administration and world-wide political activity at the height of a war
and in the face of serious internal problems. The immigrants were in
the camps, the ship commanders and most of the escorts had been
evacuated; the captains of the *Pan York* and *Pan Crescent* were left in
charge of valuable vessels without receiving sufficient attention from
the people who in normal times would have been responsible for them.
The ships languished in Cyprus for nearly seven months.

During those seven long months the ships were held under a special
Defence Detention Order issued by the Cyprus authorities. This order
was made by means of a retroactive law passed by the government of
Cyprus on the day the disembarkation was completed, which stated
that the government of Cyprus²⁴ "was entitled to arrest any ship

carrying passengers planning to enter Palestine in contravention of the immigration laws".[25]

The legal status of the ships was dealt with by the lawyer Yaakov Shimshon Shapira who later became Minister of Justice in the Israel Government. The case involved contacts with the government of Panama because of its withdrawal of the right to fly the Panamanian flag, and with the governments of Italy and France about foreign crew members. The files of documents from the ships show that the volume of cables, reports and letters sent during the seven months of arrest was several times greater than during the months that had passed between the purchase of the ships, the journey to Europe, the fitting, preparation for the voyage and the voyage itself.

The captains, Gad Hilb and Ike Aharonowitz, left alone on the open sea off the small village of Bugaz, fifteen kilometers north of Famagusta, had to deal with an embittered foreign crew whose pay had not yet been settled and who had only been given advances.[26] There were incidents of smuggling, strikes by the foreign crew, repeated friction with the British watches on the ships, constant demands by the few remaining Israeli crew members to go home and, of course, the proper maintenance and preparation of the ships for their future missions to deal with.

The endurance required during this period of enforced calm was greater than during the operation itself. On the initiative of the captains, the British soldiers on watch were paid to carry out maintenance work. Tons of high-quality wooden bunks were sold and, with the money, more comfortable compartments were built, the ventilation system improved and the ships repainted. It was not a rewarding task. This was a critical period for Gad Hilb and Ike Aharonowitz: their comrades were being appointed to the most senior positions in the army, others had become ambassadors, heads of important departments in the developing establishment, or emissaries in the Mossad which was engaged in secret operations in the field of intelligence and in enemy countries. Ike and Gad often felt uneasy. Although they were refitting the ships, idling in the quiet waters of the bay did not suit them. Again and again they asked to take the ships out secretly, to sail, to do something!

When the signal was given to move, it came suddenly. On 18th June, 1948, more than a month after the establishment of the State of Israel, the ships stole out of Cyprus and reached Haifa where they were held by the port commander, still at that time a British officer, who arrested

Gad Hilb.[27] They returned to normal operation at the beginning of July, serving as the principal immigration ships of the State of Israel. From Genoa, Marseilles and Constantsa they carried tens of thousands of Jews, for whose safe delivery Ike and Gad are to be thanked.

It was clearly the earlier activities of the immigrant ships that made mass immigration possible. In a final discussion on the *Pans* it was held that it would not have been possible to set up, on such short notice, the complex shipping system that brought the immigrants to Israel. Unauthorized immigration prepared the radio operators and sailors and it helped establish personal contacts in Europe for the acquisition of arms, through preliminary negotiations and the secret transfer of weapons to Israel.

The process of evacuation from Cyprus was long and exhausting, and as it continued it seemed to sap the strength and conviction with which the emissaries had faced up to Great Britain and the rulers of three continents. The War of Independence, which had diverted attention from individual exploits to the battle for national existence, shifted the focus of the emissaries' activities. They did not rest on their laurels – it was not in their character. Shaul Avigur was active in the organization of the Ministry of Defence; Ehud Avriel was sending the Czech rifles which were to defend the road to Jerusalem; Venia Hadari was making contacts in France which would result in the shipment of guns and tanks at the critical moment for the defence of Degania in the north; Benyamin Yerushalmi underwent a change of name and identity and was "planted" in enemy countries; Geda Shochet was one of the founders of Israel's air force; Avraham Zakai was in the navy; Paul Shulman was commander of the navy; Shaike Dan and Moshe Auerbach continued to bring Jews to Israel, sometimes secretly and sometimes openly, and Pino Ginsburg continued to find the money for it.

They all continued to play important roles in the struggle for Israel's independence. Some of them were recalled for missions during critical periods in later years. Yossi Harel, who was asked to command a special intelligence unit in the Israel Defence Forces and went on to carry out additional government functions, said: "But the climax, for all of us, was there in Romania, at the end of 1947, when we decided to sail . . ."

CHAPTER TEN

On the Threshold of Light

"This is the hour of change
when we shall stand dumb
on the threshold of light – "
(Leah Goldberg, "On the Threshold of Light")

On the first morning of the year 1948, when a bright wintry sun illuminated the harbour of Famagusta in Cyprus and thousands of Jewish refugees began to descend from the ships in silence, a few dozen British officials were standing on the quay: intelligence officers, Foreign and Colonial Office officials and, of course, officers from the Admiralty. They looked with curiosity at the bridge of the *Pan York* where the Mossad emissaries were gathered: the Gideons, men of the Palyam and Palmach and members of the Mossad Le'Aliya Bet.

Both sides had nothing to do. The disembarkation was running smoothly, there was no noticeable tension, no signs of anger or hostility. The spotlights that had been turned towards the anticipated confrontation had already been shifted elsewhere, to the war between the Jews and the Arabs now being fought in Israel.

The immigrants coming up from the crowded holds to the deck saw the group of operatives who had organized their departure from Romania for the first time. They could be recognised by their distinctive dress, which was deliberately untidy, although to their surprise the songs they were singing on the bridge were familiar. The Hebrew words were strange but the tunes were Slavic, full of longing and nostalgia. The British who were waiting below, on the quay, were polite and businesslike. The sudden easing of tension was attested to by the military equipment piled up at the side of the harbour, the large number of empty ambulances and the trucks loaded with soldiers leaving the port. The immigrants, the Israeli emissaries, and the British, eyed each other with curiosity in a situation where relief and frustration were combined. An overt confrontation had suddenly been turned into what appeared to be not more than a businesslike exchange.

The frustration was due to the strange position of the British officers. They had pursued the people responsible for illegal immigration to Palestine over continents and oceans; and now, on the bridge of the ship, there was a large group of their leaders who were responsible for a long series of operations against Great Britain. These men had been sought for a long time, but the hands of the British were tied by the agreement which prevented any confrontation with them.

This agreement had been obtained by an intermediary which was, ironically, responsible for one side in the conflict and for the immigrants – the Jewish Agency. The four groups that had taken part in the affair of the *Pans* – and put up a powerful struggle – the immigrants, the Mossad Le'Aliya Bet, the British authorities and the Jewish Agency Directorate – had drawn up an agreement. This many-sided struggle was now over. The *Pans* operation had been more successful than its opponents had thought but had not achieved what its organizers had hoped – to reach Palestine.

The immigrants could feel satisfied. Many of them had left with their families in an orderly manner, there were many of them and there were hopes that the cooperation of key members of the Romanian government would allow continued immigration from that country. In their view, there were prospects of reunification with relatives and friends who had remained behind. Their optimism was due to the smooth voyage, the speed of the operation and, above all, the fact that their dream of leaving Romania for Israel was coming true. On the other hand, there was no joy – they were disembarking in a strange, hostile port, in Cyprus, and being taken to a detention camp under British control for an unknown period.

The British had cause to feel relieved because they were spared a violent clash with thousands of refugees at sea. All the desperate proposals raised by the special committees to prevent illegal immigration were impractical. It would have been impossible to return the ships to Romania; there was no reason to take them to Germany, like the *Exodus*, and there was no country that would agree to accept so many Jews. A frontal battle at sea between a Royal Navy flotilla and two banana boats loaded with refugees would have ended in such a terrible disaster that public opinion, even in Great Britain, would have been outraged.

The agreement which prevented a clash was an easy way out for the

British but it had a reverse side. It constituted an admission of British inability to prevent the immigration of Jews to their country since Cyprus was only a way-station on the road to Israel. In this respect, the agreement encouraged the Mossad which continued to provoke the British and succeeded in creating a mass movement of immigrants who came to Israel from all over the world. The British were afraid that the agreement to divert the ships to Cyprus would become a precedent which would fill the camps that had been prepared on the island. This would create pressure to evacuate the people to Palestine and the British would then become actively involved in it.

For the members of the Jewish Agency directorate, Ben-Gurion, Golda, Nahum Goldmann and of course Sharett, the solution was convenient. They were not obliged to fight openly against the immigration of Jews. The agreement to divert the ships to Cyprus blurred the significance of the Mossad emissaries' disobedience and turned it into a "one-off" occurrence which could be easily covered up. At this time, just prior to the establishment of the state, when the drive for national sovereignty had become the central issue and there was a fear that Etzel and Lechi might obtain control of the Yishuv, independent activity by the Mossad emissaries, who were considered an elite group by the young Israelis, could endanger the efforts to bring together the various forces in the Yishuv into a united army under the command of the state.

However, the feeling of relief was mixed with anxiety. A small group of young men performing a national mission had established links with a large Jewish community and the authorities of a state, had determined, on their own initiative, a policy with far-reaching implications, and had carried it out on feeble pretexts and by deceiving their superiors. The Mossad operatives and ship commanders sitting on the bridge of the *Pan York* at the end of the voyage were aware that the existence of leadership and national institutions depended on willingness to accept their authority. This willingness was a condition of the protracted struggle to establish a Jewish state in the Land of Israel, but they, who had been active in promoting the authority of the leadership, had felt that it was rejecting them.

Their education and social heritage stressed creativity and self-realization. They did not believe that a Jewish state would rise out of U.N. decisions. They were "the national arm" and the immigrants were "the new workers" who were coming "with firm resolve". They believed that political decisions were not worth the paper they were written on. There had been fourteen years of unauthorized immigration starting with the immigrant ship *Volos* in 1934, and the *Pans* could have changed the face of their country in one voyage – immigration would have increased by more than a whole year's quota and doubled the active part of the Yishuv. They could have achieved in one operation what it had taken the Zionist movement two generations to do. For this reason the order not to leave Constantsa had seemed catastrophic to them.

Emotional involvement in the task had created a lack of distinction between the mission itself and the personal feelings of the emissaries and brought them into confrontation with their superiors. Moved by youthful enthusiasm, dedication and belief in their mission, they had drawn on their self-confidence and the powerful desire of tens of thousands of Romanian Jews to reach their homeland, and had sailed without clear authority.

In this critical period, at the end of 1947, when fate might swing the Zionist dream from immediate fulfilment to complete rejection, the Zionist leaders suddenly discovered that two banana boats in the hands of a few young Israelis were liable to unite those forces opposed to the establishment of the state.

The obstinacy that had driven opposing forces towards confrontation had cleared at the very last moment and had been replaced by determined search for a solution. It was achieved at that moment in time because the struggle for the establishment of the state had shifted from unauthorized immigration to the War of Independence – the British, who had begun to acccept the idea of evacuating Palestine, did not want to be responsible for calamity and the Mossad emissaries, realizing they had gone too far and taken a grave risk, had looked for a compromise which represented a kind of victory.

In the course of a discussion on the whole operation a generation later, Mossad operatives expressed a range of opinions on the importance of the *Pans* affair. One thought it lay in the actual ability to organize and handle such a complex enterprise – the high level of coordination, communications, financial acumen and skill. Another pointed to the heartening effect of the large number of immigrants at a crucial and dangerous moment on the spirit of the defenders of the Yishuv. Another to the inspiration which 15,000 immigrants gave to the hundreds of thousands remaining behind in Bulgaria and Romania to gather their courage and immigrate to Israel. Others spoke of the political significance of Jewish obstinacy in the wake of the *Exodus* proving to the British that, whatever they did, they could not stop Jews going to Israel. The voyage of the *Pans* was an act of defiance by a few against the whole world. Its success depended on whether there was a strong enough sense of purpose. There was.

Notes

CHAPTER ONE: IN-BETWEEN DAYS

1. Y. Talmon, "National Frustration as a cause of Ideological Polarity," *Ma'ariv* 4.5.76 (Heb.).
2. Yosef Harel, Commander of the *Pans*, interview.
3. On the internal struggles in the Yishuv at the end of the mandate from the point of view of Etzel: S. Lev-Ami, *Struggle and Rebellion*, Ministry of Defence Publication, 1979, pp. 380-384; from the point of view of the Hagana: Y. Slutski, *History of the Hagana*, Vol. C, part 2, 1972, (to be referred to below as H.H., C/2) pp. 941-959, 1540-1558 (Heb.).
4. Bevin's remarks, 18.9.47, 129/21, CAB, Public Record Office.
5. See Anne Williams, *Britain and France in the Middle East and North Africa, 1914-1967*, Massada, 1972, pp. 42-55.
6. C. Sykes, *From Balfour to Bevin*, Ma'arachot, 1966, pp. 293-302.
7. The most extensive research on attempts at reconciliation between Jews and Arabs in Eretz Israel – in A. Cohen's *Israel and the Arab World*, Sifriat Hanpoalim, 1964 (Heb.).
8. Ben-Gurion's remarks at the Mapai Convention, August 1947. See also D. Ben-Gurion's *The State of Israel Renewed*, Vol. 1, Am Oved, 1969, pp.74-75 (Heb.).
9. See also Y. Nevo, the attitude of the Palestinian Arabs to the Jewish Yishuv and the Zionist movement in *Zionism and the Arab Question*, Zalman Shazar Centre, 1979, pp. 163-172 (Heb.).
10. For the struggle against Great Britain in the Arab Revolt 1936–1939, Y. Arnon-Ohana, *Fellahin in the Arab Revolt in Eretz Israel 1936–1939*, Tel Aviv University Students Union, 1978 (Heb.).
11. Elizabeth Wixman, *Dictators' Europe*, Zemorroc, 1977, pp. 195–207.
12. *ibid.*
13. C. Sykes, *From Balfour to Bevin*, *op.cit.*, pp. 247-290.
14. A. Ilan, *America, Britain and Eretz Israel*, Yad Ben Zvi, p.204 (Heb.).
15. *ibid.*, pp.212-218.
16. Y. Roi, "USSR – Israel relations from the end of the war to the death of Stalin", *Shvut*, No. 1, p.101 (Heb.).
17. Y. Roi, "Oppression of Soviet and Jewish entity and the Campaign against the Cosmopolitans in the second half of the 1940s", *Shvut*, No. 4 (Heb.).
18. "The French and British Withdrawal from Syria and Lebanon", speech by A. Vyshinski at Security Council, 5.2.46. Y. Roi, *From Encroachment to Involvement*, Israel University Press, 1974, pp.28-29.
19. N. Bethell, *The Palestine Triangle*, Edanim, 1979, pp.250-251.
20. A. Yodfat, *USSR and The Middle East*, Ministry of Defence, 1979, p. 15 (Heb.).
21. *ibid.*, p.16.
22. Y. Roi, "USSR-Israel Relations...", *op.cit.*, p. 102 (Heb.).
23. N. Bethell, *The Palestine Triangle*, *op.cit.*, p.164.
24. C. Sykes, *From Balfour to Bevin*, *op. cit.*, p. 257.
25. N. Bethell, *The Palestine Triangle*, *op.cit.*, pp. 162-164.

26. Elizabeth Monroe, *Bevin's Arab Policy*, St. Antony's Papers II, London 1961.
27. Y. Held, "From Black Saturday to Partition: Summer 1946 as the turning point in the history of Zionist policy", *Zion*, 43rd year, Nos. C-D, pp.331-338 (Heb.).
28. H.H., C/2, pp. 801-835.
29. *ibid.*, pp.898-905
30. Committee report from *The Anglo-American Commission of Enquiry into Palestinian Affairs*, Vol. B, Z. Leinman, pp. 700-739.
31. A large number of the immigrants from the First and Second Immigrations (up to 1914) came as "tourists". From 1901 they were required to hand over their passports on arrival and were given Turkish certificates known as "red papers". These certificates were valid for three months' stay. It became the custom to symbolize the final decision to stay in Eretz Israel by ceremonially tearing up this red paper. See M. Eliav, *Eretz Israel and the Yishuv in the 19th Century*, Keter, 1978, p.265 (Heb.).
32. Y. Wolf, (ed.), *Carta Atlas of the History of Israel from the beginning of settlement to the establishment of the state*, Carta, 1973, p.73 (Heb.).
33. *ibid.*, p.81.
34. *ibid.*, p.100.
35. This subject, a major part of the question of unauthorized immigration, is clarified in Y. Bauer's *Habricha*, Moreshet and Sifriat Hapoalim, 1970 (Heb.).
36. See Ben-Gurion's speech at this conference and also D. Ben-Gurion *Bama'aracha*, Vol. D, Mapai, pp.38-39 (Heb.).
37. On the withdrawal from the Biltmore proposal, Y. Bauer, "From Biltmore to Paris – the Influence of the Holocaust on Zionist policy 1942-1946" from the *Proceedings of the World Congress for Jewish Studies*, Vol. B, p.475.
38. *ibid.*
39. It is doubtful whether there can be a quantitative assessment of the importance of the role played by each factor during this decisive period towards the establishment of a Jewish state in Eretz Israel. This is also a sensitive issue because of the emotional and ideological ties between the political movements in Israel today and the agencies operating before the establishment of the state. The connection between the sources of the Israeli political movements and the development of their historiographic significance still awaits research. The decision regarding the role of *Exodus* is based on the importance given to this operation by the British themselves and the way it was formulated by Bevin when he proposed to the Cabinet to return the Palestine Mandate to the U.N. Cabinet meeting 20.9.49, PRO. CAB.
40. The book *Exodus* by Leon Uris and the film based on it made by Otto Preminger became very important publicity vehicles for Zionism and the establishment of the state.
41. D. Ben-Gurion, *The State of Israel Renewed*, Vol. 1, *op. cit.*, p.69 (Heb.).
42. A cartoon in this vein appeared in the French newspaper *Franc Tireur*, and see a photograph of this cartoon, H.H., C/2, 1160.
43. C. Sykes, *From Balfour to Bevin*, *op. cit.*, pp. 343-347.
44. The normal wording in British memoranda to the press and appeals to other countries spoke of "the financial dealings and trade in illegal Jewish immigration." Bevin's remarks to the Prime Minister of France, 12.7.47, PRO, FO, 371.61816.
45. The British representative to the U.N. to the Secretary General, Trygve Lee, 15.4.1947, PRO, CO 537.2345.
46. See 44 above.
47. For the intensive British attempt to portray "a wave of Communist immigration" to Palestine, see Z. Drugy, *New Light on the* Exodus *Affair*, Am Oved, 1972, pp. 283-284 (Heb.).
48. For the connection between the British Mandate for Palestine as confirmed by the

League of Nations, and the Balfour Declaration, A. Prizel, *Zionist Policy after the Balfour Declaration*, Tel Aviv University and Hakibbutz Hameuchad, pp. 286-308. (Heb.).

49. The most extensive discussion on the Balfour Declaration is that of L. Stein, *Foundation of Eretz Israel*, Shocken, 1962 (Heb.).

50. For the dynamics that made the British decide to raise the subject of Palestine in the U.N., joint research of Y. Kolat, Y. Cohen, A. Elon, G. Cohen, Y. Heller, *Cathedra*, No. 15, 1980, pp. 140-189 (Heb.).

51. N. Bethell, *The Palestine Triangle, op. cit.*, pp. 249-251.

52. Recently the question has been raised "whether the Jews were prepared to pay a high price to prevent the Palestine question coming before the U.N." See Y. Kolat, "The British Decision to leave Palestine", *Cathedra*, No. 15, pp. 189-191 (Heb.).

53. N. Bethell, *The Palestine Triangle, op. cit.*, pp. 273-283.

54. *ibid.*

55. Z. Drugy, *New Light on the* Exodus *Affair, op. cit.*, pp. 267-276 (Heb.).

56. Reports of the British ambassadors in Iraq and Saudi Arabia, N. Bethell, *The Palestine Triangle, op. cit.*, p. 252.

57. Report of the British envoy in Lebanon.

58. N. Bethell, *The Palestine Triangle, op. cit.*, pp. 280-281.

59. Documents accessible to today's researcher do not prove this assumption. In any event, in view of the chaotic situation prevailing in the country at that time, there were many people who thought that the British were deliberately creating an impossible situation so that they would have an excuse to return. See *History of the War of Independence*, Ma'arachot, 1960, pp. 65-67 (Heb.).

60. *ibid.*, pp. 85-88.

61. Ben-Gurion at the political committee of the 22nd Congress, 18.12.1946, from *Bama'aracha* Vol. 4, part B, pp. 135-138 (Heb.).

62. H.H., C/2, pp. 1457-1484 (Heb.).

63. *ibid.*, p. 1206.

64. *ibid.*, p. 1209.

65. D. Ben-Gurion, *State of Israel Renewed*, Vol. I, *op. cit.*, p. 102 (Heb.).

66. Y. Wolf, *Carta Atlas . . ., op. cit.*, p. 81 (Heb.).

CHAPTER TWO: BANANA BOATS

1. On the question of America or Eretz Israel, see D. Ben-Gurion, *Igrot*, Vol. A, Am Oved, 1971, pp. 3-60 (Heb.).

2. See also Ben-Gurion's letter to the Poalei-Zion Party Central Office in America, 18.1.1918, p. 335. For Ben Zvi's attitude, Ben-Zvi's Memoirs in B. Habess, *Ben-Gurion and his Generation*, Massada, pp. 252-253 (Heb.).

3. "American Diary" by B. Katznelson, describes the disappointment and pain in his encounter with American Jewry, *Igrot*, 1921-1930, Am Oved, 1973, pp. 93-144 (Heb.).

4. R. Bondi, *HaShaliach*, Am Oved, 1973, pp. 225-254 (Heb.).

5. The authors have in their possession some of the ships' documents including the logbook and various official papers, referred to below as S.D.

6. Final report of the voyage 11-12, Archives of the History of the Hagana (AHH), *Pans* Box No. 46, containing files No. 281-14/275 (Heb.).

7. Telegram from Ben-Gurion to Sharett 3.2.48, AHH, Ben-Gurion file 17 (Heb.).

8. A. Tal, *Navy Operations in the War of Independence*, Ma'arachot, 1930, pp. 209-247 (Heb.).

9. The financial side of the *Pans* affair, from the purchase of the ships to the large amounts of bribes, is not documented for obvious reasons. The sum for which the ships were purchased is based on an estimate from the taxes paid in the USA (registration documents in Philadelphia, 17.3.47), on Zeev Shind's report on the voyage (AHH) and an interview with the Treasurer of the Mossad at that time, Pino Ginsburg (Heb.).

10. Zeev Shind, in the name of Zemurray, report on the voyage, AHH (Heb.).

11. *ibid.*

12. Danny was the underground code-name for Zeev Shind.

13. M. Weisgal, *To Here*, Weidenfeld and Nicolson, 1972, pp. 183-184.

14. Z. Shind, Report on Voyages, AHH (Heb.).

15. *ibid.*

16. *Ha'aretz*, 1.1.48 (Heb.).

17. The Mossad Le'Aliya Bet deserves separate research in this matter, as regards the ideological argument over whether the main function of unauthorised immigration was to serve as a political and propaganda weapon or an instrument to bring as many Jews as possible to Eretz Israel. This argument had far-reaching implications for the character of the Mossad's activity. For the argument between Ben-Gurion and Shaul Avigur, Mapai Secretariat meeting, 9.12.1947, Shaul Avigur files, A.M. (Heb.).

18. Z. Shind, Report on Voyage, AHH (Heb.).

19. These meals were mentioned by M. K. Eli Moyel who was an emissary in Cyprus, interview.

20. Maurice Ginsburg, interview.

21. This conclusion is found in H.H., C/2, 1181.

22. *Pan York* Log Book, May-October 1947, A.M. Detailed report on the movement of the ships in British Admiralty papers, especially the Mediterranean H.Q. in Malta, e.g. reports from Algiers, 27.9.47, Gibraltar, 28.9.47, Tunis 29.9.47, PRO ADM 1.

23. Signal to the Mediterranean Fleet H.Q. 29.9.47, PRO ADM 1.

24. For the personality and work of Enzo Sereni, see Ruth Bondi, *HaShaliach* (Heb.).

25. Ada Sereni, *Ships without Flags*, p. 125 (Heb.).

26. Interview with Paul Shulman, "owner" of the ship, and Avraham Zakai, in charge of the fitting out of the *Pan Crescent* in Venice.

27. Ada Sereni, *Ships without Flags*, op. cit., p. 136 (Heb.).

28. Binyamin Yerushalmi, interview.

29. Ada Sereni, *op. cit.*, p. 136.

30. *ibid.*, pp. 135, 138.

31. *ibid.*, p. 136.

32. One version prevalent amongst Mossad operatives is that the mine was placed by the British frogman, Commander Crabbe, who, as an intelligence officer, disappeared later on in mysterious circumstances near a Soviet ship in a British harbour. Yossi Harel, interview. No proof of this has been found.

33. H.H., C/2 1181. B. Yerushalmi is still convinced of this. B. Yerushalmi, interview.

34. Ada Sereni, *op. cit.*, p. 136.

35. Avraham Zakai, B. Yerushalmi, interviews. Paul Shulman admitted himself in an interview that he did not see any purpose in salvaging the ship. P. Shulman, interview.

36. B. Yerushalmi, interview.

37. B. Yerushalmi has recently concluded his operational activities but emphatically refuses to link his name to the image suggested in the (few) reliable books on the Mossad.

38. Interviews with Paul Shulman, Yossi Harel, Azriel Eynav, Avraham Zakai.

39. B. Yerushalmi, interview.

40. P. Shulman, interview.
41. Ada Sereni, *op. cit.*, p. 137.
42. *ibid.*
43. P. Shulman, interview.
44. Interviews with Avraham Zakai, B. Yerushalmi, P. Shulman.
45. Cable from "Yass'ur" (Venia Hadari) to "Arnon" (Mossad office in Israel), 4.10.1947, AHH.
46. Ships on shadowing duty do not try to conceal their purpose. Instructions from H.Q. 28.8.47 PRO ADM 1.
47. Yossi Harel, interview.
48. Yossi Harel, concluding report on voyage, AHH.
49. *Pan Crescent* reached Constanta on 25.9.47; *Pan York* on 10.10.47, AHH.
50. Dov Magen, concluding report, AHH.
51. *ibid.*
52. Professor David Wolf, interview.
53. Dov Magen, concluding report, AHH.
54. *ibid.*
55. Pino Ginsburg, interview. Dov Magen, report, AHH.
56. Yossi Harel, interview.

CHAPTER THREE: WHO WERE THE IMMIGRANTS?

1. The *Pans* files in the Mossad Le' Aliya Bet Archives are very detailed. They contain reports from all the unit heads taking part in the operation and the stages of planning and execution. See AHH 14/275.281.
2. *Israel Statistical Yearbook*, 16, 1965, p. 21, table 3/4.
3. Professor David Wolf, interview.
4. Report of the "operative section", see note 1.
5. Y. Klarman, oral report, 28.9.1975; interviewer Dr. David Sha'ari, Institute of Contemporary Jewry, Oral Documentation Department, Hebrew University (Heb.).
6. Poale Agudat Yisrael complained that the quota by which they were promised 10% of the total number of immigrants was not met. They insisted on taking 1,100 of their people on the *Pans* and hinted that they suspected that the number should have been even higher. Letter from the Executive Committee of Poale Agudat Yisrael, 24.11.47, AHH (Heb.).
7. To Arnon from Agami, 21.11.47, AHH.
8. Y. Klarman, oral report, see 5.
9. List of instructors and daily routine of the courses, AHH.
10. Shaike Dan, interview.
11. *ibid.*
12. Auerbuch, final report, AHH.
13. Ben-Gurion used the code-name Dust of Man (Avak Adam) in his relations with Diaspora Jewry. See his article "Israel and the Diaspora", *Government Yearbook*, 1958, p. 19 (Heb.).
14. The Mossad's policy of selecting immigrants deserves separate discussion. Pioneering immigration was certainly given preference as were young people. There was a debate on this in the Mapai political committee, 21.11.1940, Labour Party Archives, 23/40 (Heb.).
15. Ike Aaronovitz testified that as part of "divide and rule" propaganda, the British told the *Exodus* immigrants by loudspeaker "Your leaders have brought you to

disaster". N. Bethell, *The Palestine Triangle*, Edanim, 1979, p. 262.
16. For this, Y. Marom, "Notes on some demographic statistics", from the collection on Romanian Jewry in their exile and homeland, ed. S. Amiel, *Hitachdut Olei Romania*, 1958, pp. 234-277 (Heb.).
17. Jan Ancell, "Romanian Jewry, 23.8.44–30.12.47", doctoral thesis, Hebrew University, 1979, p. 27 (Heb.).
18. *ibid.*
19. World Jewish Congress, "Romanian Jewry in the Post-War Period" (undated), p. 271.
20. T. Lavie, ed., *Pinkas Hakehillot – Romania*, Vol. A, Yad Vashem, 1970, pp. 40-47 (Heb.).
21. Jan Ancell, *op. cit.*, p. 150.
22. *ibid.* pp. 120-180.
23. World Jewish Congress, *op. cit.*, p. 9.
24. Jan Ancell, *op. cit.*, p. 226.
25. Jan Ancell claims that the Israeli argument was transferred artificially to Romania.
26. *op. cit.*, p. 250.
27. *op. cit.*, p. 255.
28. H.H., C/2, 1130–1131. J. Ancell, *op. cit.*, p. 277.
29. Shaike Dan, interview.
30. In the defence of the Zionist movement it was feared that if the process of "selction" increased, the movement would lose control over the situation and the process would lead to complete anarchy. Report of the leadership of the Romanian Zionist movement to the Jewish Agency, 1.8.47, A.Z.M. 55/810.
31. For the attitude of Marx and Marxism to the Jewish question – S. Ettinger, *Romanian anti-Semitism*, Moreshet and Sifriat Hapoalim, 1979, pp. 89-98 (Heb.).
32. Report of the British representative in Bucharest to the Foreign Office in London, 12.12.1947, PRO ADM 1.
33. For the conversation with Anna Pauker, Y. Klarman, oral documentation; M. Auerbuch (Agami), interview, S. Avigur files, A.M.
34. H.H., C/2, 1129-1180.
35. J. Ancell, p. 308.
36. *ibid.*, p. 294.
37. Report of the "operative section", AHH 2.
38. From the viewpoint of the immigrant, Prof. D. Wolf, interview. From the viewpoint of the operative, cable from Agami to Mossad, 21.11.47, AHH.
39. Prof. Wolf remembered the fear of his friend, a deserter from the army, and the sigh of relief when they crossed the border into Bulgaria. This question of deserters is hinted at in the cables sent by the operatives, warning that a delay in the sailing would uncover them and they would be condemned to death.
40. Report of the "operative section", AHH.
41. Approximate estimate based on partial reports, *ibid.*

CHAPTER FOUR: SHIPS OR A STATE . . .

1. For the wide spectrum of Zionist ideology, see S. Avineri *Harayon Hazioni*, Am Oved, 1980, pp. 247-257.
2. For Weizmann's activity on the eve of the establishment of the state: A. Eilat, *Hama'arak al Hamedina*, Am Oved and the Zionist Library, 1979 (Heb.).
3. The beginning of the argument between Weizmann and Ben-Gurion was in 1936. It reached its peak in 1946. See Y. Gorni, *Shutfut Uma'avak*, Tel Aviv University and Hakibbutz Hameuchad (Heb.).

4. S. Lev Ami (Levy), *Bama'avak Ubamered*, Ministry of Defence Publications, 1979, pp. 236-238 (Heb.).
5. *ibid.*
6. N. Yellin-Mor, *Lochamei Herut Yisrael*, Shikmona, 1975, p. 459 (Heb.).
7. M. M. Porosh, *Betoch Hachomot*, Jerusalem, 1948 (Heb.).
8. A. Eilat, *op. cit.*, pp. 387-390.
9. Y. Gorni, *op. cit.*, pp. 204-205.
10. M. Pa'il *Min HaHagana Le Zva Hagana*, Zimora Bitan Moden, 1979, pp. 248-253 (Heb.).
11. "United Nations Resolution on Partition of Palestine" from the collection of political documents on the history of the Zionist movement (ed. A. Prizel), Akdamon, 1979, pp. 265-266 (Heb.).
12. The hesitations and misunderstandings in the U.S. State Dept. began before the U.N. resolution on 29.11.1947 and were seen in the attempts to propose a truncated partition, which would exclude from the emerging Jewish state Jaffa, Beersheba and most of the Negev. *Foreign Relations of the United States*, 1947, Volume V, Washington, 1971 (hereafter referred to as *FRUS*, V), pp. 1147-1151.
13. D. Ben-Gurion, diaries, 19.12.1947, B.G.A.
14. Venia Hadari, interview.
15. The British Foreign Office files are full of appeals to other countries to stop Mossad activities. See for example Bevin's appeal to the Prime Minister of France, 12.7.1947, PRO FO, 371, 61816.
16. Interview with Frank Bateman, of Jewish origin, speaking Yiddish and Hebrew, who was on a British Intelligence mission in Italy and France in 1947.
17. Cable from Arnon to Agami (Mossad office to Auerbuch in Romania), 22.12.1947, H.H.
18. On the communications people: S. Tevet *Hagideonim*, Ma'arachot, 1968 (Heb.).
19. Frank Bateman succeeded in infiltrating the operatives and was appointed to an administrative post in the Mossad transit camp by Port de Buc. F. Bateman, interview.
20. H.H., C/3, 1779.
21. On Bevin's sensitivity and frustration, Creech Jones, Colonial Minister at the time; M. Y. Cohen, "The British Decision to leave Eretz-Yisrael", *Cathedra*, No. 15, 1980, p. 145 (Heb.).
22. F. Williams, *Ernest Bevin*, London, 1952, pp. 238-249.
23. This issue of British policy is subject to dispute in research. For the assumption quoted, see Elizabeth Monroe, *Bevin's Arab Policy*, St. Antony's Papers, II, London, 1961.
24. *Daily Telegraph*, 30.9.47.
25. The U.S. ambassador in London hinted in this letter that Bevin was inclined to be hysterical. He questioned Bevin's estimate of 18,000 immigrants. *FRUS*, V, pp. 1215-1216.
26. *FRUS*, V, pp. 1226-1227.
27. *FRUS*, V, pp. 1229-1230.
28. *ibid.*
29. Rusk, ibid. It is difficult to believe that there was a proposal from Sharett to give information on the movement of immigrant ships to the American authorities.
30. *FRUS*, V, pp. 1248-1249.
31. Marshall to Bevin, 7.11.47, *FRUS*, V, pp. 1247-1248. Also Sharett, Jewish Agency minutes, 31.12.47, A.B.G.
32. *FRUS*, V, pp. 1318-1321.
33. *Daily Express*, 1.1.48.
34. For example, the response of the Italian Foreign Ministry to the British request. Cable from Rome to London, 27.9.47, PRO ADM 1, 20793.

35. Signal from Gibraltar to Fleet H.Q., 24.9.47, *ibid.*
36. Report on conversations, 12.9.47, *ibid.*
37. Memorandum to Government of Panama, 3.10.47, *ibid.*
38. Report from *Ha'aretz* correspondent in London, A. Gelblum, 13.10.47.
39. *News Chronicle*, 21. 10.47.
40. Discussion on the legal question of removing the flags with lawyer Y. S. Shapira, AHH, *Pans* box.
41. Jan Ancell, *op. cit.*, pp. 11-12.
42. *ibid.*
43. E.g., cables dated 19.11.47, 24.11.47, 13.12.47, 23.12.47, etc., PRO ADM 1.
44. Reports dated 12.12.47, 13.12.47, *ibid.* According to the intelligence information in the possession of the British, it can be assumed that it was obtained from two sources. One was the Romanian administration, apparently the passport department of the Ministry of the Interior, since they had detailed numbers, including the places of origin and ages of the candidates. The second source was most probably from the foreign crew of the *Pan Crescent*, because of the technical information on the boats. The informant was presumably an Italian sailor. It should be pointed out that the intelligence did not uncover the internal organisation of the Mossad or the purpose of the training camps that were set up in Romania and which were attended by hundreds of local Jews.
45. Foreign Office to Washington, 23.12.47, 27.12.47, PRO ADM 1.
46. From Bucharest to the Foreign Office, 12.12.47, *ibid.*
47. J. Ancell, *op. cit.*, pp. 243-255.
48. The height of this contorted ambivalence was in the cooperation between the Communists in Eretz Israel and the Mufti to prevent the establishment of a state supported by the U.S.S.R. See also Y. A. Gilboa, "Soviet Politics on Palestine: Tradition & Change", *International Problems*, Vol. 10, No. 3-4, 1971, pp. 11-19 (Heb.).
49. From the Foreign Office to Moscow, 30.11.47, PRO ADM 1.
50. The revolution in Greece was declared on 24.12.47 by Marcos, who announced the establishment of a Communist Greek Government, *Ha'aretz*, 4.1.48 (Heb.).
51. In view of the current research situation, when the archives of Eastern European countries are closed to researchers, it is not possible to know exactly how discussions took place and what were the precise reasons of the authorities to let the immigrants through to Burgos. Furthermore, the reports of the Mossad emissaries and negotiators on behalf of the Jewish Agency are inconsistent and show a tendency by various bodies to highlight the part played by some and to minimize the role of others. For example, Y. Klarmen's comments on the contribution of Moshe Sneh in H.H., C/2, pp. 1179-1182.
52. PRO ADM 1/20793. HN 08372.
53. From Sophia to the Foreign Office, 2.10.47, PRO ADM 1.
54. From Ankara to the Foreign Office, 29.11.47, *ibid.*
55. A. Eilat, *op. cit.*, pp. 298-300.
56. For this, Y. Gorni, *op. cit.*, pp. 128-129.
57. G. Cohen, "The Withdrawal from Palestine in the Mirror of British Policy", *Cathedra* 15, pp. 176-184 (Heb.).
58. M. Cohen, *Z'manim*, Book 2, 1980, p. 99 (Heb.).
59. Bevin-Marshall conversations, 2.12.47, *FRUS*, V, pp. 1298-1299, 1301-1302.
60. *ibid.*
61. *Ha'aretz*, 31.1.48.
62. *New York Times*, 3.1.48.
63. To Yass'ur from Arnon (to Venia Hadari in Paris from the Mossad office in Israel), 10.11.47, AHH.

64. From a report of the intelligence unit of *The Economist*, 6.11.47, which came into the possession of the Hagana information service, AHH.
65. Ben-Gurion's later testimony in this sensitive issue: "I admit that I supported the Jewish State in 1937 on the basis of partition, and had it taken place, the history of our people would have been different and six million Jews in Europe would not have been destroyed; most of them would have been in Israel." Letter to Ben Zion Katz, 1.9.57.
66. Ben-Gurion's diary, 17.12.47, A.B.G.

CHAPTER FIVE: THE MOSSAD VERSUS THE ESTABLISHMENT

1. From minutes of the meeting of the Mapai Secretariat, 9.12.47, S. Avigur files, A.M.
2. Description of the course of the negotiations by Ben-Gurion at the Mapai Secretariat meeting, *ibid.*
3. Ben-Gurion's letter to Sharett, 30.6.36. D. Ben-Gurion, *Memoirs*, Vol. C, Am Oved, 1973, p. 310 (Heb.).
4. For the significance of the leadership of Ben-Gurion, Z. Tsahor, "Hahistadrut – T'Kufat Ha'itzuv", doctoral thesis, Hebrew University, pp. 162-169 (Heb.).
5. S. Avigur, at the meeting of the Mapai Secretariat, 9.12.47.
6. For an example of Ben-Gurion's method of political struggle, see Y. Gorni, *Shutfut Vema'avak*, 1976, pp. 151-159 (Heb.).
7. Ben-Gurion, Mapai Secretariat meeting, 9.12.47.
8. *ibid.*
9. *ibid.*
10. On the date and reasons for formulation in the cable "to Arnon from Agami" (to the Mossad in Israel from Auerbuch in Romania), 4.12.47, AHH.
11. Interview with Moshe Sneh from 1968, in the S. Avigur files, A.M.
12. Conclusion of meeting with representatives of Jewish organisations in Romania from 7.11.47, signed by Moshe Sneh, S. Avigur files, A.M.
13. See note 11 and compare H.H., C/2, p. 1179.
14. Testimony of M. Auerbuch and also Y. Klarman in his letters to S. Avigur. S. Avigur files, A.M.
15. S. Avigur's letter to Sharett, 4.12.47. Most of this letter appeared in H.H., C/2, pp. 1184-1185.
16. *ibid.*
17. Minutes of meeting of Jewish Agency directorate, 30.11.47, A.B.G.
18. M. Sneh, see 11 above.
19. This version in S. Avigur's handwriting, outlining Ben-Gurion's position, for the draft of the book on the *Pans*, S. Avigur files, A.M.
20. Ben-Gurion to Sharett, 1.12.47, A.Z.M., S44-647.
21. To cancel the voyage, to reduce the number of passengers (substantially) or to postpone the sailing.
22. Cable dated 1.12.47, AHH.
23. From the West – Golda did not dare to demand a cessation of immigration but proposed that it move to Italy or France. For these ideas see the concluding remarks of Moshe Sharett at the meeting of the Jewish Agency directorate, 31.12.47, A.B.G.
24. Cable dated 1.12.47 AHH.
25. Cable dated 2.12.47 AHH.
26. Cable dated 4.12.47 AHH.
27. S. Avigur's remarks at the Mapai Secretariat, 9.12.47.

28. Stephens = dollars, nickname taken from Stephen Wise, one of the leaders of U.S. Jewry, the source of most of the financial resources.
29. From Yass'ur to Arnon (from Venia Hadari to the Mossad office in Israel), 3.11.47, AHH.
30. Cable dated 4.12.47 AHH.
31. Cable dated 4.12.47, AHH.
32. Manuscript report by S. Avigur on Ben-Gurion's attitude, undated, AHH.
33. On their activity in Prague, Ben-Gurion's diary, 18.12.47, A.B.G.
34. To Ben Yehuda from Ovadia (to S. Avigur from Ben-Gurion), 1.12.47, AHH.
35. On the relations between the Hagana and Etzel and Lechi – H.H., C/2, pp. 946-959.
36. See note 15.
37. To Agami from Arnon (to Auerbuch from the Mossad), 5.12.47, AHH.
38. To Avriel, *Pitchu Sha'arim*, Ma'ariv, 1976, 262-265 (Heb.).
39. Pino Ginsburg, interview.
40. Venia Hadari, interview.
41. Ben-Gurion at the Mapai Secretariat, 9.12.47.
42. *ibid.*
43. *ibid.*
44. Description of the meeting at Ben-Gurion's home, the journey to Jerusalem, etc., Shaike Dan, interview.
45. Yossi Harel, Shaike Dan, Binyamin Yerushalmi, interviews.
46. A striking example of this is Ben-Gurion. For the importance of documentation with Ben-Gurion, see Z. Tsahor, "Ben Gurion writes autobiography", *Keshet*, Vol. 55, pp. 144-152.
47. Also S. Avigur's remarks in an interview to Yigael Dunitz of the Ben-Gurion Institute, oral documentation, p. 11, A.B.G.
48. Shaike Dan, interview.
49. *ibid.*
50. *ibid.* Ben-Gurion assumed that Shaul really intended to go the the U.S.A. Ben-Gurion diary, 17.12.47, A.B.G.
51. Ben-Gurion diary.
52. This version of Shaul's remarks by Shaike Dan, interview.
53. S. Dan, interview. P. Ginsburg remembered that there was such a plan but did not remember if it was put to Shaul.
54. Interview with S. Avigur, see note 47.
55. See the joint cable of Brodetzky and Goldmann to Sharett, 20.12.47, S. Avigur files, A.M.
56. Cable from Romania to Shaul in Israel, 13.12.47, AHH. Also Shaike Dan, interview. Compare S. Avigur's remarks in the interview in note 47.
57. Remarks of Israel Galili in an interview with Y. Ben-Gorat, *Yediot Achronot*, 5.10.78.
58. To Arnon from Maurice (to S. Avigur in Israel from M. Auerbuch in Constanta), 11.12.47, AHH.
59. To Shaul from Auerbuch, 13.12.47, *ibid.*
60. To Shaul from Auerbuch, 15.12.47, *ibid.*
61. On the argument at the time of the battle of the *Exodus*, Ike Aharonovitz, interview.
62. See H.H., 2/B, pp. 833-50.
63. The weight of leadership moderates ideological fervour. Article by Chaim Arlozoroff, "Hatekassim shel Miflagot Mediniot" *Writings*, Vol. E, Shtibel, pp.173-253 (Heb.).
64. Hint at E. Avriel's proposal in Sharett's cable to Ben-Gurion, 15.12.47, G. Yogev (ed.) *Political & Diplomatic Documents, December 1947 – May 1948*. State Archives and Zionist Archives, 1980, p.62 (Heb.).

65. Venia Hadari in a report to S. Avigur who was still in Israel, 18.12.47, AHH.
66. *ibid.*
67. To Arnon from Berg (to Shaul from Pino Ginsburg), 16.12.47, AHH.
68. To Or from Agami (to Shaul from Auerbach, in Romania), 17.12.47, AHH.
69. On Sharett's conversations in U.S.A. from the American point of view, *FRUS V*, pp. 1301-1304, 1311-1312; Sharett's report to Ben-Gurion on these talks, G. Yogev, *op. cit.* p.58.
70. From Ben-Gurion to Sharett, 18.12.47, AZM, S44/674.
71. From Sharett to Ben-Gurion, 18.12.47, A.B.G.
72. V. Hadari to S. Avigur, 18.12.47, AHH.
73. From Brodetzky and Goldmann to the Jewish Agency directorate, 18.12.47, G.M. 25/1700.
74. To Yass'ur and Berg from Or (to Venia Hadari and P. Ginsburg from Avigur), 18.12.47, AHH.
75. S. Dan, interview.
76. To Arnon, Or from Agami (to Shaul in Israel from Auerbuch), 18.12.47, AHH.
77. To Or from Yass'ur (to Shaul from V. Hadari), 19.12.47, AHH.
78. To Agami and Hass'ur from Arnon (to Auerbuch in Romania and Venia in Paris from Shaul in Israel), 19.12.47, AHH.
79. The last-minute instructions were not to use the defensive devices fitted on the ships in case of a clash with the British.
80. To sabotage the empty ships to prevent their confiscation.
81. According to previous proposals which said it was possible to remain at sea for two weeks.
82. To Arnon from Agami (to Shaul from Auerbuch), 21.12.47, AHH.
83. Operations order to commanders of the *Pans* signed by M. Auerbuch, 20.12.47, AHH.
84. On the conversation, S. Avigur in an interview with the Ben-Gurion Institute. Despite diversionary attempts, the British located the conversation, recorded and deciphered it at once. The tape is in PRO, Admiralty file 08372.
85. Moshe Perlman, interview.
86. Prof. Selig Brodetzky in *Ha'aretz*, 15.12.47.
87. H.H., C/3, 1540-1558.
88. *Ha'aretz*, 24.12.47.
89. Political correspondent of *Ha'aretz*, 30.12.47.
90. S. Avigur, interview, A.B.G.
91. A. Eilat, *op. cit.* pp. 224-228.
92. *ibid*, p.19.
93. *ibid*, p.33.
94. Cable dated 27.12.47, AHH, Verse from Genesis 32,29.

CHAPTER SIX: ROMANIANS AND BULGARIANS

1. Report of the "Operative Section", p.3, AHH.
2. Final report, p.6, *ibid.*
3. This seems to be a case where the senior commanders of the operation, led by Moshe Auerbuch, sought to keep to the spirit and letter of the agreement with the Romanian authorities whilst the local activists ignored it. Shlomo Leibovitz, interview.
4. Mossad Le'Aliya Bet Archive, containing dozens of files, is located in the Archives of the History of the Hagana (AHH).

5. For the purposes of this research, use was made of the departments for oral documentation at the Hebrew University and Tel Aviv University. In the Labour Archives in Tel Aviv there are photographs and in the Zionist Archives a collection of details and documents from the various ships. The film "The Last Sea" (Hayam Ha'acharon), recently produced, is based on material taken from various places.
6. From an interview with Israel Even, testimony files, AHH.
7. B. Arditti, *Jews of Bulgaria during the years of the Nazi regime*, 1962, p.17 (Heb.).
8. A.A. Romano, "Jewry and the Zionist Movement in Bulgaria", from *Bulgarian Jewry, Encyclopaedia of Exiles*, Vol. 10, 1967, pp. 357-409 (Heb.).
9. Yosef Ben, *To Freedom & Aliya, ibid.* p. 926 (Heb.).
10. B. Arditti, *op.cit.* pp.346-349.
11. Shlomo Dagan, interview.
12. *Bulgarian Jewry, Encyclopaedia of Exiles*, p. 962 (Heb.).
13. Testimony of Venia Hadari who arranged Ben-Gurion's visit to Bulgaria.
14. For many years afterwards, at every meeting between Shaike Dan and Ben-Gurion, the latter used to recall this interruption. Dan, interview.
15. Ben-Gurion, *Bama'aracha*, Vol. 4, pp. 193-209.
16. Yehuda Braginsky relates the affair from a different angle in his book *Am Choter el Chof*, Hakibutz Hameuchad, 1965, p.405 (Heb.).
17. The British activities in Sophia to stop the voyage constituted most of the diplomatic contacts between the countries.
18. Moshe Carmel, Pino Ginsburg, Shaike Dan, interviews.
19. Shaike Dan, interview.
20. The quotation from Ben-Gurion's diaries, noted by S. Avigur, A.M.
21. Shaike Dan, interview.
22. *ibid.*
23. Description of the organization of Second Aliya and the role of the "act" in the ideology of the Israel Labour Movement by Berl Katznelson, *Writings*, Vol II, Mapai (Heb.).
24. Shaike Dan, interview.
25. Rani Alsheikh, now Yael Shemtov, interview.
26. *ibid.*
27. Moni Diga, now Shlomo Dagan, member of Kibbutz, Yad Mordechai, interview.
28. *ibid.*

CHAPTER SEVEN: TO THE SHIPS!

1. Final report on the voyage, pp. 16-17, AHH.
2. Cable from Mossad office in Israel to Moshe Auerbuch in Romania 22.12.47, AHH.
3. Final report on the voyage, pp. 16-19, AHH.
4. Nathan Alterman, response to the Italian captain after a night of disembarkation, from *Magash Hakessef* (Silver Platter), Ministry of Defence Publications, 1970, pp.301-303 (Heb.).
5. Cable from Mossad office in Israel to emissaries in France and Italy, 20.2.48, AHH. Apparently the wage promised them was £60 per month for the captain, £40-45 for the officers and £25 for the seamen, as well as special payments and bonuses.
6. Dozens of letters and cables dealing with this subject are collected in file No. 14/275, AHH.
7. Cable to the Mossad office in France, 20.2.48, *ibid.*
8. See note 7.
9. *ibid.*

10. Report on radio communications on the ships and the work of the Gideons, 22.1.48, AHH.
11. Cable to the *Pan York* from the Mossad office in Israel, 22.1.48, AHH.
12. The American seamen received special attention from the British in their constant surveillance of the ships. See the cable from British Intelligence that came into the possession of "Shai" (Information service), 9.1.48, AHH.
13. For the scorn for the role of forward planning and professional judgment in principle in the Palestine Labour movement, Z. Tsahor "HaHistadrut, T'kufat Ha'itzuv", Doctoral thesis, The Hebrew University, 1978, pp.132-141 (Heb.).
14. Shaike Dan, Binyamin Yenishalmi, Yossi Harel, interviews.
15. Yossi Harel, interview.
16. Entry in logbook, Sat. 27.12.47, A.M.
17. Ike Aharonovitz, interview.
18. E.g., report from the British representative in Ankara to the Foreign Office, 7.11.47, PRO ADM 1.
19. Moshe Perlman, interview.
20. There were different versions, ranging from $10,000-$40,000. There is, of course, no documentation on this.
21. Final report, AHH.
22. Shaike Dan, interview. Final report, AHH.
23. Final report, AHH. Shlomo Leibovitz, interview.
24. Prof. D. Wolf, interview.
25. Shaike Dan, interview.

CHAPTER EIGHT: BLACK SEA, BLUE SEA

1. Yossi Harel, Ike Aharonovitz, Shaike Dan, interviews. National flags were flown, but on leaving Bulgarian territorial waters they were taken down on Mossad orders, because of Jewish Agency objections to the voyage. When the ships were handed over to the British, on 30.12.47, the flags were raised again. More of this later.
2. Yossi Harel, interview.
3. For one of the difficult manifestations, AHH, file 362, box 57.
4. Cable from *Pan York* to Mossad office in Tel Aviv, 2.1.48, AHH, box 46.
5. Remarks of Dov Magen, final report, p.14, AHH.
6. Jan Ancell, *Romanian Jewry 23.8.44-30.12.47*, p.64 (Heb.).
7. *ibid*. pp. 29-51.
8. Y. Tabenkin, "Kavei Yichud Shel T'nu'at Hapo'alim Ba'Aretz". Lecture in 1928, from *Devarim*, Vol. 1, Hakibbutz Hameuchad, 1967, pp.92-107.
9. *ibid*.
10. For the influence of literature on the formation of the world-view of members of the Labour movement. Z. Tsahor, "Ha Histadrut, T'kufat Ha'itzuv", Doctoral thesis, pp. 61-73 (Heb.).
11. Report of meeting chaired by Moshe Sneh, 7.11.47, S. Avigur file, A.M.
12. Problems of violence, extortion and gang rule amongst the passengers over the food stores are suggested in interviews with ship commanders and immigrants. These problems, as well as many others, have not yet been properly researched.
13. Y. Harel, interview.
14. Prof. D. Wolf, interview.
15. M.K. Eli Moyel, interview.
16. Yael Shemtov, interview.

17. Dov Magen, final report, AHH.
18. The best known was the seminar for young members of Mapai organised by Berl Katznelson in Haifa, May-June 1944. See S. Yavne'eli in his introduction to *Writings* by B. Katznelson, Vol. II, 1948, pp.5-6 (Heb.).
19. It is worth pointing out that there is a considerable difference in the historical approach of Katznelson, as in note 18, and that of Tabenkin, as in note 8, despite their closeness in age, period of immigration and positions of leadership. It is easy to imagine how their versions differ from that of Hashomer Hatza'ir and how the three streams differ in their description of the operation from the viewpoint of the Revisionist movement.
20. Thus the conclusion of M. Sneh with the heads of movements and organisations in Romania on 7.11.47, S. Avigur files, A.M.
21. Immigration was not the exclusive domain of the labour movement. During the first period, from 1934 to the outbreak of the Second World War, other political parties were actively involved in it as well. The Revisionist movement and Betar together planned and arranged the sailing of eighteen ships, with 9,000 immigrants. Even during the war Betar had been able to organize four ships (one of them in cooperation with Hashomer Hatza'ir). There were also special arrangements made by the General Zionists and even private groups that operated ships for profit. After the Second World War, however, nearly all immigration was handled by the Mossad. Out of the sixty-six ships that sailed for Israel, only one, the *Ben Hecht*, was the result of Revisionist initiative. During this period the labour movement was the dominant force in the country and its enterprises were at the height of their power. Its ability to construct an integrated system in which the kibbutzim, the Histadrut, the Hamashbir (retailing organization), the Kupat Cholim Sick Fund, the Palmach and Bank Hapoalim (Worker's Bank) formed one organization whose mission was the establishment of a state served to strengthen each one of these bodies. One of their offshoots was the Mossad Le'Aliya Bet - the unauthorized immigration agency. See Y. Wolf, *Carta Atlas . . ., op.cit.*, pp.73–81.
22. Moni Dagan, Prof. D. Wolf, Shlomo Leibowitz, interviews.
23. Yael Shemtov, interview.
24. Moshe Perlman, interview. Jan and David Kimche, *Darkei Seter*, Jerusalem Post publications, 1954, pp. 199-200 (Heb.).
25. Yossi Harel, interview.
26. *ibid.*
27. Reports of the surveillance in the Admiralty files. E.g., report from Gibraltar to Malta, 28.9.47, giving direction of voyage, cargo, speed and possible ports, PRO ADM 1.
28. Shlomo Leibonik, Prof. D. Wolf, Hanna Weiss, interviews.
29. Shlomo Dagan, interview.
30. Shlomo Dagan, Roni Shemtov, interviews.
31. Yossi Harel, Ike Aharonowitz, interviews.
32. Z. Drugy *New Light on the* Exodus *Affair, op.cit.*, pp.137-152 (Heb.).
33. Ike Aharonowitz, Venia Hadari, joint interview.
34. Ike Aharonowitz, interview.
35. Logbook of *Pan Crescent*, 27.12.47.
36. H.H., C/1, 155.
37. Yossi Harel, interview.
38. PRO ADM 1, 20793, correspondence April-December 1947.
39. Cable, 27.12.47, PRO ADM 1.
40. *ibid.*
41. Naval command to ship commanders, 29.12.47, 12.14 hours, PRO ADM 1.
42. Cable from Foreign Office to Rome, 5.10.47, PRO ADM 1.

43. Cable from Sophia to Foreign Office, 2.10.47, *ibid.*
44. Report of Peter Duffield, *Daily Express*, 1.1.48.
45. Warning on this in cable from Mossad office, Tel Aviv, to Venia Hadari in Paris, 10.11.47, AHH.
46. From C. to C.S.I., 29.12.47, PRO ADM 1.
47. Cable from Mossad office to Venia Hadari, via Italy, 29.12.47, AHH.
48. Communications report from Yishai, undated, AHH 14/277.
49. For hints about the proposal – Ben-Gurion's diary, 26.12.47, A.B.G.
50. Cable from M. Auerbach, 21.12.47, AHH.
51. *ibid.*
52. Final report on voyage, p.15, AHH.
53. From Auerbach to Mossad office, 9.10.47, AHH 14/A 275.
54. Communications report from Yishai.
55. Cable to Venia Hadari from S. Avigur, 22.12.47, AHH, *Pans* box. "Agami's vessels" means Auerbach's ships.
56. From Auerbuch to Mossad office, 21.12.47, and from Venia Hadari, 23.12.47, *ibid.*
57. From S. Avigur to Mossad, 30.12.47, *ibid.* Amittai is Ben-Gurion; Ben Kedem is Moshe Sharett.
58. From Hadari to the ships, 30.12.47, *ibid.* Arnon-Mossad office, *ibid.*
59. From Mossad to the ships, cable No. 1, 31.12.47, *ibid.*
60. *ibid.*
61. Written order from M. Auerbach to "Pikud Elion shel Ha'achot ve Chevreman", 20.12.47, S. Avigur files, A.M.
62. Y. Harel, interview.
63. From C. to C.S.I., 27.12.47, PRO ADM 1.
64. Direct cable to flotilla commander, 31.12.47, *ibid.*
65. Transcription of messages, AHH 14/277.
66. From Y. Harel to Mossad, 1.1.48, 14.34 hours, AHH.
67. Y. Harel, interview.

CHAPTER NINE: CYPRUS

1. AHH, *Pans* box.
2. *ibid.*
3. Logbook of *Pan Crescent*, 31.12.47. Report signed by Goldman, i.e. Ike Aharonovitz.
4. Shlomo Leibovitz, Hanna Weiss, Yael Shemtov, interviews.
5. Cable to Mossad office from *Atzma ut*, 1.1.48, 00.40 hours, AHH.
6. *ibid.*
7. *ibid.*
8. Article by Peter Duffield, *Daily Express*, 1.1.48.
9. E.g. correspondence between Admiralty and Ministry of Transport, 17.2.48, PRO ADM 1 08372.
10. AHH, *ibid*, "Hagoyim" – foreign crew.
11. A report by Captain Linklater came into the possession of the Hagana information service, AHH, 14/275.
12. From the provisional report on the disembarkation of immigrants, *ibid.*
13. Final report of voyage, AHH.
14. Dov Magen, final report of voyage, *ibid.*
15. Capt. Linklater's report, 2.1.48, AHH, 14/275.
16. Cable dated 9.1.48, 08372 PRO ADM 1.

17. *Newsweek*, 23.2.48.
18. *News Chronicle*, 1.1.48. On the negotiations between the Foreign Office and the Government of Panama, F.O. Report dated 10.1.48, 08372 PRO ADM 1.
19. AHH, *Pans* box.
20. Arnon – Yossi Harel.
21. Conclusion of Hagana information service, 9.1.48, AHH, 14/275.
22. *ibid*.
23. Report of voyage of *Nesher* to Cyprus, 14.1.48, AHH.
24. Photostat of arrest warrant, 9.1.48, AHH.
25. Copy of special edition of *The Cypriot*, 3.1.48, AHH.
26. The discussion on salaries for foreign seamen went on for months. There is a complete file on this in AHH, 14A/276.
27. Letter from Advocate Ya'akov S. Shapira to Foreign Minister Moshe Sharett, 19.6.48, AHH, 14/276.

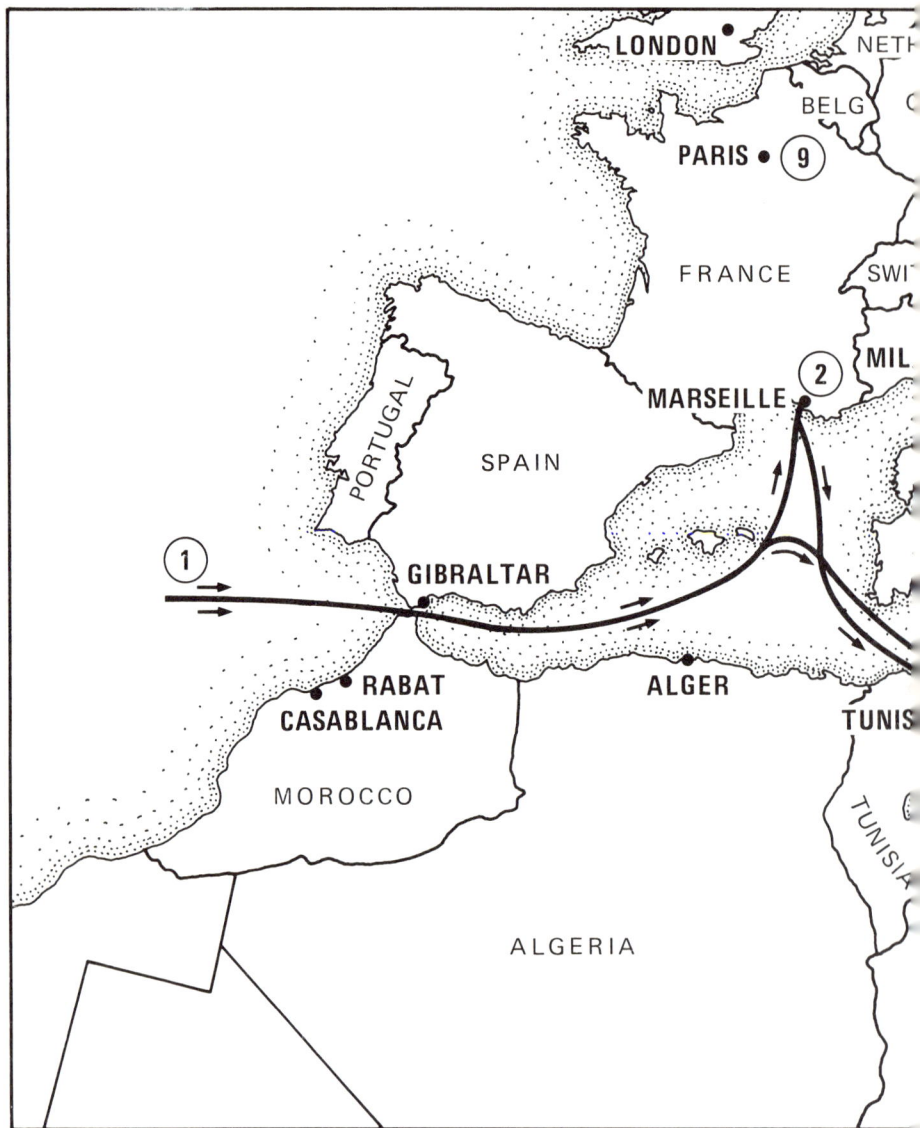

1. July 1947. *Pan York* and *Pan Crescent* leave U.S.A. Destination: the Mediterranean.
2. August–September 1947. *Pan York* on the French coast. Preparations for "commercial" sailing.
3. 30.4.47. Sabotage of *Pan Crescent* in the harbour at Venice.
4. September 1947. The ships sail to Constantza, Romania.